대지의 시간   Time of the Earth

대지의 시간　　　　　Time of the Earth

발간사

윤범모
국립현대미술관장

'인류세(Antrophocene Epoch)'는 코로나19(COVID-19) 팬데믹 시기에 가장 많이 언급된 용어 가운데 하나입니다. 이는 지질 시대상 현세에 해당하는 홀로세(Holecene Epoch) 중에서 인간의 활동으로 인한 지질 흔적이 확연하게 발견되는 시대를 의미하는 말로, 몇 세기 전 인류의 항해와 이동이 본격화되면서 감염성 질병이 따라 움직이고 천연두 확산으로 수많은 생명이 목숨을 잃었던 역사를 기억하기에 팬데믹 시기에 이 용어가 사람들의 입에 오르내리고 있는 것일지 모릅니다.

지질 시대를 구분하는 동력이 인간이 되었다는 사실은 많은 의미를 내포합니다. 인류의 개체 수와 그 활동이 지구상에서 지배적으로 변하면서 이전 지질 시대와 확연히 구분되는 플라스틱, 알루미늄, 콘크리트 같은 기술 화석이 퇴적층에 쌓이기 시작했고, 직·간접적인 상관관계에서 비롯한 기후 변화와 해수면 상승, 바다 사막화 같은 현상이 지구 곳곳에서 진행되고 있습니다. 인류세의 특징이라 일컬어지는 요소와 현상이 바로 인류의 생존을 위협하고 있는 역설입니다.

인류 자신의 욕망과 팽창의 결과가 낳은 비극적 위기 앞에서 많은 사람이 근본적 변화가 필요하다는 데 뜻을 모읍니다. 이때 사람들의 태도와 행동의 변화를 이끄는 것은 관점과 가치관입니다. 국립현대미술관 과천관에서 개최하는 《대지의 시간》은 바로 이 가치관을 예술의 언어로 말하고 있습니다. 김주리, 나현, 백정기, 서동주, 장민승, 정소영, OAA(정규동) 작가의 신작들은 새로운 관점에 대한 고민과 지향을 담고 있습니다. 올라퍼 엘리아손, 장뤽 밀렌, 주세페 페노네, 크리스티앙 볼탕스키, 히로시 스기모토의 작업은 생태적 공존과 새로운 시각을 말하고 있습니다. 또한 1970년대 중반부터 지금까지 묵묵히 생태적 가치에 대한 실험과 실천을 이어 온 국내의 작가와 단체를 살펴보는 한국 생태미술 아카이브를 전시 형식으로 구현해, 한국 미술사에서 생태미술의 지형도를 그려 보고자 했습니다.

전시를 기록하고 논의를 확장하고자 펴내는 이 도록에는 해양환경 활동가, 다큐멘터리 PD, 생태미학자, 식물학자, 기자 등 현재의 생태 위기와 관련해 활발히 활동하고 발언하는 전문가들의 원고를 수록했습니다. 전시에 참여한 작가들과 필진의 통찰력과 제안이 근본적 대전환을 촉구하는 계기와 자극이 되기를 바라며, 《대지의 시간》 전시가 생태학적 세계관에 관한 공감과 생태적 실천으로 나

Preface

Youn Bummo
Director, National Museum of Modern and Contemporary
Art, Korea

The "Anthropocene Epoch" is among the terms most frequently mentioned during the COVID-19 pandemic. Part of the Holocene Epoch, it refers to the unit of geological time that started when human activities began to leave distinct geological traces. When human voyages and migration began in earnest a few centuries back, so did the movement of infectious diseases; we remember the historic spread of smallpox that took countless lives. The fact that humanity has become a distinguishing factor of geological epochs signifies many things. As the human population and its domain of activity grew dominant, technofossils formed by materials such as plastic, aluminum, and concrete began to accumulate, forming a sedimentary stratum unlike those of previous geological eras. This has indirectly contributed to climate change, rising sea levels, and other phenomena around the globe such as desertification. We are now faced with the paradox that the elements and occurrences characteristic of the Anthropocene are the very threats to our kind's survival.

In the face of a tragic crisis attributable to human greed and expansion, many agree that fundamental change is imperative. And what drives changes in attitude and behavior are perspective and values. The MMCA exhibition *Time of the Earth* talks expressly about our value system in an artistic language. New installations by Kim Juree, Na Hyun, Beak Jungki, Seo Dongjoo, Jang Minseung, Chung Soyoung, and OAA (Jung Kyudong) demonstrate the artists' deliberation on the crisis and their search for alternative perspectives and possibilities. Works by Olafur Eliasson, Jean-Luc Mylayne, Giuseppe Penone, Christian Boltanski, and Hiroshi Sugimoto address ecological coexistence from alternative viewpoints. The exhibition also incorporates an archive of Korean ecological art, offering an overview of the ecological experiments and practices silently conducted by Korean artists and groups since the mid-1970s to map out the domain of ecological art in Korean art history.

This catalog, which both documents and expands on the topics of the exhibition, contains essays by experts—a marine environmental activist, a producer of Anthropocene-related documentaries, an eco-aesthetician, a botanist, and a social journalist—who are actively voicing their opinions on the current ecological crisis. It is my hope that the participating artists' and experts' insight and propositions kickstart a fundamental and radical transformation, and that this exhibition serves as a pub-

아가기 위한 공론의 장으로 기능하기를 희망합니다.

끝으로, 전시를 위해 애쓰고 협조해 주신 모든 분께 깊은 감사의 인사를 전합니다, 특히 비타민 크리에이티브 스페이스, 주세페 페노네 스튜디오, 스튜디오 올라퍼 엘리아손, 히로시 스기모토 스튜디오, 에바 알바란 앤 컴퍼니, 갤러리 고야나기, 스프루스 마거스, 고(故) 정재철 작가 유족, 바깥미술, 사단법인 한국자연미술가협회-야투(野投), 대안공간 소나무, 마감뉴스, 양구군립 박수근미술관, 서울시립미술관, 정익명 작가, 생태미학예술연구소에 진심으로 감사의 뜻을 전합니다.

lic forum in which we can discuss and establish a consensus on an ecological worldview, leading to related practices.

Lastly, I would like to extend my gratitude to everyone who contributed to the exhibition. I express special thanks to the Vitamin Creative Space, Giuseppe Penone Studio, Studio Olafur Eliasson, Hiroshi Sugimoto Studio, Eva Albarran & Co., Gallery Konayagi, Sprüth Magers, the bereaved family of artist Jeoung Jae Choul, Baggat Art, Korean Nature Artists' Association-YATOO, Alternative Art Space Sonahmoo, MAGAMNEWS, Park Soo Keun Museum in Yanggu-gun, Seoul Museum of Art, artist Jung Ik Myeong, and Center for Eco Aesthetics and Art Research.

모든 생명의 시간과 공동의 집을 지켜 내는 일

김경란
국립현대미술관 학예연구사

내가 보기에 근대 체제 전체가 잘못된 인간관에 기초하고 있다. … 인간성에는 지나친 자신(自信)이 있어서, 그 본래의 성향대로 내버려둔다면 필연적으로 지금껏 지구상에 유례없는 깊고 넓은 비참을 인류에게 가져다 줄 것이다.―리처드 헨리 다나(1853)[1]

당연함의 역설

산업혁명에 동력을 제공한 석탄과 현대 기술문명을 이끈 석유 등의 화석연료는 수천만 년에 걸쳐 땅속에 저장되었지만 우리가 매우 짧은 시간 동안 상당한 양을 태우는 과정에서 현재의 기후위기가 초래되었다.[2] 지구 생태계 위기를 초래한 자본주의는 산업의 지구화, 생활의 도시화, 가치의 금융화를 통해 복합적으로 가속화되었고 코로나19(COVID-19) 사태는 그 결과 중 하나로 볼 수 있다.[3] 우리는 더러운 공기, 오염된 물, 매일 배출되는 쓰레기양 등을 통해 오늘날의 환경 문제를 어느 정도 피부로 직접 느끼며 살아가고 있지만, 여전히 많은 사람은 당장 생명을 위협하지 않는 여러 사회문제 중 하나로 인식하거나 순간의 편의를 위해 무시해 왔다.[4] 팬데믹으로 인간의 활동이 잠시 멈춘 시간은 역설적이게도 재앙과 같은 비극이 발생한 원인을 생각해 볼 계기가 되었다. 코로나19의 전파 속도에 따라 인간과 물류의 이동이 강제로 멈춰진 기간 동안 우리는 환경과 우리가 얼마나 촘촘히 연결되어 있는지 체감할 수 있었고, 기존의 방식대로 살아서는 안 된다는 위기의식을 절감했다. 각종 소비재의 물질 쓰레기가 늘어난 만큼 가치관과 정신은 설 자리를 잃었다. 그 어느 시대보다 정신적으로 빈곤한 지금에서야 우리가 그동안 맹목적으로 추구한 풍요와 부, 그리고 여유의 실체를 들여다보게 된 것이다. 당연하다고 여기며 반성 없이 해 온 생각과 행위가 결코 당연해서는 안 되는 것이었음을 깨닫는 동시에, 모두가 잘 살아야 내가 잘 살 수 있다는 당위를 생명의 위협 속에서 힘겹게 체득하고 있는 것이다.

To Protect the Time of All Living Things and Our Common Home

Kim Kyoungran
Curator, National Museum of Modern and Contemporary Art, Korea

The whole modern system seems to me to be grounded on a false view of man ... There is a spirit of self-confidence in it, which, left to its natural tendencies, will inevitably bring a deeper and wider woe upon man than earth has ever yet known. -Richard Henry Dana, 1853[1]

The paradox of 'taking for granted'

The present climate crisis has been created over a very short period by the process we have burnt significant amounts of fossil fuels such as coal that powered the Industrial Revolution and oil that led to modern technological civilization have been stored in the ground for tens of millions of years.[2] Capitalism, which caused the global ecological crisis, was accelerated in a complex way through the globalization of industries, urbanization of life, and financialization of values, and the COVID-19 crisis can be seen as one of the results.[3] Although we are living by directly feeling today's environmental problems to some extent through dirty air, polluted water, and the amount of garbage emitted every day, many people still perceive it as one of many social problems that do not threaten life right away, or ignored them for convenience's sake.[4] Paradoxically, the time when human activities were halted due to the pandemic gave us an opportunity to think about the cause of such a catastrophe. During the period when the movement of humans and logistics was forcibly stopped according to the speed of transmission of COVID-19, we were able to feel how tightly connected we are with the environment, and we felt a sense of crisis that we should not live they way we used to. As the material waste of various consumer goods has increased, the values and human spirit have lost their place. It is only now that we are mentally poorer than ever before, that we start to look into the true nature of abundance, wealth, and leisure that we have blindly pursued. At the same time, realizing that the thoughts and behaviors that

1. 모리스 버먼, 『미국은 왜 실패했는가』 김태언·김형수 옮김(녹색평론사, 2015), 5 참조.
2. 루이스 다트넬, 『오리진』 이충호 옮김(흐름출판, 2020), 380-381 참조.
3. 홍기빈, 「포스트 코로나(4): 새로운 체제」, 『코로나 사피엔스』 정관용 외 지음(인플루엔셜, 2020), 107-110 참조.
4. 배리 카머너, 『원은 닫혀야 한다』 고동욱 옮김(이음, 2014), 280 참조.

1. Morris Berman, *Why America Failed*, trans. Taeon Kim and Hyeongsoo Kim (Green Review, 2015), 5.
2. Lewis Dartnell, *Origins: how earth's history shaped human history*, trans. Chungho Lee (Heureum, 2020), 380-381.
3. Gibin Hong, "Post Corona (4): A New System," *Corona Sapience*, Kwanyoung Chung et al. (Influential, 2020), 107-110.
4. Barry Commoner, *Closing Circle: nature, man and technology*, trans. Dongwook Ko (Eum, 2014), 280.

공동의 집을 지켜 내기 위한 '당연함'의 재정의

모든 것의 연결성을 전제로 균형의 회복과 진정한 공진화를 지향하는
생태학적 세계관이 새로운 시대정신으로 급부상했다. 그러나
2015년 파리협정(Paris Agreement), ESG 경영, 탄소중립 같은
국가 차원의 정책 방향이나 국제 협의는 여러 징후가 심각해진 최
근에서야 등장했을 뿐, 지구 환경 위기에 대한 각성을 촉구하는 여
러 이벤트나 국제 협약은 1960년대부터 꾸준히 이어져 왔다.[5] 하
지만 반성과 개선, 행동을 촉구하며 반 세기 넘게 외쳐 온 목소리
들은 자본주의의 개발과 성장 속도를 따라갈 수 없었다. 쉬지 않고
가속 페달을 밟으며 주변을 돌아볼 겨를 없이 질주했던 날들은 우
리를 가속화된 시간 속에서 살게 했고, 그 속에서 온전히 감각하는
일은 불가능하다. 경험과 사고는 분절되고 파편화된 순간으로 부
유했다. 팬데믹은 그 질주의 궤도에서 강제로 멈춰 서 질주의 목표
와 잊어버린 의미를 돌아보게 한다. 이미 너무 늦었지만, 더 이상
늦어서는 안 되는 지금의 전환기는, 적어도 우리에게 이미 얻은 것
이나 앞으로 얻을 것보다 무엇을 잃게 될 것인지를 분명히 보여 주
고 있다.[6]

사회의 많은 요소가 급변하는 시대에 살고 있지만 관점과 인식의 변화
는 결코 쉽지 않기에 생태라는 주제를 전시로 풀어내는 데 고민이
많았다. 기존의 인간 중심적 시각에서의 '당연함'을 재정의하고 변
화된 태도와 실천으로 나아가기 위해, 생태학적 세계관에 관한 공
감대를 형성하는 일을 전시 기획의 큰 방향으로 잡았다. 전시의 여
정은 모든 생명이 살아가는 '공동의 집'[7]을 온전히 지키기 위해 다
양한 존재와 저마다의 관점을 인정하고 거대한 전체 속에서 공생
을 위한 시각을 새롭게 모색하는 과정이었다. 작품과 전시의 내용
적인 측면뿐 아니라 전시를 위한 소통 과정과 전시 조성 방식 등
전시에 관한 태도와 형식에서도 생태적 실천을 시도했다. 전시장
에 가벽을 제거하고 작품, 관객, 공간의 열린 생태계를 구현하는
것은 가벽이 당연시된 기존의 전시 관행에 질문을 던지는 일이었

we took for granted and conducted without reflection
should never have been taken for granted, we are strug-
gling to understand the inevitableness of the principle
that one can live well only when everyone is well, under
the recent threat of life.

Redefining 'taking for granted' to keep our common home
An ecological worldview that aims for the restoration of balance and veritable co-evolution on the premise of the
connectivity of everything has emerged as a new spirit of
the times. Although the direction of policies and international consultations at the national level such as the Paris Agreement on Climate Change, ESG management, and
carbon neutrality are only what we have recently begun
to pay attention to when various signs have become serious, a number of events and international conventions
calling for awareness of the global environmental crisis
have been steadily continuing since the 1960s.[5] However,
these voices, which have been shouting for more than
half a century, calling for reflection, improvement, and
action, could not catch up with the speed of development and growth of capitalism. The days when we have
stepped on the accelerator pedal without a break made
us live in accelerated state. It is impossible to fully sense
in this accelerated time-space. Experiences and thoughts
drifted in broken and fragmented moments. Fortunately,
the time when I was forced to stop in the orbit of the sprint
made us look back on the purpose of the speed and the
forgotten meaning. It is already too late, but it should not
be no longer too late because the current shift shows us
at least what we will lose more than what we have already gained or what we will gain.[6]

Although we live in an era in which many elements of society
are rapidly changing, it is never easy to change perspectives and perceptions. In order to redefine the "taking for
granted" of the existing human-centered perspective,

5.   1962년 출간된 레이첼 카슨의 『침묵의 봄』은 환경 문제에 대한 서구의 문제 의식을 촉발한
     계기로 언급된다. 1972년 스톡홀름에서 유엔인간환경회의(UNCHE)가 개최되었고 소위 '제
     네바 협약'이라 불리는 제1차 세계기후회의(WCC)가 1979년에 열렸다. 무한 성장을 경
     고하는 로마클럽 보고서 『성장의 한계』(1972)가 출간되었고, 아르네 네스는 1973년에 인간
     중심주의를 탈피하자는 '심층생태학'을 발표했으며, 제임스 러브록은 1978년에 '가이아 이
     론'을 주장한다. 예술에서 중요한 시도가 이어졌는데, 1982년 요제프 보이스가 시작한
     〈7,000그루의 참나무〉 프로젝트는 환경 문제를 예술을 통해 발언하는 생태-사회적 조각이
     라 일컬어진다. 1980년대부터는 세계 여러 지역에서 커뮤니티 기반의 실천 운동이 활발해
     졌고, 1988년에 기후변화에 관한 정부간 협의체(IPCC)가 설립되어 이후 유엔기후변화협약,
     교토의정서, 리우선언, 발리 로드맵, 칸쿤 회의를 거쳐 파리협정에 이르는 다양한 국제 협약
     이 이어졌다. 국립현대미술관, 『한국생태미술의 흐름과 현재: 자연미술에서 생태미술에 이르
     기까지』(국립현대미술관, 2021), 20-21 참조.
6.   토머스 프리드먼, 『늦어서 고마워』, 장경덕 옮김(21세기북스, 2017), 669 참조.
7.   공동의 집(Casa comune)은 프란치스코 교황이 저서 『찬미받으소서: 공동의 집을 돌보는
     것에 관한 회칙』(한국천주교중앙협의회, 2015)에서 지구·지구 생태계·지구 공동체 등을 포
     괄하는 의미로 사용한 단어이다.

5.   Rachel Carson's Silent Spring, published in 1962, is mentioned as a trigger
     to spark Western awareness of environmental issues. In 1972, the Unit-
     ed Nations Conference on the Human Environment (UNCHE) was held in
     Stockholm, and the First World Climate Conference (WCC), the so-called
     'Geneva Convention', was held in 1979. The Roman club report, "Limits to
     Growth" (72), which warned of infinite growth, was published, and in 1973,
     Arne Ness insisted on 'deep ecology' to break away from anthropocentrism.
     James Lovelock then advocated the Gaia theory in 1978. An important at-
     tempt was also made in art; The 7,000 Oak Trees project started by Joseph
     Beuys in 1982 is said to be an eco-social sculpture that addresses envi-
     ronmental issues through art. In the 1980s, community-based movements
     became active in various regions of the world, and the Intergovernmental
     Panel on Climate Change (IPCC) was established in 1988. Since then, var-
     ious international agreements were followed such as the United Nations
     Framework Convention on Climate Change, Kyoto Protocol, Rio Declaration,
     Bali Roadmap, Cancun Climate Change Conference After the meeting, and
     came to the Paris Agreement. MMCA, The Progress and State of Korean
     Ecological Art: From Nature Art to Ecolgocal Art, (2021), 20-21.
6.   Thomas Friedman, Thank you for being late, trnas. Kyungdeok Chang
     (Book21, 2017), 669.

고, 전시 종료 후 폐기물과 탄소발자국을 최대한 줄이는 것 또한 중요한 실천 과제였다. 여기에 더해, 1975년부터 국내에 나타나는 다양한 자연미술 관련 시도 중에서 생태학적 관점에서 재조명할 수 있는 단체, 작가, 전시·프로젝트를 조사·연구하는 사업과 아카이브 전시를 병행해 그동안 주목받지 못한 한국 생태미술을 들여다보는 계기를 마련했다. 존재하지만 가려지거나 잊혀진 존재를 생각하는 행위는 모든 요소의 연결을 지향하는 생태적 가치이기도 하다. 이렇게 해서 과천관 1전시실에서는 인식의 변화를 촉구하는 생태적 세계관을 중심으로 공론의 장을 펼치고, 중앙홀에서는 이러한 관점으로 재조명한 한국의 생태미술사를 살펴보는 전시 구성을 취했다.

전시라는 하나의 생태계

1전시실은 김주리, 나현, 백정기, 서동주, OAA(정규동), 장민승, 정소영의 신작과 올라퍼 엘리아손, 장뤽 밀렌, 주세페 페노네, 크리스티앙 볼탕스키, 히로시 스기모토의 구작으로 구성했다. 평소 사용하는 재료나 선보여 온 주제, 연구 영역 등에서 생태학적 접근을 해 온 작가들을 선정해 전시의 방향성을 공유하고 신작을 제작했다. 재료 조달과 운송 과정에서 발생하는 탄소를 줄이기 위해 국내 거주 작가를 중심으로 신작을 의뢰하고, 초기 구상 단계에서부터 '가벽이 제거된' 전시장 구성 계획을 공유하며 제작부터 철수까지 전 과정에서 폐기물을 만들지 않는 선택을 해 줄 것을 요청했다. 전시 디자인이 구체화된 시점에서는 전시 담당자와 디자인 팀 그리고 작가들이 모여 새로운 시도가 적용된 전시 디자인을 공유하고 합의하는 과정을 거쳤다. 서로의 입장과 의도를 설명하고 공감하는 과정 또한 생태학적 태도의 일부라고 보았다. 전시장은 모든 요소가 상호 작용하는 하나의 생태계로 구성했다. 모든 작품이 작가 개개인의 생태학적 연구와 문제의식 및 지향점을 내포하고 있기 때문에 어디부터 관람을 시작해도 문제될 것은 없지만, 기본적으로는 전시장 입구를 기점으로 작품의 주제와 메시지 중심의 내러티브를 형성하면서 작품을 배치하고 관람 동선을 기획했다.

전시는 자연을 타자화하며 인간 중심적 시각을 공고히 하고 세대를 거쳐 이를 학습하는 과정을 드러내는 정소영과 히로시 스기모토의 작업으로 시작한다. 세상을 인간의 시각으로 수집, 분류, 전시하는 박물관학의 관습에서 벗어난 두 작업은, 기존 시각을 비워 내고 새로운 관점으로 전향할 수 있는 가능성을 보여 준다. 생태학적 세계관에 관한 공감은 '상호연결성'을 인정할 때 시작하므로, 그 연결성을 구체화하는 개념으로 '시간'에 접근했다. 지구 역사의 장대한 흐름에서 인간의 시간은 작은 구간에 불과함을 성찰하게 하는 올라퍼 엘리아손의 설치와 김주리의 젖은 흙 작업은 작은 재료 속에 압축된 시간성과 거대하게 축적된 땅과 생명의 시간을 대조적으로 보여 주며 생태학적 사유를 유도한다.

and to move forward with changed attitudes and practices, the major direction of the exhibition planning was set to form a consensus on the ecological worldview. The process of acknowledging the diversity of existence and each point of view and seeking new perspectives for symbiosis in a huge whole became the journey of the exhibition to keep our common home where all living things live.[7] Therefore, ecological practice was attempted not only in terms of the semantic context of works and exhibitions, but also in the attitudes and formalities of the exhibition, such as the communication process and construction of the exhibition. Removing drywalls in the exhibition hall and creating an open ecosystem consisting of artworks, audiences, and spaces can be said to throw a question on the convention of making drywalls in the process of exhibition preparation. Also, it was an important task to minimize industrial waste and carbon footprint from the artwork installations and exhibition construction after the exhibition was over.

In addition, among various natural art-related attempts since 1975, meaningful approaches of groups, artists, and exhibition projects that can be re-examined from an ecological point of view are investigated and researched and thus an archived exhibition is held to look into Korean ecological art which has not been noticed until now. Contemplating an existence that exists but is hidden or forgotten is also an ecological value-oriented toward the connection of all elements. In this way, Gallery 1 became a forum for public discussion on the ecological worldview that urges a change of perception, and the Main Hall functioned as a fountain to reflect the history of ecological art in Korea re-examined from ecological point of view.

Making an exhibition as another ecosystem

Gallery 1 consists of new artworks by Kim Juree, Na Hyun, Beak Jungki, Seo Dongjoo, Jang Minseung, OAA (Jung Kyudong), and Chung Soyoung, and existing artworks by Olafur Eliasson, Jean-Luc Mylayne, Giuseppe Penone, Christian Boltanski, and Hiroshi Sugimoto. Artists who have taken an ecological approach for the materials and subjects in their research and artwork making process were selected to participate in the direction of this exhibition by creating a new body of works. In order to reduce carbon footprint generated in the course of material procurement and transportation, we asked to make new works from artists residing in Korea, sharing the intention of the exhibition design with "removing drywalls"

---

7. The term 'common home (Casa comune)' was used with reference to *On Care for Our Common Home: The Encyclical Letter Laudato Si'* published by Pope Francis in 2015 and means inclusively the earth, its ecosystem, and earth community etc.

주세페 페노네의 대리석 조각은 표면에서 뻗어 나오는 새로운 생명의 가능성을 암시하며 순환과 연결이라는 생명의 원리를 환기한다. 흑연이 지나간 흔적으로 미술관 전시 역사를 드러낸 벽면 위에 대리석에 응축된 시간을 중첩시켜 새로운 생명 탄생의 배경으로 삼았다. 평생을 새와 교감하며 생활해 온 장뤽 밀렌은 새와 함께한 시간을 새의 시점으로 기록했는데, 대상화의 대표적인 도구인 사진을 자연과의 교감을 기록하는 수단으로 사용하면서 따뜻한 울림을 전한다. 여러 생물의 시각 인지 진화 과정을 연구한 서동주의 작업은 모든 생물은 저마다의 관점으로 생존하고 진화하고 있다는 사실을 체험적으로 구현한다. 거대한 안구 공간 속에서 수많은 생물의 눈동자에 포착된 자신을 마주하는 역전된 상황은 인간의 시각이 얼마나 편협한지를 깨닫게 한다.

'본다'는 행위에 관한 연구는 백정기의 점토 부적과 자연 색소로 인화한 사진으로 이어진다. 점토로 만든 육각 타일 작업은 사막화의 위기를 미신처럼 대하는 우리의 태도를 상기시키고, 무의식 중에 소비하고 학습해 온 가공된 자연의 이미지를 자연 색소를 사용해 재구성하는 시도는 자연을 바라보는 우리의 시선이 어떠했는가를 성찰하게 한다. 나현은 대만 원주민에 관한 연구를 바탕으로 식물 사진과 선반 조형물을 선보이는데, 자연을 경외하며 서로의 영역을 지키는 원주민의 삶은 자연과 인간의 균형의 깨진 지점을 들여다보게 만든다. 아슬아슬하게 균형을 맞추고 있는 선반은 단호하게 금기를 지켜내는 것이 바로 모두가 함께 사는 비결이라는 메시지를 전달한다. 크리스티앙 볼탕스키는 바람이 일깨워 주는 영혼의 종소리로 사람, 대지, 하늘, 그리고 눈에 보이지 않는 모든 요소가 하나 되는 경지를 연출한다. 눈에 보이는 것뿐 아니라 보이지 않는 모든 요소가 서로 연결되어 영향을 주고받는 상태가 바로 생태다. OAA(정규동)는 전시장 끝에 촘촘하게 연결돼 서로 의지하는 빛의 기둥을 설치했다. 팽팽하게 당겨진 가는 실이 만들어 낸 큰 빛의 기둥은 생명의 구조와 균형의 원리를 직관적으로 보여 준다. 마지막으로, 중앙홀 블랙박스 안 360도 원형 스크린에서는 대공원-동물원-경마장-미술관을 축으로 과천의 생태를 재해석한 장민승의 영화가 상영된다. 근과거와 현재의 기록을 바탕으로 한 입체 영상은 인간의 계획과 행위의 결과가 다시 인간을 향하는 순환 고리 속에 우리를 위치시킨다. 이처럼 1전시실에서는 이번 전시를 위해 제작된 국내 작가들의 신작과 해외 작가들의 작품이 어우러져 인간과 자연의 관계를 상호 존중과 교감의 관점으로 제시하며, 이를 통해 균형과 조화를 추구하는 진정한 공진화(供進化)에 관한 공감대를 유도한다.

잊혀지고 소외된 부분과의 연결

한국 미술계에도 앞서 살핀 생태학적 태도를 일찍이 실천한 작가들이 있다. 1970년대 국내 미술계에는 모더니즘이나 기존 질서에서 벗

from the initial conception stage while generating no waste in the entire process from production to withdrawal. Once the exhibition design was ready, the curatorial team, design team, and participating artists met up online to discuss and agree on the design concept to which the new attempt was applied. The process of explaining and empathizing with each other has also become a part of the ecological attitude. The exhibition hall is structured as an ecosystem in which all elements interact, and since the works contain the ecological research, problematics, and direction of each artist, it does not matter which work you start with, but we made the entrance of the Gallery 1 as a start point and arrangement and layout of artworks have been made according to the narrative of the exhibition centered on the subject and message of each work.

The exhibition begins with artworks by Chung Soyoung and Hiroshi Sugimoto that delineate the process through which people have learned to otherize nature based on a human-centric viewpoint. Starting from the custom of museology to collect, classify, and display the world from a human perspective, these two works show the possibility of emptying out the old viewpoint and turning to a new perspective. Since empathy for the ecological worldview begins when we acknowledge 'interconnection,' we approached 'time' as a concept that embodies that connectivity. The artworks by Olafur Eliasson and Kim Juree locate the visitors within the context of the earth's time and remind them of the insignificance of the time of mankind as a segment of the planet's extensive history. Eliasson's sculpture and Kim's wet soil installation contrast and emphasize the compressed temporality in small materials and the vastly accumulated time of land and life.

A marble sculpture by Giuseppe Penone hints at the possibility of new life sprawling from its surface, calling to mind the cyclical and interconnective nature of life. The time condensed on marble is superimposed on the gallery wall that reveals the history of the museum's exhibition by frottage technique which shows traces of the passing of graphite, and used as the background for the birth of a new life. Jean-Luc Mylayne, who has spent his life communing with birds, documents moments of kinship from an avian perspective. By using photography, a representative tool of objectification, as a means of recording the time of communion with nature, it conveys a warm resonance. Seo Dongjoo's work is a study on the evolutionary process of visual perception of various living things, and it empirically embodies the fact that all living things are surviving and evolving from their own point of view. The inverted situation in which we enter the space of a huge eyeball and see ourselves caught in the eyes of countless creatures makes us realize just how narrow our vision is.

The act of "seeing" continues through Beak Jungki's natural

어나 새로움과 대안을 모색하는 다양한 시도가 존재했다. 지금처럼 환경 문제가 가시화되지도 않았고 '생태'라는 용어도 일반적으로 사용되지 않았지만, 1970년대 중반부터 생태학적 법칙과 세계관을 내포하거나 실천한 의미 있는 작업들이 등장하기 시작했다. 이번 전시를 계기로 그러한 작업을 전개해 온 단체와 작가 및 전시, 프로젝트를 수집·정리·분류하는 사업을 시작해 그동안 주목 받지 못했던 한국의 생태미술사 연구를 위한 기초를 다지고자 했다.[8] 중앙홀에는 그 사업의 첫 성과를 바탕으로 공존과 공생의 가치를 구현한 작업들을 살펴보는 아카이브 전시를 마련해, 전시장을 벗어나 야외로 나갔던 자연미술과 환경미술의 궤적 속에서 한국 생태미술의 시작점과 흐름을 추적한다. 1960년대부터 환경 위기에 관한 각성을 촉구하는 세계적 이슈가 대두되기 시작했고 1970년대 전세계적으로 자연과 인간의 공존에 관한 논의가 시작되는 시점에 한국에서도 바깥을 향해 기존과 다른 가치를 좇는 움직임이 포착된다는 사실은 매우 유의미하다.

그중 흰 광목을 바위 허리에 둘러 하늘-땅-사람이 하나되는 경지를 구현한 전국광의 〈수평선〉(1975)을 재현한 퍼포먼스 기록은 한국 생태미술의 정신적 기원을 보여 준다. 자연과 야생이라는 바깥을 향해 질문을 던지고 의미를 되받는 취지를 새겨 '야투(野投)'라는 실험 단체를 이끈 임동식은 한국 생태미술의 시작점에서 큰 줄기를 형성하는 작가로,[9] 원본 기록이 없어 작품의 진가를 알리기 어려웠던 전국광의 〈수평선〉을 재현하는 퍼포먼스를 총감독했다. 임동식의 〈선사시대 다가가기〉(2005)는 어두운 동굴을 벗어나 빛과 본질을 향해 화면 가운데로 나아가는 사람들의 순수한 지향에 관람객을 동참시킨다. 끊임없이 서로 영향을 주고받는 자연의 일부로 인간을 위치시키고 공생의 참뜻을 모색하는 임동식의 작업은 한국 생태미술의 정신적 본류를 형성한다.

정재철의 작업은 작가가 여행과 이동의 수행적 과정에서 남긴 수집품과 기록을 중심으로 구성했다. 정재철에게 작업과 삶은 스스로 많은 것과 연결되는 과정인 동시에 흩어지고 잊혀진 것을 연결해 주는 과정이었다. 작가는 국경과 경계를 넘나들며 현지인들과 직접 소통하는 과정을 작업의 중심에 두었고, 목적과 결과를 향한 이동이 아닌 여행의 과정 그 자체를 작업으로 삼았다. 전시에서는 과천을 근거지로 오래 작업했던 작가가 과천의 재개발 지역에서 수집한 돌과 이를 바탕으로 한 드로잉, 재개발 과정을 담은 기록과 지도를 통해 우리가 잊고 지내던 기억을 되살린다. 기후위기에 관해 적극적으로 발언해 온 활동가이기도 한 이경호의 영상은 여러 도

---

8. 결과물은 『한국 생태미술의 흐름과 현재: 자연미술에서 생태미술에 이르기까지』(국립현대미술관, 2021)로 출간되었다.
9. 류철하, 「임동식_동방소년 탐문기」, 『임동식_동방소년 탐문기』, 전시 도록(대전시립미술관, 2016), 19-21 참조.

dye photographs and talisman made of clay. The work reflects on our attitude toward superstitious treatment even towards the crisis of desertification, and attempts to reconstruct processed images of nature that are consumed and learned using natural pigments leave questions about how we have seen nature and related us to it. Na Hyun presents photographs of plants and a shelf installation based on his research on the Formosans of Taiwan, whose lives, in which nature is revered and others' territories are respected, awaken us to the wisdom and balance between nature and humans we have lost. The spiritual bell sound in the video work by Christian Boltanski allows visitors to experience a spectacle in which everything from people to the land, sky, and even invisible elements come together as one. Ecology is a state in which all elements, both visible and invisible, are interconnected and influence each other. OAA (Jung Kyudong) presents tightly interconnected and interdependent columnal structures that convey messages of harmony, balance, respect, and consideration. The large pillars of light supported by the tautly pulled thin thread intuitively suggest the structure of life and the principle of balance. Lastly, inside the black box located in the Main Hall, a movie by Jang Minseung unfolds on a cylindrical 360-degree screen, reinterpreting the ecology of Gwacheon region, which is surrounded by the Seoul Grand Park, SEOUL ZOO, LetsRun Park Seoul, and the museum. Based on the documentary records of the past and present, the work places us in a cycle in which the results of human plans and actions return to humans. The interplay among new works of Korean artists as well as the works by overseas artists allows us to contemplate the relationship between humans and nature in mutual respect and sympathy, seeks balance and harmony, and shares the bond of co-evolution.

Connecting with forgotten and marginalized areas
Some artists put into early action of the ecological worldview. In the Main Hall, an archive exhibition shedding new light on works that embody the value of coexistence and symbiosis under the category of "Korean ecological art" is being held. The Korean art world in the 1970s saw various attempts to seek novelty and alternatives to modernism and the existing order. Among them, we analyzed the starting point and tendency of Korean ecological art in the flow of nature art and environmental art which took nature as an element and subject away from the white cubes. Although the term "ecology" was not commonly used at that time, the purpose is to lay the foundation for the description of ecological art history in Korea by collecting, organizing, and classifying the operations, works, and group activities that connote or embody ecological principles and worldviews.[8] It is very meaningful that the seriousness of environmental destruction began

시를 배경으로 현대사회의 대표적인 석유계 플라스틱 제품인 비닐 봉지를 등장시키면서 지금 마주하는 환경 파괴의 심각성을 직시하고 추적하는 적극적인 행동의 필요성을 역설한다. 지구 어디서나 발견되는 비닐 봉지처럼 인간의 무의식적인 행위가 야기한 파괴의 결과는 지역과 국가의 경계를 초월해 우리 자신에게 되돌아오기 때문이다. 김보중은 도시의 공원이나 도시 주변에 형성된 숲을 거니는 경험을 그리는 도시 생태 부문의 작가다. 도시의 숲은 개발에 훼손된 자연이거나 이식된 형태로 남은, 온전한 자연이 아니다. 비정형으로 분절되고 어슷하게 조립된 캔버스는 자연을 부분적으로 감각하는 도시인의 경험을 옮긴 것으로 이는 우리 대부분이 자연을 접하는 방식이기도 하다.

중앙홀 가운데에는 1980년대 초부터 지금까지, 자연미술에서 생태미술에 이르는 범주 에서 활동을 이어오고 있는 여러 단체와 작가, 주요 전시와 프로젝트에 관한 자료와 함께 이번 전시 준비 과정에서 참고한 생태 관련 도서를 비치했다. 유연하게 흐르는 생태계처럼 구조물 없이 중앙홀의 벽과 바닥을 활용한 아카이브 구성은 관람객이 주체가 되어 작품과 자료 사이의 의미를 잇도록 유도한다. 끊임없이 서로 영향을 주고 받는 생태의 특징을 전시의 형식으로 취하면서 다양한 층위의 소통을 가능케 하는 방식으로 생태미술에 관한 관심을 확장시키고자 했다.

생태학적 대전환을 향하여

인간 중심적 관점을 극복하고 생태학적 사유와 실천을 모색하는 생태미술을 조명하는 것은 미술의 언어로 동시대와 미래를 향해 새로운 가능성을 여는 일이다. 큰 의미에서 생명은 한 개체의 탄생과 죽음 사이의 시간을 의미하는 것이 아니라 개체의 생사가 반복되며 흘러가는 영속성을 뜻하므로,[10] 생태 가치의 회복은 각 개체를 넘어 연속된 시간의 축에서 고려하는 것이 마땅하다. 유장한 대지의 역사에서 한 종만 앞서 나가는 진화란 존재하지 않는다. 공생을 전제로 한 진화만이 지속될 수 있는데, 서로가 서로를 향상시키는 진화를 지향할 때 비로소 공생이 가능한 것이다.[11] 많은 전문가가 이 생태학적 세계관을 바탕으로 한 생태적 대전환의 필요를 역설한다. 일상에서 플라스틱 빨대나 일회용 종이컵 사용을 줄이는 것도 의미 있는 실천이지만, 다양한 생명이 함께 살 수 있는 근본적인 변화를 이끌어 내기 위해서는 무엇보다 산업의 전환과 단호한 결단이 실행되어야 한다. 사회생물학의 창시자인 에드워드 윌슨(Edward O. Wilson)은 생태 회복을 위해 지구의 절반을 자연 보호 구역으로 지정하자는 '지구의 절반(Half Earth)' 운동을 시작했다.[12] 파리협정이나 탄소중립에 관한 국제 협의도 순조롭게 이행되지 않는 상황에서 '지구의 절반'은 먼 길처럼 보이지만, 그렇더라도 우리는 부단히 변화해야 한다. 생태적 재난의 시대에 우리가 다음 세대에 물려줄 행동 양식은 소비와 소유가 아니라 배려와

to rise in the 1960s, and at a time when discussions about coexistence with nature began to be discussed around the world in the 1970s, the fact that Korean artists also pursued values that are different from the existing ones.

For this archive exhibition, we tried to find the spiritual origin of Korean ecological art through the performance record that has been made in the course of representation of Chun Kook-Kwang's *Horizon* (1975). The work remained unknown because of the absence of the original photograph and Rim Dong Sik who witnessed the work himself directed the representational performance and produced a video and photographs which embody the realization of the oneness of sky, earth, and people by wrapping a white cotton cloth around the waist of a rock. Rim, who also led an experimental group called 'YATOO,' with the intention of asking questions to nature and receiving the meaning that the wild throws back, is a figure who forms a big stem at the beginning of Korean ecological art.[9] His *Approaching Prehistoric Times* (2005) invites viewers to join in the pure intention of people walking towards light and essence in the middle of the painting, out of the dark cave. Rim's work, which places humans as a part of nature that is constantly influencing each other, and seeks the true meaning of symbiosis, forms the spiritual mainstay of ecological art.

Jeoung Jae Choul's work consists of collections and records left behind in the performative process of travel and movement. The artist has taken the process of communicating with local people across borders and has focused on the process of travel itself. The redevelopment process that took place in Gwacheon region, where the artist stayed for a long time, revives our forgotten memories through the collection of stones and discarded flowerpots, drawings, records, and maps produced by the artist. For Jeoung, work and life were a process of connecting with many things and at the same time connecting things that were scattered and forgotten through his bodily engagement. Lee Kyung Ho, an activist-artist who speaks on climate change, uses plastic bags, a representative petroleum-based plastic product of modern society, in the landscapes of various cities. It also emphasizes the need for active action to face and track the current seriousness of environmental destruction, rather than avoid it. This is because the repercussions of our unconscious actions, such as plastic bags found everywhere on Earth, transcend regions and borders, and return to

8.   The result of research and collection of materials is published as a source book *The Progress and State of Korean Ecological Art: From Nature Art to Ecological Art* (MMCA, 2021).
9.   Cheolha Ryu, *Rim Dong Sik _ Interrogatory records of a boy from East* (Daejeon Museum of Art, 2016), 19-21.

존중을 바탕으로 한 균형·공생·연대의 가치이며, 이 관점이 세대를 거쳐 학습될 때 비로소 건강한 긴장 관계를 바탕으로 한 생태학적 대전환이 가능할 것이다. 쉽고 빠르고 풍요로웠던 어제에서 불편하고 느리고 가난한 오늘로 전환하는 것만이 모두가 함께 사는 내일로 가는 유일한 길이다.

ourselves. Kim Bo Joong is an artist in the urban ecology sector, depicting the experience of walking in a city park or forest formed or left around the city. The forests that city dwellers visit are not pure nature but they exist in the form of natural elements left behind or transplanted by human needs. The atypically segmented and obliquely assembled canvas conveys the experience of city dwellers partially sensing nature and represents the way we interact with nature.

In the center of the Main Hall, archive materials and publications related to various groups and artists active since the early 1980s and books on ecology topics referenced in the preparation of the exhibition are on display. Like a flexibly flowing ecosystem, this archive exhibition used only the walls and floor of the architecture without any artificial structures in order to allow the viewer to take the lead and connect the meaning between the works and the documents. It was intended to expand interest in ecological art through a method that enables communication at various levels while taking the characteristics of ecology that constantly influence each other as a formal language of the exhibition.

Towards ecological shift

Ecological art, which overcomes the anthropocentric perspective and seeks ecological thinking and practice, opens up new possibilities for the present and future with the language of art. In a large sense, the term 'life' does not mean the time between the birth and death of an individual, but the permanence that repeats the cycles of the life and death of an individual,[10] the restoration of ecological value should be considered on the continuous axis of time beyond each individual. There is no evolution in which only one species advances in the rich history of the earth.

Only evolution on the premise of symbiosis can be sustained, and symbiosis is possible only when each of them pursues an evolution that improves each other.[11] Many experts are saying that a great ecological shift is necessary based on an ecological worldview. Reducing the use of plastic straws and disposable paper cups in our daily life is also a meaningful practice, but above all, industrial transformation and fundamental and decisive decisions will be needed to bring about a change in which various lives can live together. Edward O. Wilson, the founder of sociobiology, started the 'Half-Earth' movement, which argues the need to designate half of the earth as a nature

10. 에두아르도 콘, 『숲은 생각한다』, 차은정 옮김(사월의 책, 2018), 370-373 참조.
11. 다카기 진바부로, 『지금 자연을 어떻게 볼 것인가』, 김원식 옮김(녹색평론사, 2006), 165-167; 최재천, 『손잡지 않고 살아남은 생명은 없다』(샘터, 2014), 64 참조.
12. 에드워드 윌슨의 『Half-Earth: Our Planet's Fight for Life』는 2016년 미국에서 초판이 출간됐고, 국내에는 『지구의 절반』(사이언스북스, 2017)이라는 제목으로 번역 출간됐다.

10. Eduardo Kohn, *How forests think: toward an anthropology beyond the human*, trans. Eunjeong Cha (April Books, 2018), 370-373.
11. Takagi Jinzaburo, *How to see nature now*, trans. Wonsik Kim (Green Review, 2006), 165-167; Jaechun Choi, *There is no life that survived without holding hands each other* (Samtoh, 2014), 64.

reserve for ecological restoration.[12] 'Half-Earth' seems like a long way to go because the Paris climate agreement and international negotiations on carbon neutrality are not going ideally, but we have to constantly change now and there is no other way. In the era of ecological disaster, the behavior we should pass on to the next generation is not consumption and possession, but the values of balance, symbiosis, and solidarity based on consideration and respect. Learning this perspective from generation to generation will eventually lead to a great ecological transformation based on healthy tensions. The shift from the easy, fast and prosperous yesterday to the inconvenient, slow and poor today is a shortcut to a tomorrow in which everyone lives together.

12.   Edward Wilson's *Half-Earth* was first published in 2016, and a Korean translation was published by Science Books in 2017.

《대지의 시간》 전시 형식에 관하여

김용주
국립현대미술관 전시운영디자인기획관

《대지의 시간》은 '공생, 연결, 균형'을 중심 개념으로 둔 기획으로, 이
    전시 기획의 출발점으로 삼은 것은 바로 '생태적 세계관'이었다.
    인간 중심적 사고에서 벗어나 지구상에 공존하는 다른 생명체로
    시선을 확장하고, 우리가 지구에 머무는 시간의 유한함과 더불어
    인간은 광대한 우주의 시간 속에 잠시 머물다 가는 공생자임을 전
    하려 했다. 그렇다면 이러한 생태적 관점을 담는 전시의 '형식'은
    어떠해야 할까?

1전시실
《대지의 시간》은 전시가 끝나면 공간을 채우고 있던 구조물이나 가구
    가 고스란히 폐기물이 되는 상황을 벗어나기 위해 그 출발에서부
    터 전시로 인한 폐기물을 최소화한다는 기준을 세웠고, 그에 따라
    '공기막 구조'라는 새로운 구조체를 도입했다. 공기막 구조는 표피
    를 형성하는 얇은 탄성 재질과 내부를 채우는 공기가 그 재료로,

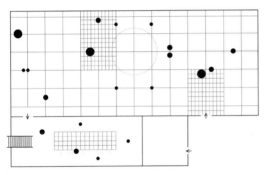

graphic image©Yoon Jiwon

On the Format of the Exhibition *Time of the Earth*

Kim Yongju
Director for Design & Management team, National Museum
    of Modern and Contemporary Art, Korea

Adopting "symbiosis," "connection," and "balance" as key
    concepts, the format of the exhibition *Time of the Earth*
    starts with an "ecological worldview" that expands be-
    yond an anthropocentric point of view to consider the
    perspectives of organisms coexisting with humans on
    the planet. At the same time, it encourages us to think
    about the finiteness of the time humans spend on Earth
    and our role as symbiotes who have arrived to share a
    single moment of time within the vastness of the uni-
    verse. Through what format might this exhibition most
    effectively reflect its ecological worldview?

Gallery 1
First, the exhibition adopts a concept similar to recycling;
    from the outset, it has taken an approach to reduce the
    amount of waste produced and avoid the unnecessary
    disposal of exhibition items when the event is over. In de-
    veloping this approach, one idea that arose was that of a
    pneumatic structure. This structure consists of a thin,
    elastic membrane filled with air. Once the exhibition is
    over, the air ball can be deflated, allowing the structure
    that served as the exhibition's space configuration to be
    entirely stored inside a small box measuring 1.5 cubic
    meters. The pneumatic structure was designed to form a
    sphere when inflated, a shape that calls the mind the
    ways in which all life originates in small circles. For the
    surface, reflective materials such as mirrors are used to
    visualize the key concepts "symbiosis," "connection,"
    and "balance" as they reflect you, me, and us.
By objectifying the artwork and viewers alike, the reflective
    spheres in the exhibition setting help viewers perceive
    how they are both part of the ecosystem and agents with
    a voice, just like artists.[1] The exhibition floor plan uses a
    grid system to assign positions and areas to the artworks,
    with spherical pneumatic structures placed among them
    like commas in a sentence. In this way, the design of the
    space creates flows of movement and unit areas of dif-
    ferent sizes without any physical partitions. The round
    pneumatic structures are assigned three different levels
    by height: those at ground level (level zero) serve to mark
    pathways within the space, while one-meter-high spheres
    create visual connections and flows of movement among
    the works and two-meter-high spheres illuminate their
    surroundings through reflected rather than directly pro-
    duced light. The pneumatic structures have individual air
    pressure autoregulation systems that allow each of them

전시 후 공기를 빼면 전시실의 공간 구조를 형성했던 크고 작은 구조체들은 1.5×1.5×1.5미터의 상자 안에 오롯이 담기게 된다. 공기막 구조의 형태는 모든 생명체가 작은 원으로부터 출발한다는 점에 착안해 구형으로 계획했고, 그 표피는 거울과 같은 반사 재질을 사용해 이 구조가 너, 나, 우리를 반사하도록 만들어 공생 관계와 연결, 균형의 메시지를 시각화했다.

전시장에 배치된 구형의 반사체들은 작품과 관객을 한데 묶어 대상화함으로써, 관객 스스로가 생태의 한 부분이며 작가와 같은 발화의 주체임을 인지토록 한다.[1] 전시 평면은 그리드 좌표를 통해 작품이 놓이는 위치와 면적을 배분하고, 마치 문장에 쉼표를 위치시키듯 작품들 사이에 구형 공기막 구조를 배치함으로써 전시 공간은 물리적으로 분절되지 않으면서도 다양한 크기의 단위 영역과 흐름을 만들어 낸다. 또한, 구형 공기막 구조의 높이를 3단계로 나누어 그라운드(0) 레벨에 위치한 볼은 공간에서 동선을 구획하는 역할을 담당하고, 레벨 1미터 높이의 볼은 작품과 작품 사이의 시각적 연결과 흐름을 만들어내며, 레벨 2미터 높이의 볼은 일종의 반사체로서 직접 조명이 아닌 반사광으로 주변의 조도를 확보하는 역할을 수행하도록 했다. 특히 공기막 구조는 각각 공기압 자기 제어 장치를 통해 스스로 부피 값을 조절하며 전시 기간 동안 서서히 공기 주입 양을 줄여 생명체가 겪는 형상의 변화를 표현한다. 이는 공기로 가득 채워져 가벼운 물리적 질량을 갖는 이 구들이 역설적이게도 가장 무거운 의미적 질량을 내포하며 전시장에 입체적 지형을 형성한다.[2]

제로(0) 레벨 아카이브

이번 전시에서 국립현대미술관 과천의 중앙홀은 '한국 생태미술의 흐름과 현재'를 보여주는 아카이브 영역으로 기획됐다. 특히 《대지의 시간》 아카이브는 전시 후 폐기물이 되는 좌대나 가구를 따로 제작하지 않는다는 전제하에 '펼치고 보다'라는 아카이브 전시에 필요한 기본 행위를 자유롭게 행할 수 있도록 열린 개념의 동적 장으로 설계했다. 즉, 장소라는 개념을 생성하는 것은 공간을 나누는 구조체나 가구가 아니라 인간의 행위임을 설계의 출발점으로 삼았다. 이에 따라 반사도가 다른 두 재질(카펫과 미러 패널)을 단 차이 없이 중앙홀 바닥에 시공해 재질의 반사도 차이만으로 영역의 성격을 구분하는 이른바 '제로(0) 레벨 아카이브' 전시 방식을 새롭게 선보였다. 미러 패널과 같이 반사도가 높은 재질로 마감한 영역은 심리적 집중도와 접근의 조심성이 생기기에 자료와 아카이브 작품을 배치했고, 반사도가 낮고 폭신한 매트 영역에는 낮은 방석들을 배치해 자료를 살펴보는 관람자의 영역이 되도록 했다. 또한 물리적 경계 없이 펼쳐진 제로(0) 레벨 아카이브에 사용한 재료는 지난 전시에서 사용했던 패널을 재사용한 것으로, 전시 후 새활용 센터로 보내 또 다른 용도로 활용될 수 있도록 재료의 순환을

to adjust their volume level. Over the course of the exhibition, the amount of air in the balls will be gradually reduced, representing the changes in form that organisms undergo. Despite having lighter physical mass due to being filled with air, the globes ironically carry the heaviest weight in terms of meaning, forming a three-dimensional landscape in the exhibition space.[2]

Zero Level Archive

The design of this exhibition positions the Main Hall at MMCA Gwacheon as an archival space that presents trends and current developments in Korean ecological art. In particular, the *Time of the Earth* archive forgoes the creation of pedestals or exhibition furniture that would be disposed of as waste after the exhibition. Instead, the design achieves a dynamic, open-concept place to allow the basic activities conducted an archival exhibition, namely "displaying" and "viewing," to be performed freely. As a starting point, the design adopts the notion that assigning something as a "place" is a human act rather than a matter of structures or fixtures partitioning an area. Executing this idea involves placing two materials with different reflectivity (carpet and mirror panels) on the Central Hall's floor, a designated space without heightening, to present a new exhibition approach: the "zero-level ar-

graphic image©Yoon Jiwon

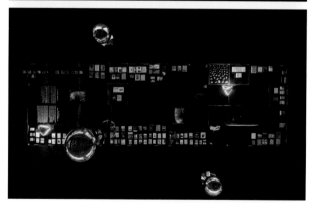

photography©image Joom and Jang Jun-Ho

계획하고 있다.

'제로(0) 레벨 아카이브'에서 관람자들은 스스로의 행위를 통해 공간의 성격과 기능을 규정하게 되며, 관람 시간이 끝나고 사람들이 머물지 않을 때의 중앙홀은 그 자체로 비어 있는 '광장'과 같은 '공간'이 된다.

chive" in which areas are distinguished solely by differences in the floor's reflectivity. The use of highly reflective materials such as mirror panels grants a section a sense of psychological focus and caution when visitors approach it. Informational and archival work is presented in these sections, while the softer and less reflective carpeted areas are outfitted with low cushions to provide a space for viewers to examine the material. The physically unbounded spread zero-level archive uses materials recycled from panels from past exhibitions, and the exhibition plan calls for them to recycled for reuse again by being sent to an upcycling center after the event.

In the zero-level archive, viewers determine the character and functions of the space through their own actions, and once the viewing period is over and visitors are gone, the Central Hall will become something akin to an empty "plaza" in its own right.

1.   서현, 「전시 디자인이 생태를 이야기하는 방식」 2021년 12월, https://brunch.co.kr/@oser/10.
2.   같은 글.

1.   Seohyeon, "Exhibition Design—Methods that Address Ecology (exhibition critique)," December 15, 2021, https://brunch.co.kr/@oser/10.
2.   Ibid.

대지의 시간

정소영	Chung Soyoung
히로시 스기모토	Hiroshi Sugimoto
올라퍼 엘리아손	Olafur Eliasson
김주리	Kim Juree
주세페 페노네	Giuseppe Penone
서동주	Seo Dongjoo
장뤽 밀렌	Jean-Luc Mylayne
백정기	Beak Jungki
나현	Na Hyun
크리스티앙 볼탕스키	Christian Boltanski
OAA(정규동)	OAA (Jung Kyudong)
장민승	Jang Minseung

Time of the Earth

우리가 발 딛고 살아가는 지질 구조에 대한 관심에서 비롯된 연구를 기반으로 작업하는 정소영은 최근에 그 관심을 해저로 확장했다. 작품 제목 〈미드나잇 존〉은 태양의 빛이 미치지 않는 심해의 영역을 지칭하며, 작가는 의도적으로 바다 혹은 수족관 같은 이미지로 설치를 했다. 작품은 크게 4개의 진열장, 4개의 영상, 2개의 설치물과 QR코드로 구성되어 있다. 신작을 구상하는 과정에서 작가는 국립현대미술관 과천관 수장고 복도에서 폐기되기를 기다리며 보관되어 있던 진열장을 재활용했다. 작가는 이 진열장이 자연을 타자화하여 발굴, 수집, 조사, 분류한 후 전시를 하는 일련의 행위를 압축하고 있기 때문에, 기존의 인간 중심적 시각을 잘 보여 준다고 보았다. 그렇게 인간의 시각으로 체계화되고 박제된 대상은 진열장에 놓여 여러 세대에게 이러한 관점을 학습시키는 역할을 수행해 왔다. 작가는 이 일련의 행위와 관점으로부터 벗어나고자 진열장 안에 아무 대상 없이 흰 염화나트륨만 얕게 깔아 두었다. 진열장 옆에 있는 영상에는 심해의 지형을 탐사하는 과정이 담겨 있다. 이 영상은 실제로 심해를 탐사하는 모습이 아니라, 작가가 해양시료도서관에서 대여한 작은 망간, 해저화산암, 열수암석 등을 정밀 촬영해서 마치 탐사선을 타고 심해를 비추며 항해하는 것처럼 편집한 영상이다. 수집, 분류, 전시의 대상이 사라지고 그간 쉽게 상상하지 못했던 저 깊고 어두운 심해와 심야의 미술관 풍경으로 들어선 관람객은 자연스럽게 자신과 심해를 연결시키게 된다. 저 먼 우주와 마찬가지로, 이 심해의 풍경도 우리 모두가 살아가는 생태계의 구성 요소이기에, 심해를 상상하는 행위는 우리를 보다 큰 맥락 속에 위치시키는 일이 된다.

Chung Soyoung. The artist, whose works are founded on her inquisitive studies into the geological structures that we stand on, has recently expanded her inquiry to the seabed. The title *Midnight Zone* refers to the deep sea where sunlight doesn't reach, and the overall appearance of the installation calls to mind the sea or an aquarium. The work largely consists of four display cases, four videos, two installations, and a QR code. While conceptualizing the work, the artist found and reused these display cases in the hallway outside of a storage area in MMCA Gwacheon, waiting to be disposed of. Chung thought that the display cases symbolized the human-centric process of othering, excavating, collecting, studying, sorting, and exhibiting nature. Systemized and taxidermized from the human perspective, nature has long been showcased in these cases as subjects of learning. But here, the artist uses them as a setting for the new perspectives while showing only seabeds made of sodium chloride, the main component of salt also used for deicing, ridding the expected objects from the cases. From this point, our visual attention shifts to the submarine topography in the videos. What seems like rare footage of the ocean floor captured during an underwater exploration is, in fact, an edited procession of close-up images of manganese, underwater volcanic rocks, and hydrothermal rocks the artist borrowed from the Library of Marine Samples. With the subject of collection, categorization, and exhibition absent, we are left with the landscape of the dark and atemporal seabed and the image of the museum at night. *Midnight Zone* brings our eyes to the furthest reaches of the deep sea to locate ourselves in broader context by expanding the scope of our view.

정소영

Chung Soyoung

(1-1)

(1-1)

정소영   Chung Soyoung

25   정소영   Chung Soyoung

정소영　　　　　　Chung Soyoung

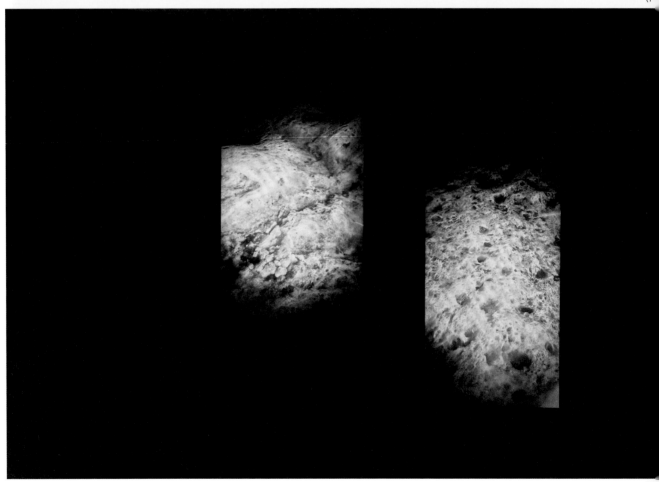

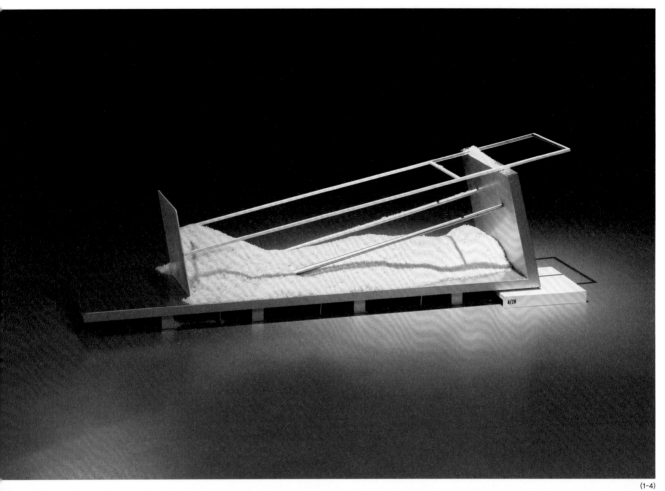

(1-4)

(1-4)

정소영   Chung Soyoung

(2-1) 〈흰 코뿔소〉
1980
젤라틴 실버 프린트
66×84×3cm(액자 포함)
작가 소장
©히로시 스기모토

(2-2) 〈흰 망토 콜로부스 원숭이〉
1980
젤라틴 실버 프린트
66×84×3cm(액자 포함)
작가 소장
©히로시 스기모토

(2-3) 〈겜즈복〉
1980
젤라틴 실버 프린트
66×84×3cm(액자 포함)
작가 소장
©히로시 스기모토

(2-4) 〈알래스카 늑대〉
1994
젤라틴 실버 프린트
66×84×3cm(액자 포함)
작가 소장
©히로시 스기모토

(2-5) 〈바다소〉
1994
젤라틴 실버 프린트
66×84×3cm(액자 포함)
작가 소장
©히로시 스기모토

(2-1) *White Rhinoceros*
1980
Gelatin silver print
66×84×3cm (framed)
Courtesy of Hiroshi Sugimoto
©Hiroshi Sugimoto

(2-2) *White Mantled Colobus*
1980
Gelatin silver print
66×84×3cm (framed)
Courtesy of Hiroshi Sugimoto
©Hiroshi Sugimoto

(2-3) *Gemsbok*
1980
Gelatin silver print
66×84×3cm (framed)
Courtesy of Hiroshi Sugimoto
©Hiroshi Sugimoto

(2-4) *Alaskan Wolves*
1994
Gelatin silver print
66×84×3cm (framed)
Courtesy of Hiroshi Sugimoto
©Hiroshi Sugimoto

(2-5) *Manatee*
1994
Gelatin silver print
66×84×3cm (framed)
Courtesy of Hiroshi Sugimoto
©Hiroshi Sugimoto

현대 사진작가이자 건축가인 히로시 스기모토(杉本博司)는 흑백의 사진 속에 공간의 시간성과 사유를 담아낸다. 이 5점의 사진은 작가가 1980년과 1994년에 촬영한 '디오라마' 시리즈 중 일부이다. 자연사박물관에서 만날 수 있는 디오라마는 주로 이국적 동물들의 생활 환경을 연출하고 그 속에 박제한 동물을 설치해 북극, 아프리카, 원시림의 한 장면을 들여다보는 듯한 착각을 불러일으키는 입체 모형을 말한다. 작가는 1974년 처음 뉴욕에 도착했을 때 자연사박물관에서 본 디오라마 풍경에서 영감을 받아, 이후 그 디오라마를 촬영해 실제 동물을 포착한 것 같은 사진을 남겼다. 박제된 가짜 풍경에서 진짜 동물의 모습을 포착해 낸 작가의 새로운 시각과 더불어, 지금의 생태학적 위기 속에서 우리는 사진 속 동물을 또 다른 관점에서 바라보게 된다. 디오라마 자체가 동물과 자연을 타자화하고 관찰과 학습의 대상으로 보는 지극히 인간 중심적 관점의 산물이기 때문이다. 기존의 세계관과 새롭게 요구되는 생태학적 관점 사이에서 혼란과 진통을 겪고 있는 우리는 사진을 보며 박물관학의 관습을 따라 그동안 의심하지 않고 받아들인 지식 속에서 놓치고 있던 중요한 가치에 관해 반문할 수 있다.

Hiroshi Sugimoto is a contemporary Japanese photographer and architect whose practice explores memory and time in space. These five photographs are from the 'Diorama series' produced in 1980 and 1994. The diorama of the Natural History Museum often refers to a three-dimensional model that represents scenes such as the Arctic, Africa, and primeval forests, mainly by decorating the living environment of exotic animals and installing stuffed animals in them. When the artist first arrived in New York in 1974, he visited the American Museum of Natural History, where he encountered animal dioramas and later he photographed them to seem authentic from those replicated subjects. His photographs not only allow us to see the artist's new perspective of capturing scenes in different way from the stuffed fake landscape, but also make us to look at the animals in the photographs from a different point of view in the current ecological crisis because they epitomize the human-centric perspective which sees animals and nature as subjects for observation and study. We, who are experiencing a vibration from the long-held anthropocentric view to the newly required ecological view, can raise a question about the important value we have missed in the knowledge we have accepted without question, through museological custom.

히로시 스기모토

Hiroshi Sugimoto

(2-4)

히로시 스기모토   Hiroshi Sugimoto

(2-5)

(2-1)

히로시 스기모토   Hiroshi Sugimoto

(2-3)

(2-2)

(2-4) (2-5) (2-1) (2-3) (2-2)

(3) 〈시간 증폭기〉
2015
유목(流木), 검은 돌, 크리스털 구(부분
은도금), 철
18×118×14cm
개인 소장
ⓒ올라퍼 엘리아손

(3) *Time amplifier*
2015
Driftwood, black stones,
partially silvered crystal
sphere, steel
18×118×14cm
Private Collection
ⓒOlafur Eliasson

아이슬란드계 덴마크 작가인 올라퍼 엘리아손(Olafur Eliasson)은 기후와 환경 위기에 대해 적극적으로 발언하는 작가로, 나무 선반, 작고 검은 돌멩이, 그리고 원형의 크리스탈로 구성된 〈시간 증폭기〉(2015)라는 설치를 통해 시간의 의미를 확대한다. 나무 선반은 시베리아 혹은 더 먼 곳에서 아이슬란드로 떠내려오는 과정에서 북극에서 떠오른 유목의 부분이고, 돌멩이는 오랜 시간 파도의 물 도리질에 의해 연마되어 작고 둥근 형태에 이르렀다. 오래된 나무가 바다에 표류하던 시간, 작고 둥글게 연마될 때까지 돌멩이가 견뎌낸 시간은 인간의 시간과 비교할 수 없을 것이다. 나무 선반 위에는 12개의 위치에 작은 돌멩이와 크리스털 공이 놓여 있는데, 각각 1월부터 12월이라는 인간의 시간 개념을 상징한다. 그중 크리스털 공은 우리가 작품을 대하는 시점의 달에 위치하는데, 그 달에 해당하는 돌멩이를 대신하여 현재의 시점을 직관적으로 알려줄 뿐 아니라, 크리스털 뒷면의 거울에 관람객과 공간의 모습을 거꾸로 비춘다. 시공간을 반전시켜 보여주는 크리스털은 지금의 시점을 강조하면서 동시에 새로운 관점의 가능성을 열어 준다. 작가는 단순하지만 엄청난 시간이 압축된 재료를 이용한 〈시간 증폭기〉를 통해 우리를 기나긴 지구의 시간 축에 위치시키고 거대한 생태계로 연결시켜 준다.

Olafur Eliasson, an Icelandic-Danish artist whose works often address climate change and the environmental crisis, extends the meaning of time though *Time amplifier*, which consists of a wooden shelf, small black stones, and a crystal sphere. The shelf is a piece of driftwood that once floated around the Arctic, travelling all the way to Iceland from Siberia or further away, and the small round stones have been scoured and polished by the waves over an extended period of time. The lengths of time that the old wood spent drifting in the sea and the stones endured as they became smaller and smoother transcend the time of human existence. The 12 positions for the stones on the shelf symbol- ically represent the 12 months of a year in "human time." The position of the crystal sphere in the row represents the month in which we are viewing the work. It not only intuitively signifies the present moment in the place of the stone that represents the corresponding month, it also has a mirror on the back that reflects the viewer and the space upside down, emphasizing the here and now while simultaneously opening up another perspective. The artist places viewers, who are busy living in the present, within eternally cyclical and extensive deep time, linking us to the vast ecosystem. The simple materials of *Time amplifier* compress an immensity of time.

올라퍼 엘리아손

Olafur Eliasson

(3)

올라퍼 엘리아손   Olafur Eliasson

올라퍼 엘리아손　Olafur Eliasson

(3)

올라퍼 엘리아손   Olafur Eliasson

올라퍼 엘리아손 Olafur Eliasson

(3)

(4) 〈모습 某濕 Wet Matter 5〉
2021
젖은 흙, 혼합 매체, 연필나무 향
1270×770×330cm

(4) *Wet Matter 5*
2021
Wetter soil, mixed media,
scent of cedarwood
1270×770×330cm

장소가 매개하는 시간과 기억의 영역을 흙을 이용한 설치로 선보이는 김주리 작가의 신작 〈모습 某濕 Wet Matter 5〉은 거대한 젖은 흙덩어리이다. 생명을 구성하는 가장 기본적인 원소인 물과 흙을 주재료로 하는 이 작업은 젖어 있는 상태의 어떤 모호한 형상을 취하면서 공간을 점유하고, 나무와 흙의 냄새를 머금고 있어 주변을 서성이는 관람객들을 작품의 시공간으로 끌어들인다. 〈모습〉 연작은 압록강 하구 습지의 유연한 땅에서 시작했다. 인간은 국경과 같은 여러 경계와 구분을 만들지만 강바닥의 흙은 끊임없이 경계를 허물고 서로 연결되는 생태적 특징을 담고 있다. 다시 말해, 물과 결합된 흙의 이 '젖은 상태'는 고체와 액체 사이의 유연한 상태의 물질로, 생명의 가능성과 자연의 순환이 축적된 시공간이 된다. 고운 흙 입자가 되기까지 오랜 풍화작용의 시간을 품고 있는 이 거대한 젖은 흙덩어리는 수많은 생명 작용의 장소로 환기되며 인간이 등장하기 이전부터 존재했던 모든 생명의 시간에 대한 시각적 은유로 다가온다. 이 장대한 대지의 시간 주변을 거닐며 인간의 시간을 생각하는 일은 자연의 한순간이자 생명 순환 고리의 일부로써 우리의 존재를 들여다보게 하는데, 이 지점에서 생태학적 사유가 시작될 수 있다.

Kim Juree makes wet soil installations that probe time and memory, mediated by certain sites. Composed mainly of water and soil, the most basic elements of life, this wet, ambiguous form emits a woody and earthy smell as it occupies its space, attracting nearby visitors into its unique spacetime. The solid soil and liquid water are intermixed to dismantle the boundary between the materials, and the indistinguishably melded materials attest to the nature of ecology. Kim's *Wet Matter* series began at the supple wetland at the mouth of the Yalu River, and it is an eco-logical statement that while humans continue to create more divisive boundaries such as national borders, the soil on a riverbed constantly erases boundaries to connect the lands together. Where the soil meets the water in the river's estuary, various living and non-living things live as well as die. *Wet Matter 5*, a massive chunk of wet soil, something that promotes count-less biological processes, embodies the time of all life that precedes humans, not to mention the time it took for the soil to be weathered into such fine particles. This exhibition was organized under the belief that when we place the time of humankind within the time of the earth and see ourselves in connec-tion to the history of all biological processes, we may be able to view the world from a slightly different angle.

김주리

Kim Juree

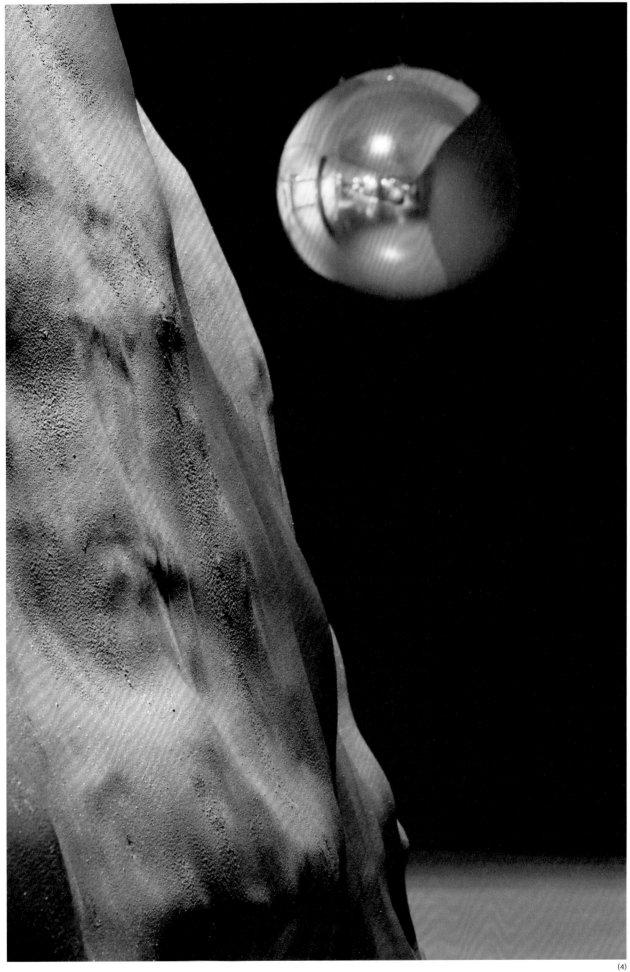

47   김주리   Kim Juree

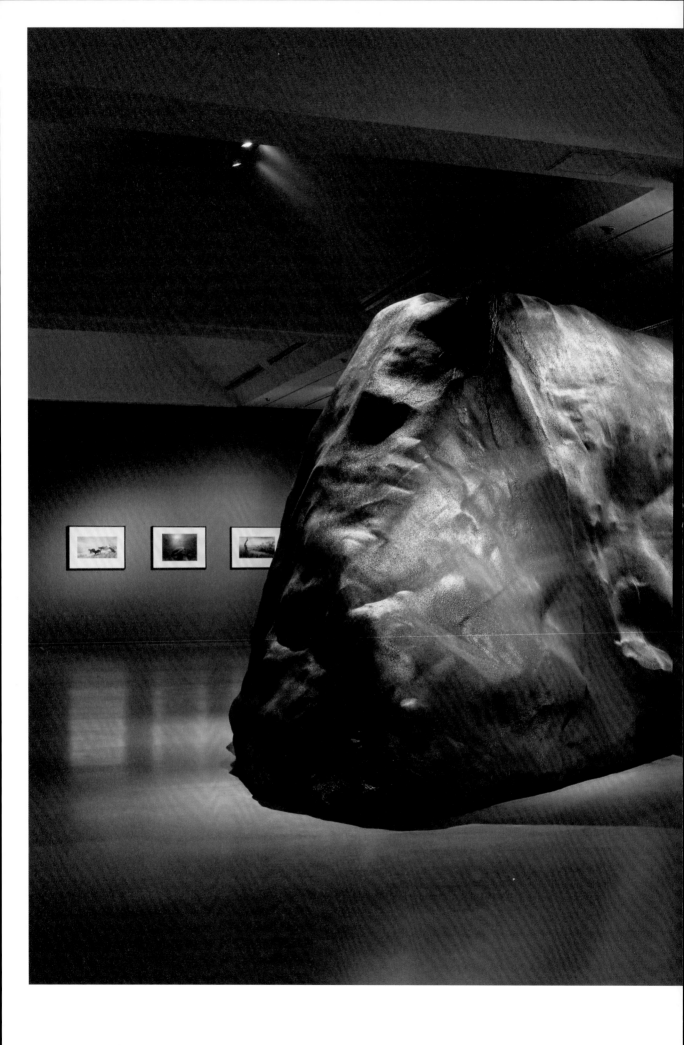

　　　　　　　김주리　　　　　　　Kim Juree

(4)

51 김주리 Kim Juree

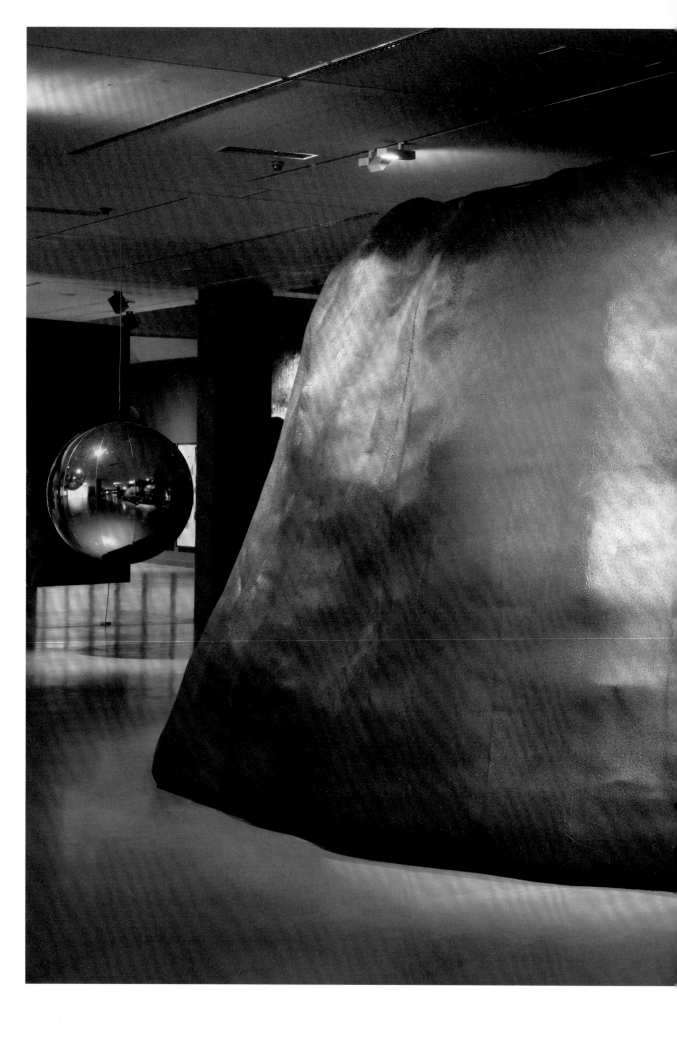

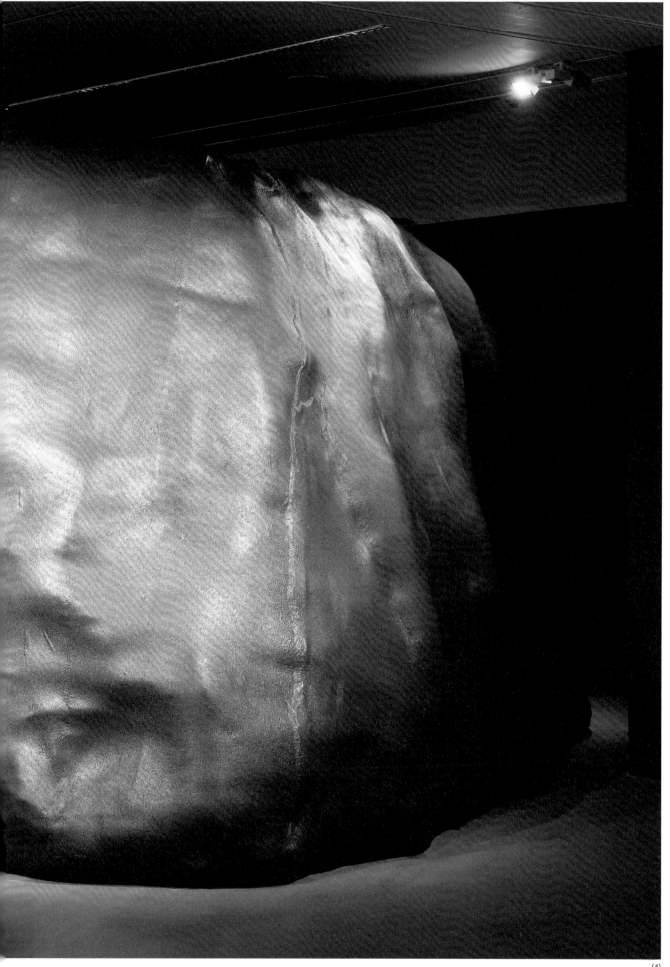

김주리　　　　Kim Juree

(4)

이탈리아의 미술가 주세페 페노네(Giuseppe Penone)는 1970년대 이후 '아르테 포베라(Arte Povera)' 운동의 중심 인물이었고 주로 숲, 나무, 대리석과 같은 주변의 환경을 이용해 인체와 정신성에 대한 작품을 제작해 왔다. 전시에 선보인 〈돌의 몸―라미(cod 2033)〉와 〈불분명한 경계들―트레비아(cod 1673)〉는 흰 대리석이 주재료인 조각이다. 인테리어 내장재로도 인기가 많은 비앙코 카라라, 즉 이탈리아 카라라 지역에서 나는 흰색 대리석은 건축 자재로 세계 각지에 수출되는데, 페노네는 산업용으로 채석되는 과정에서 버려진 자투리 대리석을 이용해 조각을 만들었다. 〈돌의 몸―라미(cod 2033)〉는 흑연으로 긁는 '프로타주' 기법으로 표면의 시간성을 드러낸 전시장 벽면에 설치되어 있다. 버려진 대리석의 표면 패턴을 마치 피부의 핏줄처럼 부각하고 그 위에 작은 청동의 나뭇가지가 솟아나는 모습을 표현하는데, 이 작업을 통해 작가는 대리석 패턴 속에 응축된 시간의 흐름과 미술관이 가진 전시의 역사 위에 새로운 가능성이 움트는 순간을 한 편의 시처럼 구현했다. 그 앞에 놓인 조각 〈불분명한 경계들―트레비아(cod 1673)〉는 버려진 작은 대리석을 받침대로 삼아 나무줄기의 형태를 올려 두고 거기에서 또다시 새로운 가지가 뻗어 올라가는 모습을 보여 준다. 대리석과 청동이라는 전혀 다른 물성의 매체, 저마다의 시간이 경계를 허물고 융합되면서 새로운 자연의 조형을 보여주는 이 조각은 제목처럼 불분명한 경계들이 유연하게 맞닿아 끊임없이 상호작용하는 생태 작용을 은유한다.

Italian artist Giuseppe Penone was a lead figure in the 1970s Arte Povera art movement and has mostly produced works that investigate spirituality and the human body using materials from nature such as wood and marble. Bianco Carrara, a white marble from the Carrara region of Italy popularly used in interior design, is exported around the globe as a building material, but Penone's sculptures use pieces of the industrial marble discarded in the quarrying process. The first work Corpo di pietra—rami (cod 2033) is installed in the center of an eight-meter-wide wall, the surface of which has been scraped with graphite using the frottage method as an ode to a gallery wall that has hung countless artworks to inspire generations of people. The surface patterns of the marble are emphasized to look like veins underneath the skin, and sprouting from these veins are small tree branches. In this poetic scene, new branches of possibility bud from marble, whose patterns are symbolic of the accumulation of time, and are hung on the time-honored gallery wall representative of the history of museum exhibitions. The three-dimensional sculpture presented in front of this work conveys a similar message. A new branch grows from a tree trunk placed on top of a scrap piece of marble. This sculpture, titled Indistinti confini—Trebia (cod 1673), allows the disparate properties and temporalities of marble and bronze to break down boundaries and become a single form. Like its namesake, the work is a metaphor for an eco-system in which different elements receptively and perpetually interact with one another.

주세페 페노네

Giuseppe Penone

(5-1) (5-2)

주세페 페노네   Giuseppe Penone

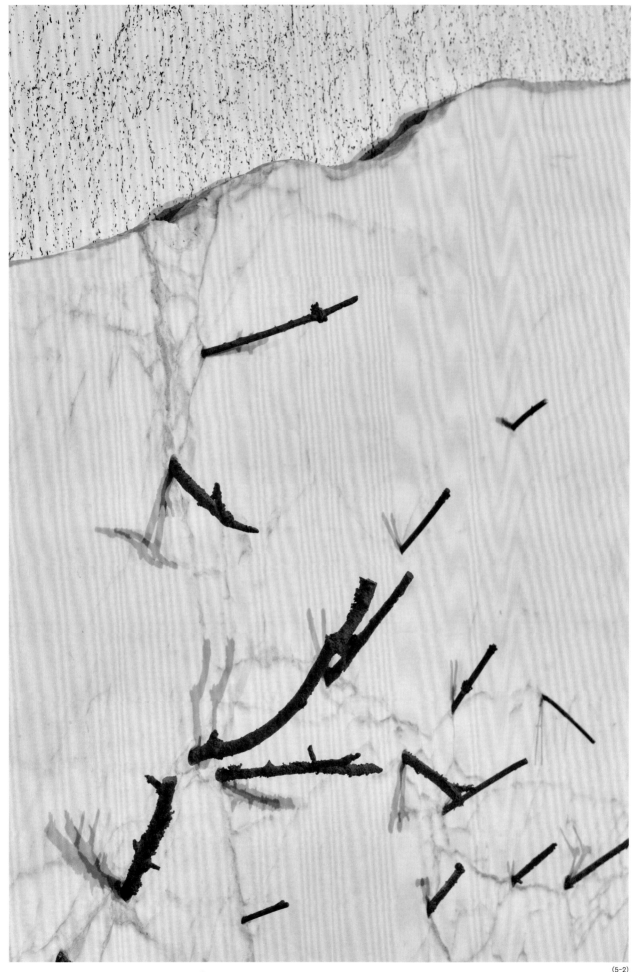

(5-2)

주세페 페노네 Giuseppe Penone

(5-2)

주세페 페노네　Giuseppe Penone

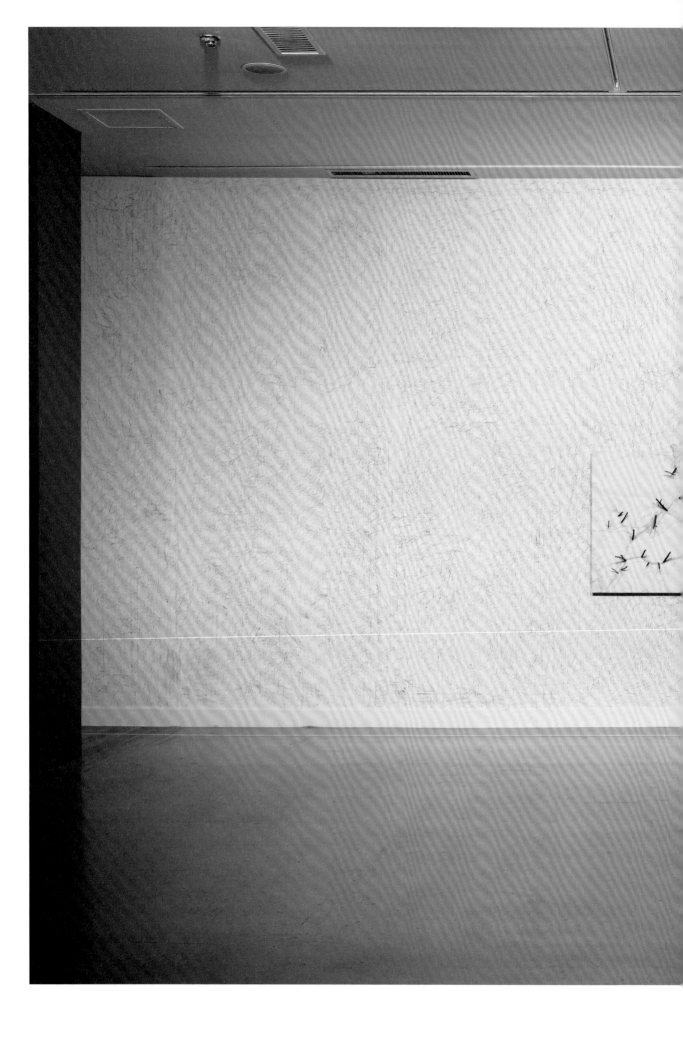

(5-1) (5-2)

(6) 〈비전〉
2021
단채널 LED 비디오, 3채널 HD 비디오,
컬러, 10채널 오디오(머신러닝 이미지
생성, 실시간 카메라 캡처, CG, 데이터
음향화 및 시각화), 시아노타입 프린트,
디지털 잉크젯 프린트
가변 설치

(6) Vision
2021
Single-channel LED screen,
three-channel HD video
projection, color, ten-channel
audio (machine learning image
generation, real-time camera
capture, CG, data audio-
visualization), cyanotype
photograph, digital inkjet print
Dimensions variable

인류학적 관점에서 미디어와 디자인 작업을 교차시키는 서동주는 빛과 생명체의 시각 메커니즘을 통해 종의 다양성, 개별성, 공통성을 체험적으로 구현한 신작 〈비전〉을 제작했다. 빛의 통로이자 조절 기관인 눈동자 역할을 하는 대형 LED 패널에서는 다양한 생명체의 눈이 머신러닝을 통해 끊임없이 새로운 이미지로 생성되어 제시되는데, 이를 통해 오랜 시간에 걸친 각 생명의 시각인지 진화 과정을 요약적으로 보여 준다. 동공에 들어온 수많은 빛의 정보가 망막에 맺히는 과정은 3개의 곡면 스크린에 투사된 영상으로 비유된다. 현미경으로 들여다본 미시적 장면도 있고, 거시적 시점에서 바라본 우리 주변의 모습도 등장하는데, 이런 장면들이 곤충이나 갑각류의 시점을 재구성한 이미지 등으로 구성되어 있어서 인간 뿐 아니라 수많은 생명체가 저마다의 방식으로 세상을 인지하며 살아가고 있음을 실감하게 된다. 태양 광량 스펙트럼 데이터와 태평양의 해양 색상 변화 데이터를 연동해 생성하는 빛의 시그널과 생명의 에너지는 소리로 변환해 작품의 배경음으로 사용하고, 우리 주변에 존재하지만 일상에서 듣지 못한 자연 현상의 소리들은 무선 헤드셋을 통해 집중적으로 들을 수 있게 하는데, 이 역시 미처 인식하지 못한 영역과 우리를 연결하는 작업이다. 예컨대, 잠자리의 시지각이 인간과 다르다는 것은 너무나 당연한 이야기다. 하지만 편협하고 자기중심적인 시각으로 세상을 접하기에 바쁜 우리에게 〈비전〉은 더 다양한 생명체가 지닌 저마다의 관점과 시각을 소리와 이미지의 질감과 패턴 등을 통해 공감각적으로 체험하도록 하며, 그 과정에서 다양성, 상대성, 상호연결성과 같은 통합적 사유와 전망을 제안한다.

Seo Dongjoo, whose researches and works inter-sect new media and design, produced a new work *Vision* to implement empirically the concept of diversity, individuality, and commonality of all species through a visual perception mechanism of living things. While an eye is a sensory organ, this work magnifies the ocular structure to present it as a space. The LED screen shows an image of an eye that is constantly regenerated by an AI machine learning algorithm. Projected onto the three curved screens are images of macro and micro worlds as seen from various creatures' perspectives, combined with the texture and movement of light. The images that explore the process of light information entering the pupil and being converted into neural signals at the retina allow us to realize that countless creatures—besides humans—view the world from their own perspectives, which they have used to survive and evolve. Viewers can sense the presence of light through the "sound of light," created by linking 10 channels of solar irradiance spectrum data and Pacific Ocean color change data to fill the space, while the sounds of natural phenomena are also played through wireless headsets to link us to sounds that exist around us but are seldom heard. The back sides of the curved screens representative of the outermost surface of the eye have cyanotype-printed patterns, and the evolutionary similarity between the plant and animal kingdoms is visualized through light imaging to capture imperceptible biological phenomena. Largely composed of video, sound, and graphic elements, this architectural space reminiscent of the ocular structure amplifies and heuristically renders the process of visual perception to reflect on the act of seeing while reminding us that humans aren't the only agents of perception—all creatures perceive the world in their own ways. By magnifying the small sensory organ into a space, the work makes us walk into an experience of perception in which the human-centric perspective is overturned as we are watched by the constantly regenerating eyes of other creatures to remind us that humans are also mere subjects of their sight. Diversity, relativity, and interconnectivity are ecological principles that are essential in overcoming the current ecological crisis and building solidarity for symbiosis.

서동주

Seo Dongjoo

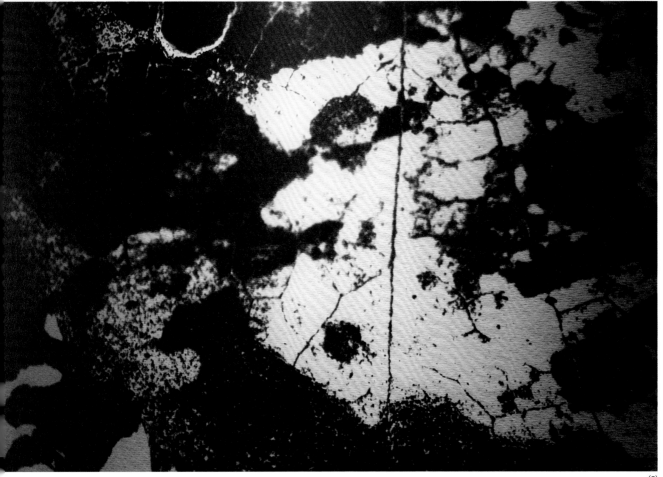

(6)

65 서동주 Seo Dongjoo

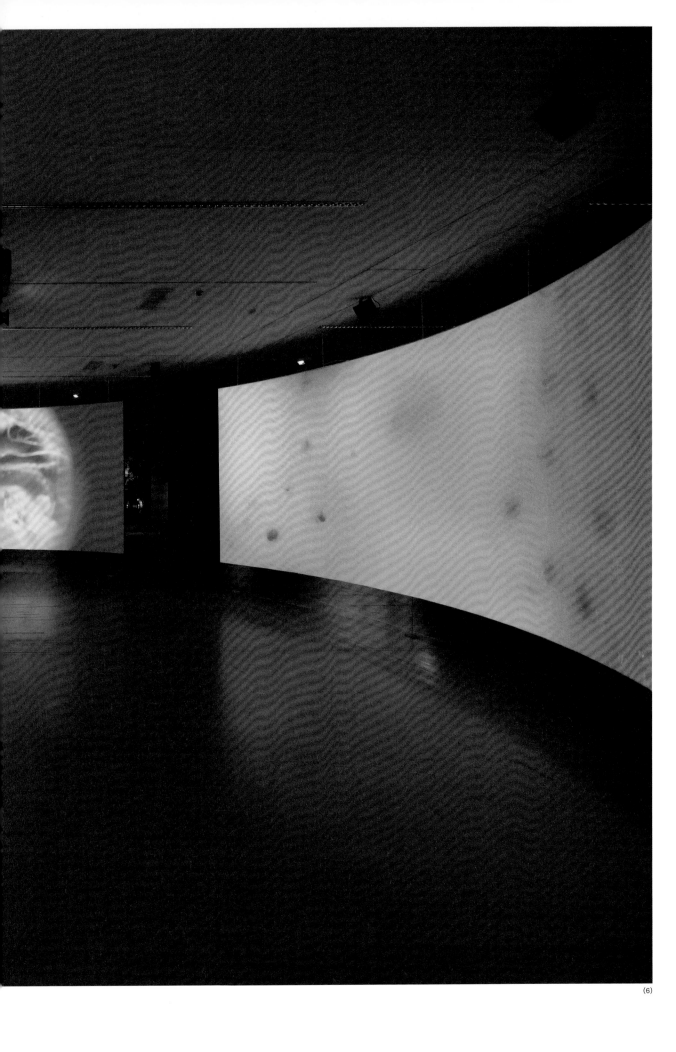

(6)

67   서동주   Seo Dongjoo

69 　　　　　서동주　　　　　　　　Seo Dongjoo

(7-1) 〈№ 60, 1987년 1월 2월〉
1987
크로모제닉 컬러 프린트
50×50cm, 88×88cm(액자 포함)
밀렌 앤드 장뤽 밀렌, 스프루스 마거스
소장
©장뤽 밀렌

(7-2) 〈№ 61, 1987년 1월 2월〉
1987
크로모제닉 컬러 프린트
50×50cm, 88×88cm(액자 포함)
밀렌 앤드 장뤽 밀렌, 스프루스 마거스
소장
©장뤽 밀렌

(7-3) 〈№ 304, 2005년 3월 4월〉
2005
크로모제닉 컬러 프린트
123×123cm(액자 포함)
밀렌 앤드 장뤽 밀렌, 스프루스 마거스
소장
©장뤽 밀렌

(7-4) 〈№ 377, 2006년 4월 5월〉
2006
크로모제닉 컬러 프린트
230×185cm(액자 포함)
밀렌 앤드 장뤽 밀렌, 스프루스 마거스
소장
©장뤽 밀렌

(7-5) 〈№ 434, 2006년 12월-2007년 1월〉
2006-2007
크로모제닉 컬러 프린트
123×153cm(액자 포함)
밀렌 앤드 장뤽 밀렌, 스프루스 마거스
소장
©장뤽 밀렌

(7-6) 〈№ 520, 2007년 2월 3월 4월〉
2007
크로모제닉 컬러 프린트
185×230cm(액자 포함)
밀렌 앤드 장뤽 밀렌, 스프루스 마거스
소장
©장뤽 밀렌

(7-1) *№ 60, Janvier Février 1987*
1987
Chromogenic color print
50×50cm, 88×88cm (framed)
Courtesy of Mylène & Jean-Luc
Mylayne and Sprüth Magers
©Jean-Luc Mylayne

(7-2) *№ 61, Janvier Février 1987*
1987
Chromogenic color print
50×50cm, 88×88cm (framed)
Courtesy of Mylène & Jean-Luc
Mylayne and Sprüth Magers
©Jean-Luc Mylayne

(7-3) *№ 304, Mars Avril 2005*
2005
Chromogenic color print
123×123cm (framed)
Courtesy of Mylène & Jean-Luc
Mylayne and Sprüth Magers
©Jean-Luc Mylayne

(7-4) *№ 377, Avril Mai 2006*
2006
Chromogenic color print
230×185cm (framed)
Courtesy of Mylène & Jean-Luc
Mylayne and Sprüth Magers
©Jean-Luc Mylayne

(7-5) *№ 434, Décembre 2006–Janvier 2007*
2006-2007
Chromogenic color print
123×153cm (framed)
Courtesy of Mylène & Jean-Luc
Mylayne and Sprüth Magers
©Jean-Luc Mylayne

(7-6) *№ 520, Février Mars Avril 2007*
2007
Chromogenic color print
185×230cm (framed)
Courtesy of Mylène & Jean-Luc
Mylayne and Sprüth Magers
©Jean-Luc Mylayne

장뤽 밀렌(Jean-Luc Mylayne)은 프랑스의 미술가로, 새를 촬영한 사진으로 그 이름이 알려져 있다. 그의 작품은 새가 등장하는 평범한 사진처럼 보이지만, 새를 수동적 피사체로 설정하고 특정 구도와 미학적 성취 등 사진의 기술적 효과를 추구하기 위한 목적에서 촬영하지 않는다는 점에 주목할 필요가 있다. 평생을 자연과 벗 삼아 살아가면서 야생의 새와 교감하는 과정을 즐기는 은둔자이자 자연인인 작가는 자신이 몇 달 동안 함께 생활하고 소통한 새와 보낸 시간을 기록하기 위해 사진이라는 매체를 사용한다. 야생의 새는 경계심이 강해 쉽게 다가가기 어렵다는 점을 떠올려 보면, 여러 계절마다 찾아오는 새들과 친밀하게 소통한 작가가 스스로를 자연의 일부로 인식하고 위치시켜 왔음을 짐작할 수 있다. 1987년 1월과 2월에 눈 위에서 놀던 1쌍의 검은 새가 담긴 사진부터 2005년에서 2007년까지 촬영한 4점의 사진에 이르기까지, 작가는 각기 다른 계절의 풍경 속에 자신의 삶의 일부였던 새와 함께한 시간을 기록했다. 작가의 사진 속에 남은 친구이자 동반자인 새의 모습은 기다리고 배려하고 소통하는 상호 존중의 태도와 생태학적 가치관의 실천을 보여 준다.

Jean-Luc Mylayne is a French artist known for his bird photographs, but to him, photography is not a means to capture a subject. As an artist leading a reclusive life in commune with wild birds in nature, the artist uses the medium of photography to document the months of time he has spent interacting with the birds. As with any other wild animals, wild birds are known to be extremely alert and difficult to approach. The fact that the artist is able to intimately communicate with the different species of birds that fly in by season signifies that the birds have accepted him as part of a safe environment. Mylayne blends in with the natural environment and waits for the birds to approach him in order to initiate communication, and this considerate and respectful attitude is reflected in the photos. Here, a couple of blackbirds that spent January and February of 1987 with the artist are frolicking in the snow. The four photographs from 2005 to 2007 also capture the birds that were part of Mylayne's life with different seasonal landscapes as their backdrops. From these pictures, we can sense the artist's intention and effort to photograph from the birds' point of view. Photos of people, flowers, architecture, and objects often represent the human perspective that covetously consumes and objectifies nature from the other side of the lens. Mylayne's photos propose a different perspective of the world in that they document his periods of communion and mutual respect.

장뤽 밀렌

Jean-Luc Mylayne

장뤽 밀렌
Jean-Luc Mylayne
N° 60, 1967년 1월 2월
N° 60, Janvier Février
1967
C-print
C-print
88×88cm

장뤽 밀렌 Jean-Luc Mylayne

(7-1) (7-2)

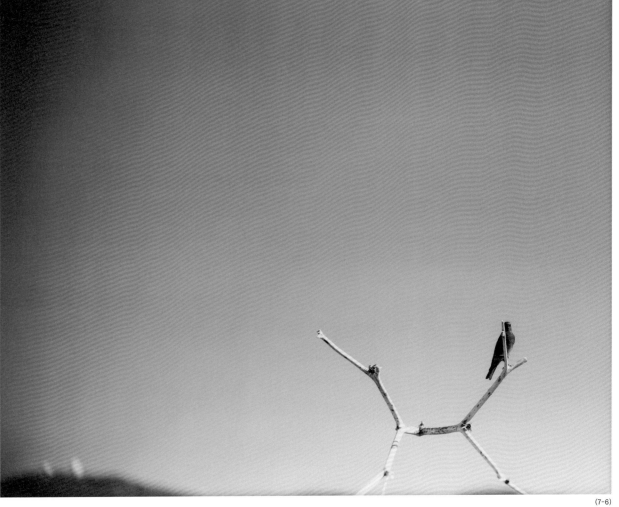

(7-6)

장뤽 밀렌 Jean-Luc Mylayne

(7-4)

(7-3)

(7-5)

장뤽 밀렌   Jean-Luc Mylayne

(7-1) (7-2) (7-6) (7-4) (7-3) (7-5)

장뤽 밀렌   Jean-Luc Mylayne

(8-1) 〈육각부적〉
2021
점토, 에폭시 레진, 시멘트, 혼합 매체
42×36×1.2cm(81)
가변 설치

(8-2) 〈ISOF 시리즈〉
2021
식물 색소 잉크젯 프린트, 에폭시 레진,
합성 목재, 스테인리스 스틸 파이프,
혼합 매체
62×92×5 (1)
82×122×5 (2)
92×137×5 (3)

(8-1) Hexagonal Talisman
2021
Clay, epoxy resin, cement,
mixed media
42×36×1.2cm (81)
Dimensions variable

(8-2) ISOF Series
2021
Plant pigments inkjet print,
epoxy resin, WPC, stainless
steel pipes, mixed media
62×92×5 (1)
82×122×5 (2)
92×137×5 (3)

백정기는 현대와 전통, 과학과 종교, 물질과 정신 등 이분법적 가치의 틈새를 물이나 전기 등의 유동적인 흐름으로 연결하는 작업을 해 왔다. 작가는 점토로 만든 육각 타일 형태의 작업인 〈육각부적〉과 〈ISOF 시리즈〉를 신작으로 제작했다. 〈육각부적〉은 점토가 마르면서 생긴 균열을 투명 에폭시로 채운 육각형의 타일로 모서리마다 한자로 물을 뜻하는 '水(수)'가 새겨져 있다. 목재 기둥에 육각 타일의 모서리를 맞닿게 설치하면 세 모서리에 새겨진 3개의 '水' 자가 합쳐지면서 '아득할 묘(淼)'가 되어 큰 물을 의미하게 된다. 작가가 리서치 과정에서 경복궁 근정전에서 발굴된 각 모서리에 '水' 자가 새겨진 육각판이 물을 기원하는 부적이었다는 것을 알게 되면서 그 의미와 형태를 차용했다고 한다. 작가는 갈라지도록 말린 점토 표면을 투명 에폭시로 채워 가뭄으로 균열된 땅을 물이 촉촉하게 적시는 모습으로 제작했다. 이를 통해 급속히 진행되는 사막화가 완화되기를 바라는 마음과 더불어 기후 변화와 물 부족 위기의 심각성을 절감하지 못하고 마치 기우제 부적 같은 미신으로나 여기는 듯한 우리의 모습을 중첩시켰다. 2011년부터 이어지고 있는 〈ISOF 시리즈〉는 흔한 자연 풍경 사진을 작가가 자연에서 직접 추출한 색소로 인화해 설치한 작업이다. 꽃잎 등의 식물에서 추출한 자연 색소로 이미지를 인화하면 색소가 즉시 갈변될 뿐 아니라 시간이 흐름에 따라 자연스레 색이 바랜다. 우리가 일상에서 무의식 중에 소비하고 학습하는 자연 풍경 사진의 쨍하고 유혹적인 색상이 아닌, 변하고 흐려지는 자연 색소로 구현한 자연의 풍경이라는 역설적 순환 구조를 통해 작가는 자연에 대한 우리의 인식이 어떠한 것인지 근본적인 질문을 던진다.

Beak Jungki produces works that bridge the gap between dichotomous values—such as modernity and tradition, science and religion, and materiality and spirituality—using the flows of water and electricity. The installation *Hexagonal Talisman* is made of the dried and crackled tiles which have been glazed using clear epoxy to seem as though the cracks are filled with water, and the corners of the tiles are inscribed with the Chinese character meaning "water." This corner design, derived from the hexagonal talisman found in Gyeongbokgung Palace, is intended to form a Chinese character meaning "a wide expanse of water," when three corners come together. At the time of Gyeongbokgung Palace's construction, this type of talisman was often used to ward off fire from wooden buildings and wish for rain at apposite times. Beak draws upon this tradition to present this talisman as a metaphor for his hopes to mitigate today's rapid desertification and climate change. At the same time, he satirizes our abstract and shamanistic view of the real threat of the environmental crisis. His second installation *ISOF Series* consists of photographs of natural landscapes. They are printed using natural pigments hand-extracted by the artist, thus they are not the sharp and colorful landscape pictures that we are used to. Developed in this unique way, the photographs immediately begin to lose color after printing, taking on colors reminiscent of autumn leaves that gradually fade over time. Through the paradoxical cycle of printing images of natural scenery using natural pigments instead of the alluring artificial pigments that we generally consume, this work makes us reflect on how we perceive nature as well as our relationship with it.

백정기

Beak Jungki

(8-1)

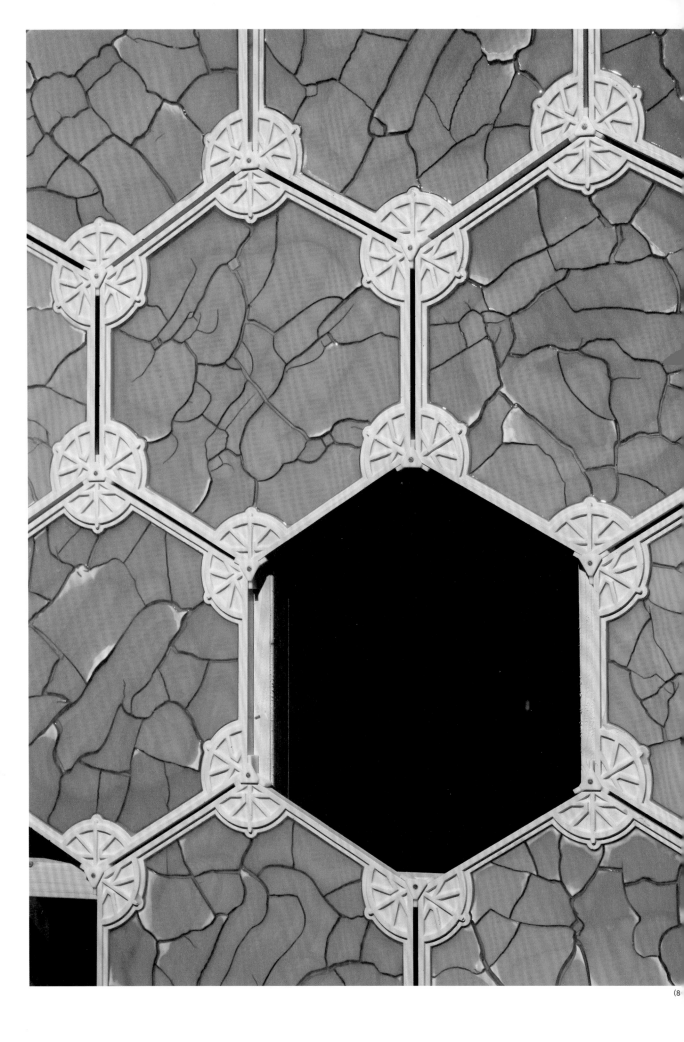

(8-2)

(8-2)

백정기 Beak Jungki

(8-2)

백정기 Beak Jungki

(9-1) 〈오년제〉
2018
자료 영상
단채널 비디오, 컬러, 무음
8분 46초
장즈산 제공

(9-1) *Maljeveq*
2018
Archival film
Single-channel video, color,
silent
8 min 46 sec
Courtesy of Chang, Chi-Shan

(9-2) 〈머리사냥꾼의 선반〉
2021
나무, 철, 점토, 갈륨
240×700×100cm

(9-2) *The shelf of head hunter*
2021
Wood, steel, clay, gallium (Ga)
240×700×100cm

(9-3) 〈포모사 프로젝트〉
2021
종이에 아카이벌 피그먼트 프린트,
콜라주, 구아슈, 수채 물감, 스탬프 잉크
185×125cm(11)

(9-3) *FORMOSA Project*
2021
Archival pigment print on paper,
collage, gouache, watercolors,
stamp ink
185×125cm (11)

인류와 자연이 문명의 폭력에 노출된 곳에서 출발해 조사 연구를 기반으로 작업하는 나현 작가는 문명이 닿지 않은 곳에서 생활하는 원주민의 삶에서 인간과 자연의 이상적 관계를 모색하는 신작을 제작했다. 〈포모사 프로젝트〉는 파이완 부족과 타로막 부족이라는 두 고산족이 척박한 자연 환경 속에서 어떻게 살아가는지에 대한 연구다. 포모사(Formosa)란 현재의 대만을 일컫는 옛말이다. 전시장 벽면에 걸린 11개의 사진은 작가가 두 부족의 생활반경에서 채집한 식물을 압화해 출력한 것으로, 나무나 풀과 같은 존재가 고산족의 소소한 일상생활부터 영적인 영역까지 모든 삶을 함께하는 동반자이자 인간과 동등한 자연의 일부임을 알려 준다. 사진 앞에 놓인 거대한 목재 설치물의 제목은 〈머리 사냥꾼의 선반〉인데, 파이완 부족이 상대의 목을 베어 집 앞 선반 위에 올려 두고 전시하는 관습에서 선반의 형태를 빌려 왔다. 인간의 머리 대신 선반의 한쪽 끝에는 나무의 입장에서 '머리' 와도 같은 나무 뿌리를 올려 두고, 다른 한쪽 끝에는 29.7도에 이르면 액체로 녹아 내리는 갈륨으로 제작한 카나리아가 든 새장을 올려 두어 지구의 기후 변화가 자연과 인간의 긴장감 속에서 균형을 맞추는 상황을 상징적으로 연출했다. 작가는 야생의 자연에서 살아가기 위해 공포스러울 정도로 단호하고 철저하게 금기를 지켜내는 고산족의 삶의 태도에서 자연과 공생하는 원칙을 보여 준다. 즉, 자연을 경외하되 서로 조화롭게 공존하는 고산족의 삶을 통해 지금의 깨어진 생태적 균형을 회복하기 위해 우리가 철저히 변화해야 함을 강조한다.

Na Hyun's research and work start from a place where humans and nature are exposed to the violence of civilization and he has conducted research on the Formosan people of Taiwan to explore the ideal relationship between humans and nature through their lives untouched by civilization. Through his two new works he seeks to tell us about the values and perspectives that are long lost or forgotten. In the *FORMOSA Project*, titled after the old name of present-day Taiwan, the artist compressively depicts how two Formosan tribes, the Paiwan tribe and Taromak tribe, live in a barren environment. The 11 photographs on the wall are pressed prints of plants botanized from the two tribes' living circles. From plants that replace toothpaste and toilet paper to sacred plants used in rituals, the various plants are companions in every aspect of tribal life from daily activities to spiritual customs. The large shelf in the front, titled *The shelf of head hunter*, draws upon the Paiwan custom of beheading enemies and displaying the severed heads on the shelf in front of one's house. With the root of a tree, which serves the role of a head from the tree's perspective, on one end of the shelf and a cage containing a canary made out of gallium on the other, the work is precariously balanced to create tension. Because of their ability to detect harmful gases, canaries served to warn of life-threatening danger in coal mines; therefore, the canary in this work is an indicator of life and death. But as it is made of gallium, a type of metal that liquefies at temperatures above 29°C, it also symbolizes global warming and rising sea levels. What we see as the Formosans' almost horrifying decisiveness and strict prohibitions are key to surviving in an infertile environment, and their respect for nature and others' territories while coexisting teaches us how balance can be restored through coevolution.

나현

Na Hyun

(9-2) (9-3)

(9-2) (9-3)

나현 Na Hyun

(9-2) (9-3)

나현 Na Hyun

(9-2)

(9-2)

나현　　　　Na Hyun

나현
Na Hyun
포모사 프로젝트
FORMOSA Project

설명 텍스트
Archival pigment print on paper, Collage,
Gouache, Watercolor, Tracing ink
각 185 × 125cm
각 185 × 125cm(조각)

(10) 〈사해의 작은 영혼〉
2017
비디오 설치, 단채널 HD 비디오, 컬러,
사운드
가변 크기
10시간 33분
©크리스티앙 볼탕스키

(10) Animitas Mères Mortes
2017
Video installation, single-channe
HD video, color, sound
Dimensions variable
10 hr 33 min
©Christian Boltanski

프랑스의 미술가 크리스티앙 볼탕스키(Christian Boltanski)는 2014년부터 2017년까지 칠레를 시작으로 일본, 캐나다, 이스라엘 사해를 순회하며 '작은 영혼'이란 뜻의 〈아니미타스〉 시리즈를 선보였다. '아니미타스(animitas)'는 아메리카 원주민이 죽은 자를 기리기 위해 길가에 두는 제단 설치물들을 의미하는 용어인데, 길목에 제단을 설치하고 사라진 존재를 염원하는 이러한 전통은 여러 문화권에서 유사하게 발견된다. 〈사해의 작은 영혼〉은 작가가 이스라엘 사해 호숫가에서 동틀 무렵부터 해 질 무렵까지 약 10시간 30분을 기록한 영상으로, 우리 주변에 보이지 않는 존재들이 있고, 바람을 통한 종소리가 그 존재들을 구체화한다고 생각한 작가의 믿음을 설치로 구현한 작업이다. 바람이 들려주는 종소리는 "별의 음악과 떠다니는 영혼의 목소리"가 되어 전시장을 채우는데, 이 영혼의 음악은 땅과 하늘과 사람, 그리고 보이지 않는 무수히 많은 존재를 하나로 모아주는 염원 그 자체라고 볼 수 있다. 눈에 보이는 것뿐 아니라 눈에 보이지 않는 수많은 요소들이 서로 연결되어 거대한 하나를 이룬다는 생태학적 세계관에 대한 아름답고 시적인 은유가 바로 이 〈사해의 작은 영혼〉이 들려주는 종소리다.

French artist Christian Boltanski toured around Chile, Japan, Canada, and Israel's Dead Sea from 2014 to 2017, presenting the series Animitas, whose title translates to "tiny souls." Also referring to the roadside shrines installed by indigenous people to commemorate the dead, animitas are in line with the tradition shared by many countries of installing shrines on beaches. Among the series of videos, each of which documents the sound of bells installed on a beach resonating in the wind along with sticks tied with hopeful messages for a day, presented in this exhibition is Animitas Mères Mortes, the series' last and the most recent piece. This video, which captures the shore of the Dead Sea for the duration of 10 hours and 30 minutes—from dawn to dusk—puts us in the artist's shoes. Boltanski believed that there are invisible beings around us, corporealized by the sound of the bell. These sounds, delivered by the wind, fill the exhibition space as "astral music and the voice of the wandering souls" that become a form of hope themselves, gathering the earth, sky, people, and myriads of invisible beings together. The silver spheres hung across the exhibition space serve both as visualizations of the bell sound of this work and as symbols of invisible souls and elements. The sound of these bells rung by the tiny souls of the Dead Sea is a beautiful and poetic metaphor for the ecological viewpoint that we are all, and should be, one.

크리스티앙 볼탕스키

Christian Boltanski

(10)

97 크리스티앙 볼탕스키 Christian Boltanski

(10)

크리스티앙 볼탕스키   Christian Boltanski

크리스티앙 볼탕스키 Christian Boltanski

(11) 〈인과율〉
2021
PET 재활용재, 실
가변 설치

(11) *Causality*
2021
PET recycled materials,
threads
Dimensions variable

건축가 정규동은 미국 건축가이자 수학자인 버크민스터 풀러(Buckminster Fuller)의 개념인 텐세그리티(tensegrity) 구조를 사용해 제작한 신작 〈인과율〉을 통해 세상 모든 것이 불가분의 관계를 맺고 있음을 건축적 언어로 보여주었다. 텐세그리티는 인장(tension)과 결합(integrity)의 합성어로 견고함과 유연함이 서로 평형된 긴장 관계를 형성할 때 확보되는 안정성을 의미한다. 열처리한 나선형의 광섬유가 빛의 건축처럼 공간에 떠 있는 모습인 〈인과율〉은 페트병을 재가공해 얻은 플레이크, 팰릿, 비닐 등의 재활용 재료와 6개의 색실 이외에 어떠한 지지 구조도 없다는 것이 특징이다. 바닥에서부터 무게 중심을 계산해 어슷하게 배치된 아크릴 관들은 가느다란 실로 팽팽하게 연결되어 있는데, 작가는 눈에 잘 띄지 않는 실의 역할과 기능을 통해 생태계의 구조를 가시화한다. 즉, 한 줄의 실이라도 끊어지면 (전체가) 균형을 잃게 되는 구조를 통해 서로 의지하고 영향을 주고받는 생태학적 관계의 순환 고리를 보여줌으로써, 모든 요소가 보이지 않는 원리에 의해 서로 불가분의 관계를 맺고 있음을 강조한다. 또한 이와 동시에 이분법적 사고를 벗어나 전체적인 관점에서 인과 관계를 인지할 때 균형과 조화의 관계를 회복하는 방향으로 나아갈 수 있음을 말하고 있다.

Architect Jung Kyudong produced this new work using the "tensegrity" structure conceptualized by American architect and mathematician Buckminster Fuller. Tensegrity is a compound word that combines "tension" and "integrity," and this work visualizes the stability achieved when rigidity and flexibility form a balanced tension. In the dimly lit exhibition space, the oblique, luminescent acrylic tubes hovering in midair catch the eye, and this effect is created by spiral heat-treated optical fibers inside each acrylic tubes. The real support of this hole installation comes from thin strings sorted by six colors. The strings connect and tightly bind the tubes, each arranged off the floor in an oblique angle based on a careful assessment of their center of gravity. The present yet barely noticeable strings and their function represent ecological structure. This fragile yet solid installation is sustained as long as every material component stays in balanced tension and plays its role according to a constant principle, but as soon as one element is derailed, the entire framework collapses. Demonstrating a seemingly impregnable yet delicate linkage, this work reminds us of today's climate crisis and our faltering state in the face of a global pandemic. Every element of *Causality* exists in an inseparable relationship with each other under an invisible rule. Thus, it urges that we escape dichotomous thinking and perceive causality from a holistic point of view to reflect on the relationship between humans and the natural environment, seek ways for coexistence, and work towards restoring a balanced and harmonious relationship.

OAA(정규동)

OAA (Jung Kyudong)

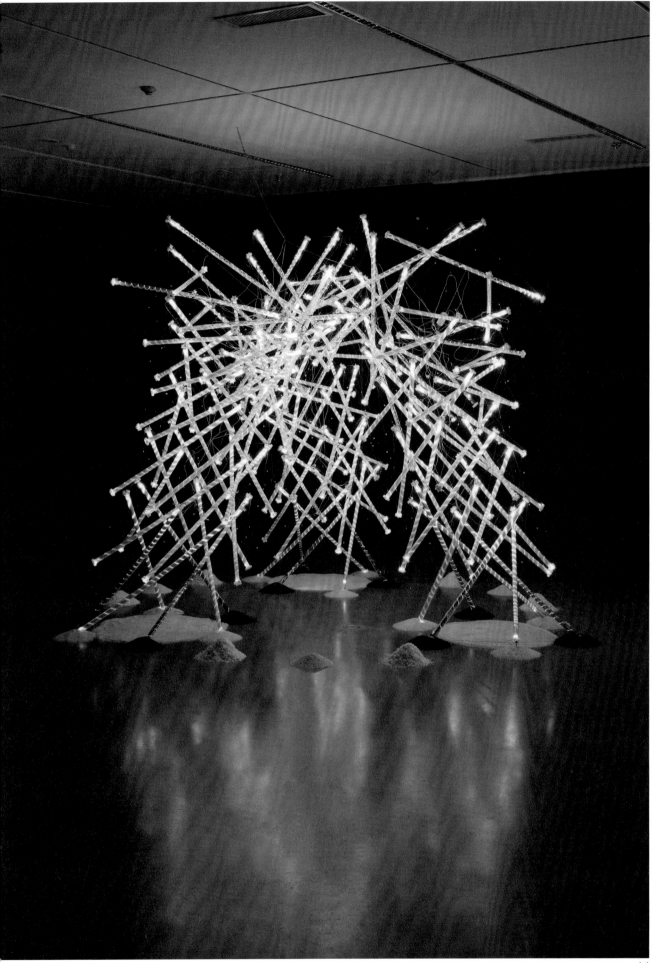

OAA(정규동)

OAA (Jung Kyudong)

(11)

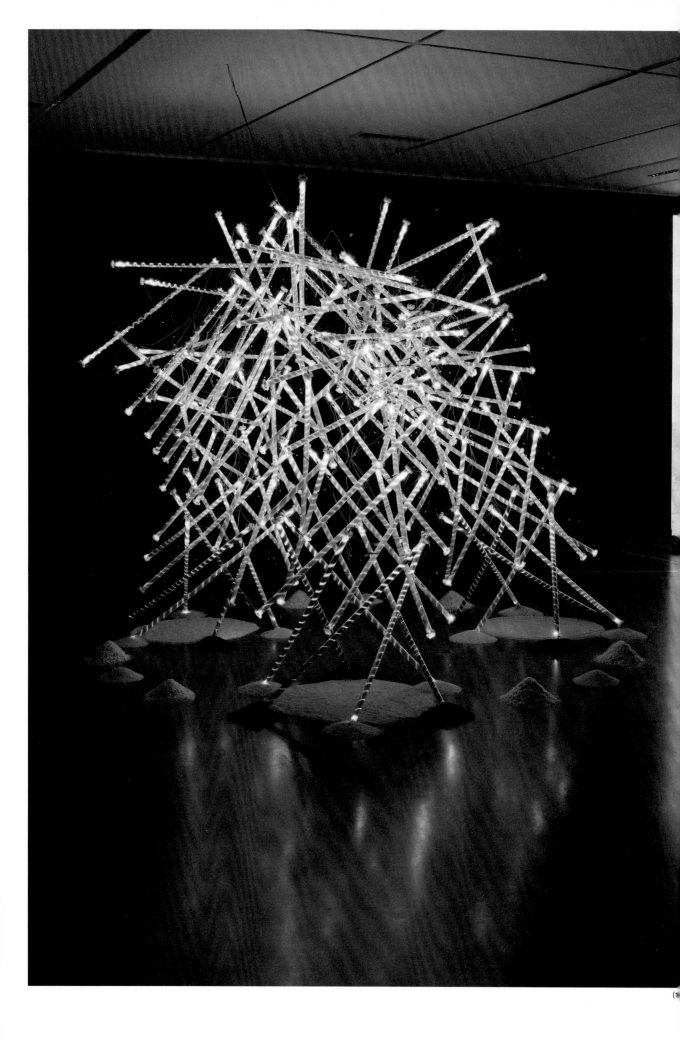

OAA(정규동)　　　　　　OAA (Jung Kyudong)

(11)

(11)

107   OAA(정규동)   OAA (Jung Kyudong)

(11)

OAA(정규동)   OAA (Jung Kyudong)

(12) 〈대공원 大空圜〉
2021
입체 영상, 컬러, 사운드
15분
국립현대미술관 커미션

감독. 장민승
음악. 정재일
편집 / 색보정. 존스톤
조감독. 이무언
프로듀서. 서광환

현장
촬영. 존스톤
시네마토그래피. 이우헌
조명. 전영석
그립. 나성식

스튜디오
촬영. 김선혁
조명. 최우혁
그립. 남현수
수중 촬영. 김동기
초고속 촬영. 옵티캠

CG 장-줄리앙 푸스
현장 녹음. 이범
음향. 김병극

제작팀
로케이션매니져. 양명헌
제작 팀장. 정희석
회계. 배희경
제작 보조. 이승룡, 한이삭

소품. 곽휘곤
말 조련사. 이천 호스파크
응사. 박용순

전시 구현
영상. 한국 AV
음향. AU 신도용
전시장 조성. 더디자인
설치 감리. 최상협

촬영 장소
청계산
관악산
국립현대미술관 과천관
서울대공원
한국마사회
서울랜드

기록 영상. 한국정책방송원

(12) carousel
2021
360° immersive video installation, color, sound
15 min
Commissioned by MMCA

Directed by Jang Minseung
Music by Jung Jaeil
Editing / Grading Johnston Warren Anthony
Assistant director Lee Mooun
Producer Seo Kwanghwan

Location
Director of photography Johnston Warren Anthony
Cinematography Lee Wooheon
Gaffer Jeon Youngsuk
Grip Na Seongsik

Studio
Director of photography Kim Sunhyuk
Gaffer Gafferwoo
Grip Nam Hyeonsu
Underwater photography Kim Donggi
HFR photography Opticam

CG artist Jean-Julien Pous
Field recording Lee Berm
Audio mixing / mastering Kim Byoungkeuk

Production Department
Location manager Yang Jisan
Production manager Jung Heeseok
Accountant Bae Huikyeong
Production assistant Lee Liong, Han Isak

Props designer Kwack Huigon
Wrangler Icheon Horse Park
Falconer Park Younsoon

Exhibition Implementation
Visual systems by AUDIO VISUAL KOREA
Audio systems by AU Shin Doyong
Space construction The Design
Installation manager Choi Perter Sanghyeob

Filming Location
Cheonggyesan Mt.
Gwanaksan Mt.
MMCA Gwacheon
Seoul Grand Park
Korea Racing Authority
Seoul Land

Archive film KTV

자연에 대한 의미 있는 영상 작업을 선보이고 있는 장민승은 과천의 과거와 현재의 시간 흐름 속에서 생태의 순환적 속성을 모색하는 신작 〈대공원 大空圜〉을 제작했다. 청계산과 관악산을 둘레로 하는 과천의 산자락에는 1980년대 초부터 동물원, 경마장, 서울랜드, 미술관 등의 시설이 자리 잡았고, 코끼리 열차의 궤도, 경마장 트랙, 동물원의 철창들 등 크고 작은 원형의 궤도가 관찰된다. 작가는 이 시설물에서 반복적으로 보여지는 원형 구조와 그 의미를 현재의 생태학적 관점에서 재구성해 360도 입체 영상으로 설계했다. 어린이날, 사생대회, 벚꽃놀이, 단풍놀이 등을 포함해 서울·경기 시민들의 여가 생활의 한 축으로 여러 세대에게 추억과 경험의 일부가 된 이곳의 건설 당시 자료와 현재 모습이 교차되는 영상을 보며 우리는 자연과 동물을 대하는 인간 중심적 시각과 행위에 관해 질문을 시작하게 된다. 작가가 비어 있다는 뜻의 '빌 공(空)' 자를 써서 '크게 빈 원'의 의미로 〈대공원 大空圜〉이라는 작품 제목을 붙인 이유는 '공존'의 감각이 부재했던 현대사의 단면을 말하기 위해서다. 즉, 이 작품은 자본주의가 만들어 낸 양극화, 전 세계적인 소비·물류의 순환 구조 속에서 소외되고 잊혀진 존재와 가치에 대해 질문을 던지는 행위다. 원형 스크린에 둘러싸여 여러 형태의 울타리를 경험하면서, 우리는 결국 누가 갇히게 되었는지를 보게 된다.

Jang Minseung, who presents meaningful video works on the subject of nature, produced this new work, exploring the city of Gwacheon's ecological environment. Surrounded by the Cheonggyesan and Gwanaksan Mountains, Gwacheon is bordered by a zoo, museum, racecourse for horse racing events, and theme park. Established in anticipation of the national event that was the 1988 Summer Olympics in Seoul, these facilities have been a major part of recreation in Seoul metropolitan area since their opening. Taking an aerial perspective, such as that of a drone, the video shows that the border of the city around the mountains forms a giant circle. Inside it, there is the circular racecourse, the circular dome of the museum, the circular carousel of the theme park Seoulland, and the circular Elephant Train track of Seoul Grand Park. Capturing these facilities, each of which is circular for its own purposes, the artist emphasizes "cyclicality" by presenting the video on a 360-degree screen. Cyclical structures that continue to revolve outside of ecological contexts don't just exist in Gwacheon; the artist is simply using Gwacheon as an example to address an aspect of modern history. He suggests that it's time we think about the polarization exacerbated by capitalism, the global cycle of consumption and logistics, and the people and values that are marginalized in the cycle. Titled carousel, as in a large, empty circle, this circular work can be interpreted not so much as criticism but as a metaphor for the possibility of the empty hole being refilled with the values lost amidst today's hectic modern life.

장민승

Jang Minseung

(12)

장민승 Jang Minseung

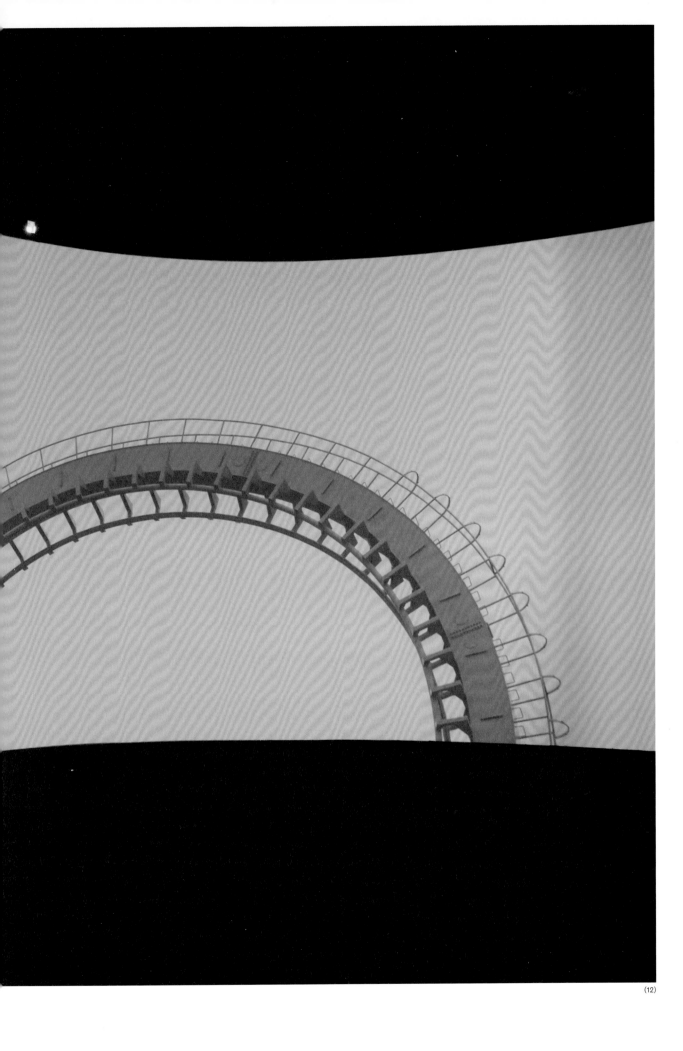

(12)

(12)

장민승   Jang Minseung

(12)

《한국 생태미술의 흐름과 현재》는 1970년대 한국 미술계에서 모더니즘과 기존 질서에 대한 새로움과 대안을 모색하는 과정에서 시도된 다양한 자연미술과 환경미술의 흐름 속에서 한국적 생태미학의 기원을 찾고 그 흐름을 추적하는 아카이브 전시다. 1970년대부터 전 세계적으로 환경과 공존이라는 논의가 본격화되던 시점에 한국에서도 개개인의 작가와 소규모 단체들이 유의미한 시도를 시작했다는 점에 주목했다.

1980년대 초에 시작되어 지금까지 존속 중인 '바깥미술'과 '야투(野投)'는 자연미술 단체로 잘 알려져 있지만, 그들의 여러 전시와 프로그램에는 현재의 생태학적 관점으로 재조명할 지점들이 상당히 존재한다. 지금의 관점에서 큰 울림을 주지만 그동안 잊혔던 작업들을 소개하는 일 역시 의미가 있을 것이다. 그중 이번 전시에서는 우선 흰 광목천을 바위에 둘러 하늘과 땅과 사람이 하나되는 경지를 구현한 전국광의 〈수평선〉(1975)을 재현한 퍼포먼스 기록을 사진과 영상으로 선보인다. 이 작업의 가치를 알리고자 애쓴 임동식은 한국 생태미술 본류의 시작점에 해당하는 인물로, 작가가 가진 세계관의 정수를 담은 〈선사시대 다가가기〉(2005)를 이번 전시에서 선보인다. 자연과 미술의 관계성과 지향을 연구한 단체 '야투'를 창립한 임동식에게 가장 중요한 것은 배려와 존중의 태도를 바탕으로 한 균형 있는 관계 맺음과 순수한 정신성의 지향이며, 이는 1990년대 '야투'에서 진행한 프로그램의 포스터에 등장하는 아기동자의 순수하고 맑은 모습에서도 확인할 수 있다.

The Progress and State of Korean Ecological Art is an archive exhibition that finds the origin of Korean ecological aesthetics and tracks the flow of various natural and environmental art attempted in the 1970s in the process of seeking novelty and alternatives to modernism and existing order. We note that artists and small groups in Korean art began to make meaningful attempts at a time when discussions on environmental coexistence began in earnest from the 1970s around the world.

Although Baggat Art and YATOO, which have begun in the early 80s and continue to this day, are well known as natural art groups, there are quite a few points that need to be re-examined from the current ecological perspective among their various exhibitions and programs. And it is also meaningful to introduce works that have been forgotten but have a great resonance from the present point of view. Among them, a performance record that re-produces Chun Kook-Kwang's Horizon (1975), which embodies the spiritual state where the sky, the ground, and people unite by wrapping a stripe of white cotton cloth around a rock, was prepared as photography and video for this exhibition. Rim Dong Sik, who tried to promote the value of this work, can be regarded as a root of the mainstream of Korean ecological art and he presents Approaching Prehistoric Times (2005), which contains the essence of his worldview. The most important thing for Rim Dong Sik, who founded YATOO, a group that studied the relationship and orientation of nature and art, is a balanced relationship based on an attitude of consideration and respect, and this can be seen from the pure and clear appearance of baby children in the 90s YATOO program posters.

한국 생태미술의 흐름과 현재

도시인으로 접하는 자연, 도시의 숲을 걷는 경험을 변형된 캔버스로 확장시키는 김보중의 회화는 부분적이고 불완전하게 부유하는 도시인과 도시 생태에 대한 감각적 사유다. 국경, 지역, 인종의 경계를 넘나들며 계속된 여행과 이동 속에서 소통과 교류로 새로운 창작의 가능성을 연 정재철 작가는 그 이동과 수행의 과정을 상세한 기록으로 남겼다. 전시에서는 작가가 자신이 오랫동안 거주하기도 했던 과천의 재개발 과정에서 남겨진 것들을 수집하고 기록한 결과물을 설치해 이미 사라진 과천의 시간과 공간을 기억해 본다. 한편, 기후 위기에 관해 적극적인 발언을 하는 활동가이자 작가인 이경호의 영상은 지구의 여러 지역에서 바람에 날아다니는 '봉다리'의 모습을 따라가며 유통과 소비의 편의를 위해 비닐봉지를 일상적으로 사용한 결과를 되짚어 보고 인간의 효용과 편익을 위해 희생된 많은 것을 생각하게 한다.

전시실 가운데에 자리한 아카이브는 한국 생태미술을 조사하고 정리하는 과정에서 참고한 작가, 단체의 전시 자료와 출판물을 그러모은 것으로 이를 통해 생태에 관한 관심을 확장하는 계기를 제공하고자 했다. 1970년대 중반부터 1980년대는 지금처럼 전 지구적 위기가 가시화된 상황도 아니었고, '생태'라는 용어도 일반적으로 사용되지 않던 때다. 그때부터 지금까지 큰 주목을 받지 못한 채 묵묵히 신념을 지켜낸 작가들의 생태학적 세계관과 태도를 아카이브 전시를 통해 알리고, 이를 바탕으로 더 활발한 조사 연구가 이루어져 한국 생태미술사 서술의 발판이 마련되기를 희망한다.

Kim Bo Joong's paintings, which expand the experience of walking through urban forests and nature as city dweller, are sensory contemplation on urban ecology in which urbanites are partially and incompletely existing while drifting. Jeoung Jae Choul, who opened the possibility of new creation through communication and exchange amid the continuous movement of travel across borders, regions, and races, has left a detailed record of the process of movement and performance. In the exhibition, it is in display what he has collected and recorded in the process of recent redevelopment of Gwacheon, where the artist lived and worked for a long time, and they help us to remember the time and space of Gwacheon that has already disappeared. Meanwhile, the video of Lee Kyung Ho, an activist-artist who speaks out on the climate crisis, follows the appearance of plastic bags flying in the wind in various parts of the earth, reflecting the results of daily use of plastic bags for convenience of distribution and consumption.

The archives located in the middle of the Main Hall are designed to expand interest on ecological themes by gathering printed materials and publications of artists, groups, and exhibition projects. From the mid-1970s to the 1980s, the global crises we experience today and even the term "ecology" had not yet emerged, but by collecting, sorting, and categorizing meaningful works and group activities that conveyed ecological principles or worldviews at the time, this archival exhibition seeks to lay the ground-work for the further documentation of Korean ecological art so that its history can be written in proper way.

The Progress and State of Korean Ecological Art

한국 생태미술의 흐름과 현재   The Progress and State of Korean Ecological Art

(13-1) 임동식
〈선사시대 다가가기〉
2005
캔버스에 유채
182×227cm
작가 소장

(13-2) 《예술과 마을》(공주 원골 마을, 2000)
도록 아카이브 재가공
2020
디아본
66×100cm
제작: 프레임바이프레임
서울시립 미술아카이브 소장

(13-3) 전국광 〈수평선〉(안면도 꽃지 해변,
1975) 재현 퍼포먼스(안면도 꽃지
해변, 2021) 기록 영상
2021
단채널 비디오, 컬러, 사운드
18분 33초
국립현대미술관 소장

(13-4) 전명은
전국광 〈수평선〉(안면도 꽃지 해변,
1975) 재현 퍼포먼스(안면도 꽃지
해변, 2021) 기록 사진
2021
크로모제닉 컬러 프린트
86×129cm(액자 포함)
국립현대미술관 소장

(13-1) Rim Dong Sik
Approaching Prehistoric Times
2005
Oil on canvas
182×227cm
Courtesy of the artist

(13-2) Reprocessed the exhibition
catalogue of *Art and Village*
2020
Acrylic frame
66×100cm
Made by Frame by Frame
Courtesy of Seoul Museum of Art
Archive

(13-3) Archival film of 2021
re-enactment of Chun
Kook-Kwang's performance
Horizon (Ggotji Beach,
Anmyeondo Island, 1975)
2021
Single-channel video, color,
sound
18 min 33 sec
MMCA collection

(13-4) Eun Chun
Archival photography of
2021 re-enactment of Chun
Kook-Kwang's performance
Horizon (Ggotji Beach,
Anmyeondo Island, 1975)
2021
Chromogenic color print
86×129cm (framed)
MMCA collection

전국광 + 임동식

Chun Kook-Kwang
Rim Dong Sik

(13-4) (13-2) (13-3) (13-1)

(13-4) (13-2)
(13-3)

123   한국 생태미술의 흐름과 현재   The Progress and State of Korean Ecological Art

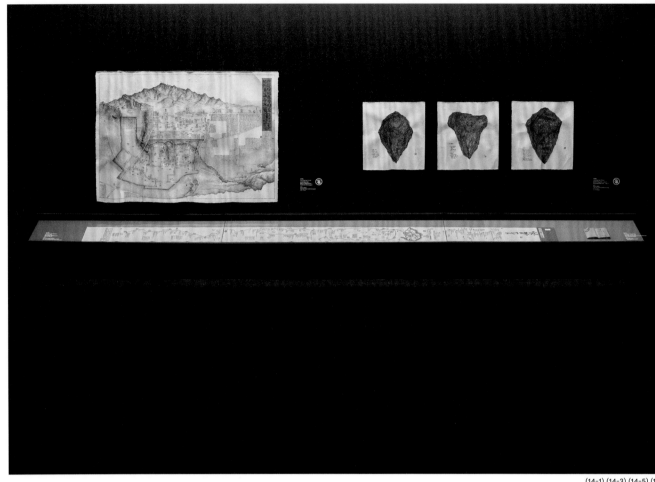

(14-1) (14-3) (14-5) (14-

(14-1) 〈관악청계분수령도〉
2017
장지에 수묵 채색
150×210cm
유족 소장

(14-2) 〈시간의 씨앗 1〉
2017
혼합 매체
가변 크기
유족 소장

(14-3) 〈드로잉 KGG 701-1, 2, 3〉
2017
장지에 수묵 채색
75×70cm(3)
유족 소장

(14-4) 〈세계일화—수집품 목록〉
2017
종이에 혼합 매체
17.5×12.5cm
유족 소장

(14-5) 〈경기천년 화첩〉
2017
종이에 혼합 매체
28×20cm, 28×535cm(펼친 면)
유족 소장

(14-1) *Map of Watershed - Gwanak
Cheonggye*
2017
Color on Korean traditional paper
150×210cm
Courtesy of the family

(14-2) *Seeds of time 1*
2017
Mixed media
Dimensions variable
Courtesy of the family

(14-3) *Drawing KGG 701-1, 2, 3*
2017
Color on Korean traditional paper
75×70cm (3)
Courtesy of the family

(14-4) *The whole world is a single
flower—List of collection*
2017
Mixed media on paper
17.5×12.5cm
Courtesy of the family

(14-5) *Gyeonggi 1000 Years sketch
book*
2017
Mixed media on paper
28×20cm, 28×535cm
(unfolded)
Courtesy of the family

정재철 Jeoung Jae Choul

124

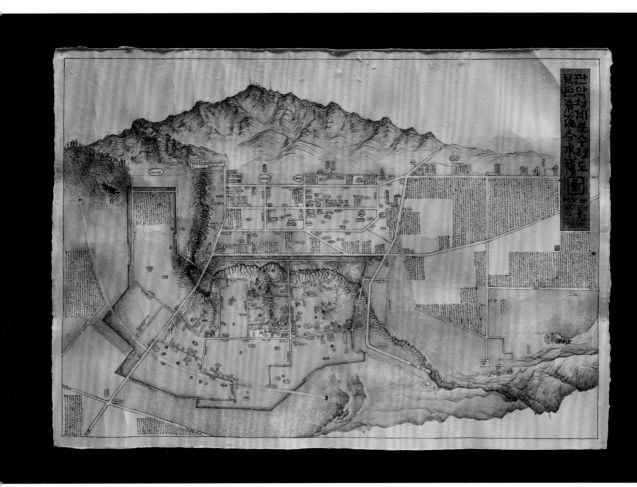

(14-1)

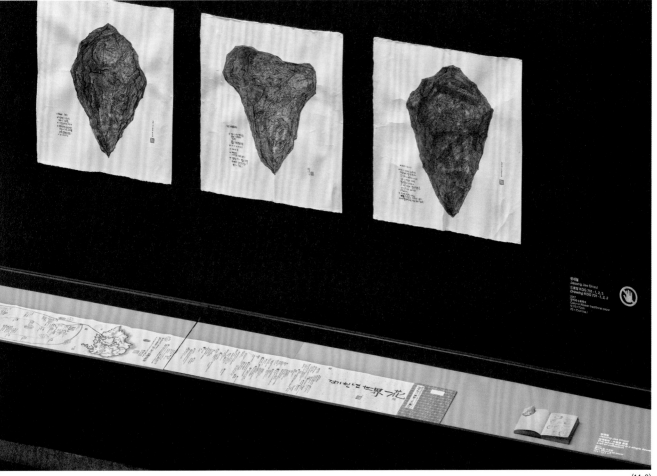

(14-3)
(14-5) (14-4)

(15

(15-1) 〈어딘가에〉
2006-2021
단채널 비디오, 컬러, 사운드
10분
작가 소장

(15-2) 〈지구와 사람〉
2019
단채널 비디오, 컬러, 사운드
10분
작가 소장

(15-1) *Somewhere*
2006-2021
Single-channel video, color,
sound
10 min
Courtesy of the artist

(15-2) *People for Earth*
2019
Single-channel video, color,
sound
10 min
Courtesy of the artist

이경호   Lee Kyung Ho

(15-1)

(15-2)

한국 생태미술의 흐름과 현재　The Progress and State of Korean Ecological Art

(16-4) (16-2) (16-1) (16-

(16-1) 〈천안—목천저수지〉
1998
변형 캔버스에 유채
130×97cm(3)
작가 소장

(16-2) 〈자라는 사다리〉
1997
변형 캔버스에 유채
234×125cm
작가 소장

(16-3) 〈숲 안의 거주지〉
2000-2004
자연목 구조물에 유채
145×130×70cm
작가 소장

(16-4) 〈빛나는 길〉
2019
자연목 구조물에 유채
162×62×28cm
작가 소장

(16-1) *Cheonan—Mokcheon reservoir*
1998
Oil on transformed canvas
130×97cm (3)
Courtesy of the artist

(16-2) *Growing ladder*
1997
Oil on transformed canvas
234×125cm
Courtesy of the artist

(16-3) *Residence in the woods*
2000-2004
Oil on wooden structure
145×130×70cm
Courtesy of the artist

(16-4) *Shining path*
2019
Oil on wooden structure
162×62×28cm
Courtesy of the artist

김보중   Kim Bo Joong

(16-4)

(16-1)

(16-2)

(16-3)

한국 생태미술의 흐름과 현재   The Progress and State of Korean Ecological Art

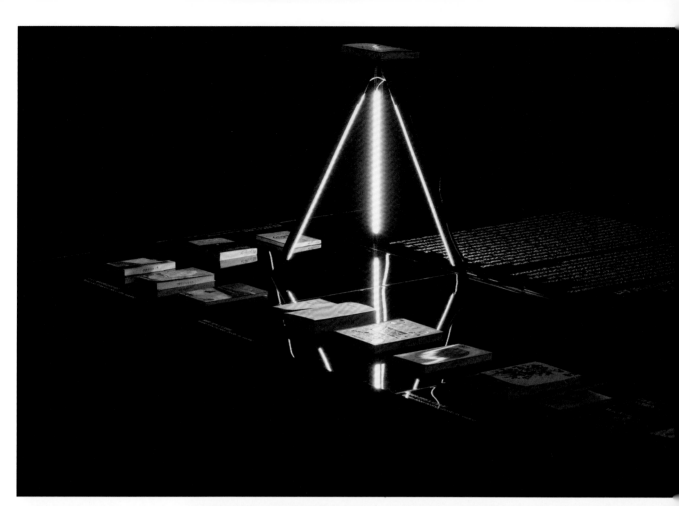

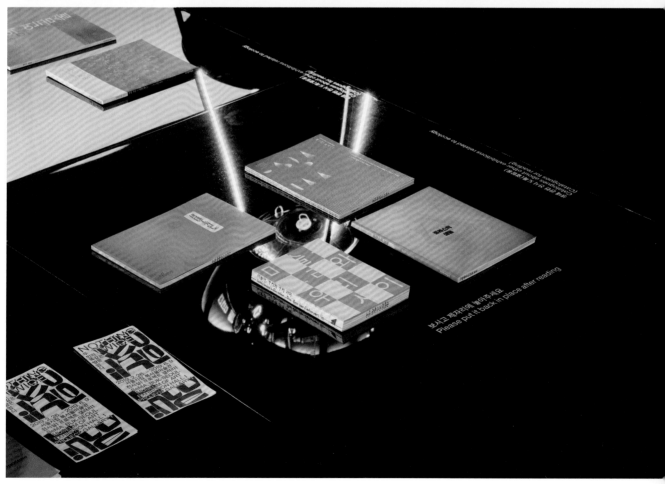

정재철의 기록이 담긴 노트

한국 생태미술의 흐름과 현재   The Progress and State of Korean Ecological Art

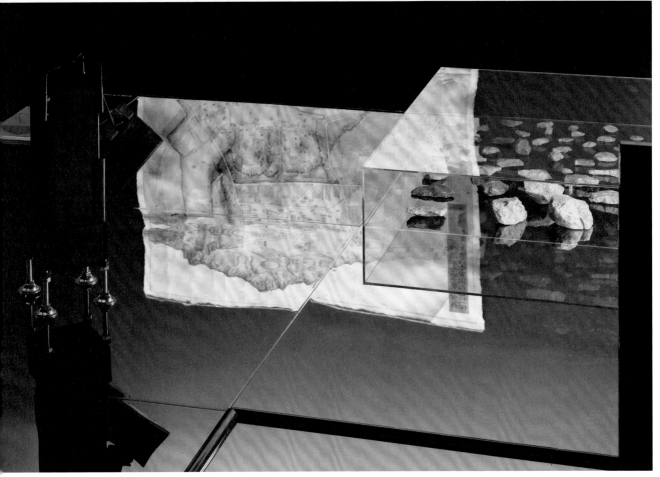

한국 생태미술의 흐름과 현재   The Progress and State of Korean Ecological Art

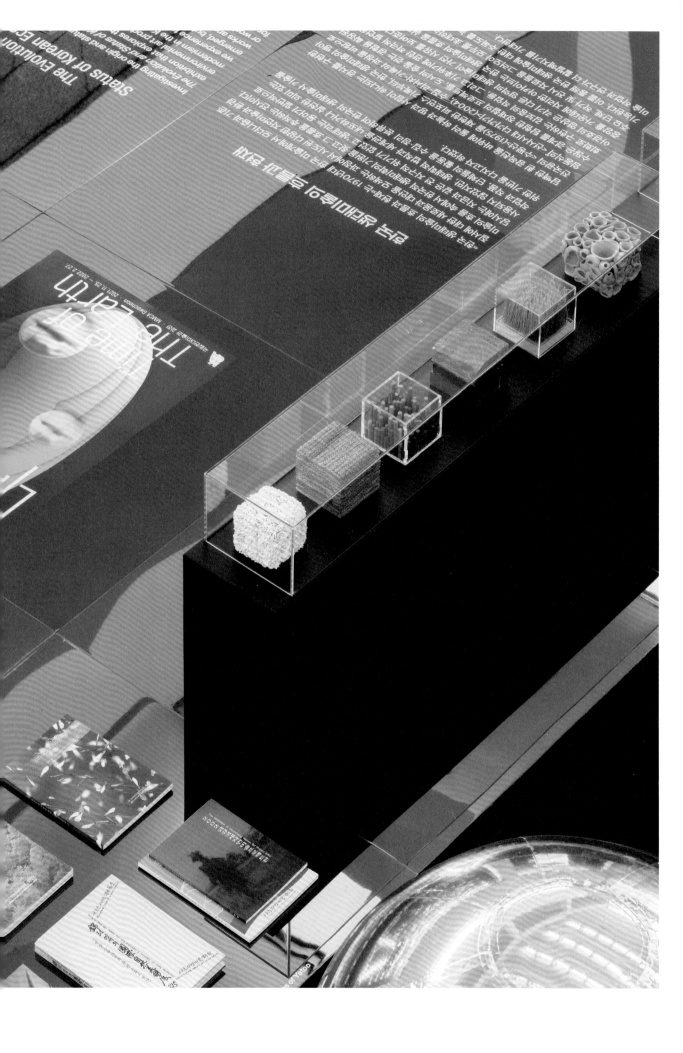

한국 생태미술의 흐름과 현재　The Progress and State of Korean Ecological Art

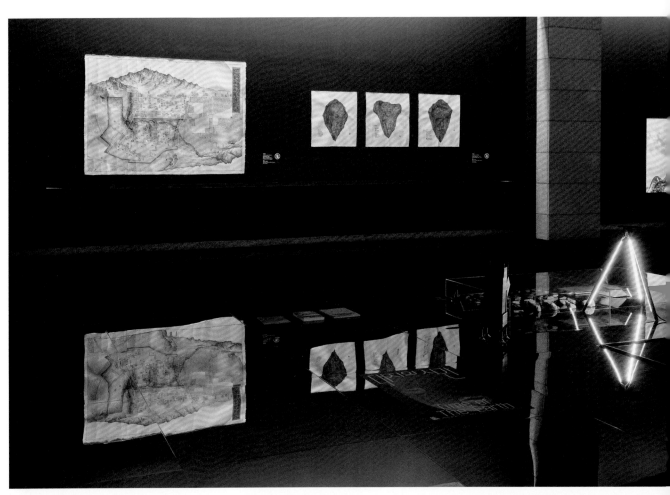

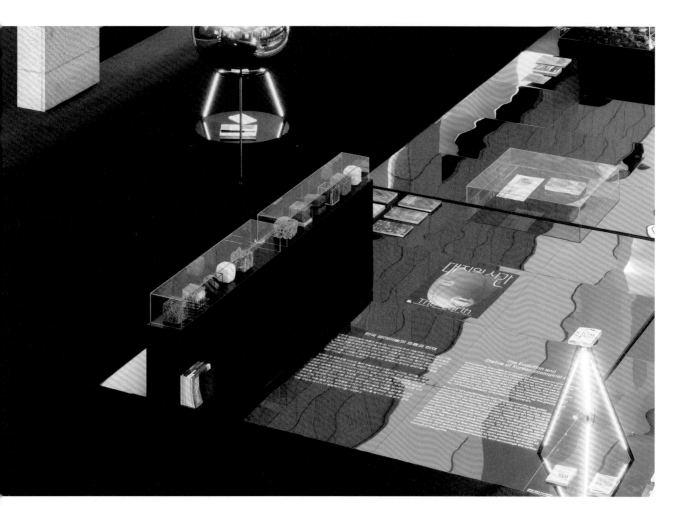

한국 생태미술의 흐름과 현재   The Progress and State of Korean Ecological Art

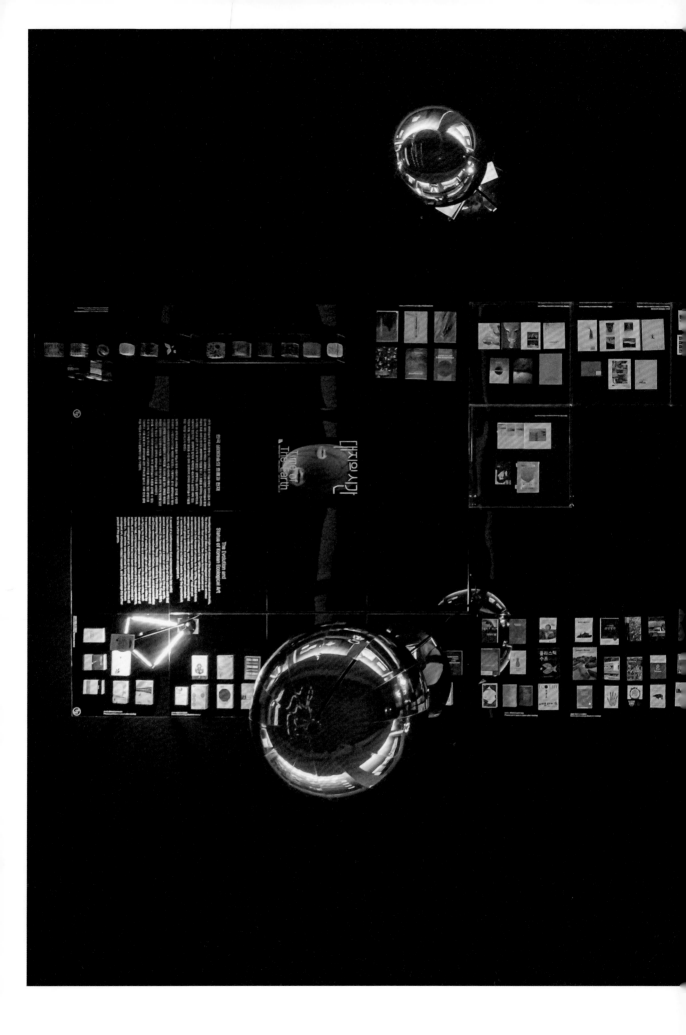

한국 생태미술의 흐름과 현재　　　The Progress and State of Korean Ecological Art

에세이   Essay

생명과 잡것의 미학

임지연
미학의 집 소장, 생명정치재단 이사

Life and the Aesthetic of Vulgarity

Im Ji-yeon
Director of House of Aesthetics; Director of Institute of Biopolitics

인간 이성과 분리 활동

"정작 생명을 알지도 못하면서 그것을 말한다." 얼마 전 개인적으로 연구하고 있는 샤머니즘 관련 인터뷰 도중 상대가 던진 말이다. 지나가듯 한 말이었지만, 나는 감추려고 했던 어리석음을 들킨 것만 같아 한차례 마음이 내려앉았다. 실상 생명에 관해서라면 한 번도 경험해 보지 못한 것을 막연한 상상 속에서 쫓고 있는 것인지도 모르겠다. 혹은 책에서 읽은 내용을 두고 비로소 생명을 알게 되었다고 생각하는 것일 수도 있다.

아리스토텔레스(Aristoteles)도 언급했듯이 인간에게 앎은 분명한 쾌감을 준다. 그러나 지금 우리가 처해 있는 상황을 떠올려 보면 단지 '앎'의 '쾌'만으로는 부족하다. 바이러스로 인한 팬데믹과 기후 위기의 상황은 인간을 비롯해 비인간 생명체의 건강과 생존도 위협하고 있다. 대규모 재난 상황과 자본의 왜곡된 힘으로 인한 경제적 불평등 및 사회적 고통은 심심치 않게 죽음을 떠올려야 하는 수준으로 가중되었다. 필요한 지식은 이미 차고 넘친다. 위험을 알리는 신호들은 수십 년 전부터 데이터 형태로 충분히 전달되었다. 지식의 양으로 치자면, 또 지식이 문제 해결의 열쇠라면, 지금과 같은 상황은 벌어지지 않아야 할 것이다. 기후 위기의 심각성을 전 세계에 알렸던 그레타 툰베리(Greta Thunberg)의 요청은 말로 떠드는 것은 그만하고 제발 행동에 나서자는 것이었다. 지금 우리에게 필요한 것은 활자와 정보값으로 저장해 두었던 지식을 체화하는 일이다. 또 작은 행동일지라도 올바른 방향 속에서 그것을 실천해야 한다. 첫 줄의 말을 화자의 취지에 따라 다시 적어보자면, '우리는 생명체임에도 그런 사실을 제대로 경험해 보지 못했다. 우리는 살아도 산 적이 없다'.

앎을 통해 세상을 인식하고 이해하는 활동은 인간 삶의 고유한 방법이다. 그러나 지식과 그것의 일반적 형태인 언어 구조는 생생하게 살아있는 삶의 현장감을 퇴색시키기도 한다. 지금 내가 있는 거실 한편에는 푸른 잎의 식물이 놓여 있다. 창문 너머로 동네 사람들의 대화가 들려온다. 나는 이 글을 쓰기 위해 책상 앞에 앉아 있다. 내가 경험하고 있는 이 모든 것은 다 무엇일까? 식물과 사람들, 나에게 공통되는 그 생명이란 것의 실체란 무엇일까? 아니, '실체', '무엇'이라는 식으로 접근하는 것이 과연 생명에 합당한 일일까? 따지면 따질수록 번잡하고 우습다는 느낌이 든다. 푸른 잎의 식물이 제 생명의 실체를 '알고서' 저리 있지는 않을 것이다. 묻는 자는 인

Human reason and separation activities

"You say that without even knowing what life really is." Not long ago, these words were spoken to me during an interview I was conducting on the topic of shamanism, something that I have been researching independently. It was an ordinary observation, said in passing, but it made my heart sink and gave me the feeling that the foolishness I had been trying to conceal had been exposed. When it comes to life, perhaps I'm chasing something I've never experienced before in a dim place in my imagination. I may have read something in a book and come to believe that I understand life.

As Aristotle observed, knowledge gives humans a definite sense of pleasure—but if we consider humanity's current situation, the "pleasure" of mere knowing does not seem like enough. The COVID-19 pandemic and the climate crisis threaten the health and survival not just of humankind, but of non-human life as well. The economic inequalities and societal suffering spawned by large-scale disasters and the twisted power of money have escalated to a point at which we have to start seriously contemplating death. We already have more than enough of the knowledge we need to reduce suffering and make a change toward the values of life. Signs of danger have been amply communicated in the form of data for decades now. Viewed simply in terms of the volume of information, our situation would not have come about if knowledge had been the key to solving problems. When Greta Thunberg speaks to the world about the seriousness of the climate crisis, her plea is for us to stop just talking about things and start taking action. What we now must do is internalize the knowledge that has been stored up in the form of letters and information values. We must take steps in the right direction, even if they are very small. If I were to rephrase the opening sentence the way the speaker intended it, I might say something like, "Even though we are organisms, we have never truly experienced the truth of life. Even as we have lived, we have never lived."

It is an inherent way of life for humans to recognize and understand the world through knowledge. But knowledge and the linguistic structure in which it is generally represented sap away the immediacy of life as it is vividly lived. In the living room where I sit right now, there is a plant with green leaves. Through the window, I hear the voices of my neighbors conversing. To write this, I sat down at my desk. What are all these things that I am ex-

간일 뿐, '생명'이니 '존재 근거'니 하는 말들도 인간이 만들어 낸 관념에 불과하다.

일찍이 니체(Friedrich Wilhelm Nietzsche)는 현실의 구조가 언어의 구조와 같다고 생각하는 데서 서구 형이상학의 가장 큰 오류가 비롯되었다고 말했다. 예컨대 '바람이 분다'라고 말하지만, 현실적으로 '바람'과 '불다'는 분리되지 않고 통일된 상태로 일어난다. 오로지 인간만이 이 단일한 활동을 주어와 술어 구조 속에서 나누어 생각한다. 성경의 그 유명한 선악과 이야기는 인류의 역사가 지성의 탄생과 함께 시작된다는 사실을 잘 보여 준다. 지식의 나무(the Tree of Knowledge)에 열린 열매를 먹은 인간은 부끄러움을 알게 된 뒤, 평화롭고 순수한 땅에서 쫓겨난다. 지식과 앎의 열매를 먹음으로써 인간은 신으로부터 전격적으로 분리되어 자신만의 힘겨운 삶을 살게 된다. '판단'을 뜻하는 독일어 'Urtiel'은 이러한 '근원적(ur-)' '나눔(Teil)'의 사건을 품고 있는 말로서, 지식 일반은 '~은/는 ~이다'라는 이 나눔의 형식, 즉 주어와 술어의 구조로 형성된다. 생명의 단일한 활동성은 언어와 사유 속에서 조각들로 흩어진다.

생명에 접근하기 위해 지식과 일반 문법에 전적으로 의존하는 것은 분명 한계를 지니지만, 현대 문명의 근간이 된 서구 근대의 인간 및 이성 중심주의는 이와 같은 한계를 더욱 고착하고 확산시켰다. 물론 그 시작은 진리를 추구하고 그에 따라 세상을 보는 새로운 방법론을 제시하는 일이었다. 데카르트(René Descartes)의 중심 명제인 '나는 생각한다. 그러므로 존재한다(cogito ergo sum)'는 자아와 신의 존재마저 인간의 이성 활동 속에서 증명하고자 했다. 존재의 참된 바는 수학적 계산과 논리적 추론 활동에 따라 획득되며, 좌표계의 값을 통해 보편적으로 전달된다. 이러한 이성적 사유 방식은 비단 학문 영역만이 아니라 일상에서도 도움이 되었다. 자신의 생명과 시간, 재능 등의 가치를 표명하자면 아득하기만 하지만, 그것을 시간당 임금으로 환산하면 거래할 수 있는 수준으로까지 명확해진다. 로크(John Locke)의 '인격(person)' 개념에 담긴 기획은 이를 그대로 반영한다. 『통치론』에서 로크는 모든 인간은 자신의 인격 안에 재산(property)을 지니며, 노동, 시간, 생명, 재능 등 그의 모든 속성이 이 재산에 속한다고 주장한다. 극단적으로 말하자면, 존재하는 모든 것은 재산 혹은 사물 차원으로 치환되었을 때 비로소 공동체의 구성원이 될 수 있다는 것이다. 인간이든 자연이든 있는 바 그대로의 상태는 없는 것과 마찬가지이며, 거래 가능한 상태로 등록되었을 때 그제야 존재하기 시작한다.

무관심한 미학과 순수하기만 한 예술

물론 이성을 통한 문명 발달의 성과를 무시할 수는 없다. 세부 전공 영역으로 분리된 학문은 많은 양의 지식을 생산했고, 인류는 더욱 풍요롭고 편리한 삶을 살 수 있게 되었다. 그러나 전쟁과 무분별한

periencing? What is the reality of the "life" that I share with such plants and people? Is it even appropriate for me to approach life in terms of words like "reality" and "object." The more I question life, the more vexing and comical it feels. The plant over there with its green leaves doesn't exist there because it "understands" the reality of its being. It is only humans who ask; terms like "life" and "basis for existence" are nothing more than concepts that we have created.

Friedrich Nietzsche once said that the biggest error of Western metaphysics originated in thinking that reality had the same structure as language. We say that "the wind blows," for example, but in reality, "the wind" and "blowing" are not separate; they occur in an integrated state. It is only humans who divide that single action up to conceptualize it within a "subject-predicate" structure. The famous story of the forbidden fruit in the Bible clearly demonstrates how human history began with the birth of knowledge. After eating fruit from the Tree of Knowledge, humans came to know shame and were driven out of their peaceful, pure land. By consuming that fruit of knowledge, they found themselves suddenly separated from God, condemned to live difficult lives on their own. The German word *Urteil*, meaning "judgment," consists of *ur-* ("original") and *Teil* ("dividing"). Knowledge ordinarily follows this structure of subject and predicate, this division between "A" and "is B." As long as humans think, they continue to break these unitary actions of life—the things that exist and happen—into scattered fragments of language.

When we deal with life, there are clear limits to our total dependance on knowledge and ordinary grammar. However, these limits are cemented and expanded by the central role assigned to humans and reason by Western modernity, which serves as the basis for today's civilization. This began, obviously, with the conception of a new methodology for seeking truth and viewing the world. With his central proposition "*cogito, ergo sum*" ("I think, therefore I am"), René Descartes even sought to demonstrate the existence of the self and God within the activities of human reason. The truth of existence is acquired through mathematical calculation and the workings of logical deduction, then conveyed universally through the values in a coordinate system. This rational way of thinking became a source of support not just for academia but for everyday life. When asked to express the values of one's life, time, abilities, and so forth, we can only be vague—but when these are converted into hourly wages, they are clarified as things that can be traded. The design in Locke's concept of the "person" offers a clear reflection of this. In *Two Treatises of Government*, Locke claims that all people possess property within their person, and that all of a person's qualities—such as their labor, time, life, and abilities—fall into the category of this

자연 개발, 사회경제적 차별로 인한 고통은 여전히 인류사에서 사라지지 않는다. 20세기 이후 인간의 도구적 이성 사용에 대한 비판이 강도 높게 제기되기도 했으나, 빠른 속도로 진행되는 대규모 자본의 형성과 새로운 기술의 변화에 대응할 현실적인 운동을 만들지는 못했다.

비판 의식의 한계는 아도르노(Theodor Wiesengrund Adorno)의 기획 속에서도 지적될 수 있다. 그는 개체의 독특한 차이들을 하나로 만드는 이성의 동일화 운동에서 전체주의적 정치 체제의 근본 원리를 발견하고, 이를 거부할 수 있는 이성의 '부정' 운동을 강조했다. 그러나 그의 사상은 끝내 엘리트주의라는 비판을 면하지 못하는데, 나는 그 이유를 집단화에 대한 그의 두려움에서 발견한다. 전체주의에 대한 비판과 회의가 깊었던 탓에, 그는 집합체로서의 대중 역시 거대한 힘에 휩쓸리는 우매한 군중으로 인식했다. 그는 스스로 대중 속으로 들어가지 않는다. 그의 음악 역시 의식이 또렷하게 깨어있도록 자극하지만, 대중의 심정을 끌어올리지는 못한다. 어쩌면 집단화 자체가 근본적 문제는 아닐 것이다. 사람들의 집단 에너지가 권력의 폭력적인 지배하에서 왜곡되는 것이 문제이며, 이 왜곡된 관계성을 해체하고 재조직할 힘이 개인 차원에서는 온전히 마련될 수 없다는 점에 어려움이 있다. 집단적인 몸체로서 사회를 다른 국면으로 전환하는 에너지는 역시 대중 속에서 형성되어야 한다. 그가 강조한 깨어있는 의식은 어느 때건 중요하지만, 정작 그러한 의식의 실행 주체가 될 사람들을 믿지 못한다면 그것은 한낱 관념의 유희에 불과하다. 그는 대중의 우매함만을 염려할 것이 아니라 그런 가운데에도 전혀 다른 운동을 일으킬 수 있는 그들의 잠재력을 보아야만 했다. 비판 의식은 나와 너의 차이를 인정하되 관계의 왜곡이라는 폭력에 함께 저항해 간다는 연대 의식과 믿음을 기초로 작동해야 한다.

한편 엘리트주의는 비단 아도르노만이 아니라 서양 근대 미학 전반에서 발견되는 기조이기도 하다. 근대 미학은 이성의 우월적 지위가 인정되던 시절, 진리를 추구하는 데에서 감성 영역의 자율적 역할을 강조하며 등장한 학문이다. 이성의 독단적 사용에 대한 비판과 이성만으로는 인간의 온전함과 세상의 진리를 다 파악할 수 없다는 시각은 당시 학문 영역에 새로운 지평을 여는 일이기도 했다. 그러나 감성과 그것의 합당한 장소로서 몸에 대한 가치를 새로이 조명할 국면을 형성했음에도 미학은 자신의 역할과 정체성을 이성 철학에 복속시키는 방식으로 타협한다. 즉, 당시 이성을 중심에 둔 계몽의 기획 속에서 미학은 감성을 기초로 인간을 이해하되, 이를 통해 역시 계몽주의적 '교양인'을 배출하는 일에 몰두한다. 특히 근대 미학의 '무관심성(disinterestedness)'은 교양인의 이상을 위한 최적의 원리로 제시되었다.

무관심성은 아름다움을 판단하는 자의 기본 태도이다. 취미판단의 순간 인간은 자신의 사적인 이해관계나 이익(interest)으로부터 거

property. In more extreme terms, this can be seen as saying that we only become part of a community when everything that exists is transposed into the dimension of property or objects. This asserts that humans and nature alike have no "proper" state; they only start to exist when registered in a state that can be transacted.

Apathetic art and (merely) fine art

Of course, we cannot simply overlook the achievements and advancements made in civilization through reason. Subdivided into detailed areas of specialization, fields of scholarship have yielded vast volumes of information, and humans have been able to live richer and more convenient lives as a result. Yet war has not vanished from human history, nor has the indiscriminate exploitation of nature or the suffering caused by socioeconomic discrimination. Since the 20th century, people have been vocally critical of the instrumental use of reason by humankind. However, they have also been unable to create a realistic movement to respond to the rapid development of large-scale capital and transformations in new technology.

The limits of critical consciousness may also be observed in Theodor Adorno's project. Adorno identified the core principles of the totalitarian political regime in human reason's tendency toward "identification," in which unique individual differences are merged into a single, abstract whole. To respond to and repudiate this, he emphasized a movement of "negating" reason. But his ideas were ultimately criticized as elitist—something that I attribute to his fear of collectivization. So critical and deeply skeptical of totalitarianism was he that he perceived the collective public as a foolish multitude trapped in the grip of vast forces. He did not place himself among the crowd. His music is stimulating in a way that allows for a clear awakened consciousness, but it fails to uplift the hearts of the masses. Collectivization, at any rate, cannot fundamentally be the problem in and of itself. If such a problem exists, it lies in the way that humans' collective energy becomes distorted under the violent dominance of the power structure, as well as in the fact that the power to deconstruct and reorganize this skewed relationship cannot be mustered fully at the individual level. The power to transform society as a collective body must inevitably take shape from within the masses. The awakened consciousness that Adorno emphasizes is always important, but when one doesn't trust the people who will be the agents of that consciousness, it ends up as nothing more than conceptual play. Rather than simply worrying about the foolishness of the masses, he should have seen their potential to achieve an entirely different movement nonetheless. Even as it recognizes the differences between "you" and "me," critical consciousness should be based on a sense of solidarity and a belief in

리를 두어 초연하고 무관심한 내적 상태에 있(어야 한)다. 그러나 사유재산과 소유에 대한 감각이 민감해지는 시대에, 무관심성에 기초한 미적 태도는 위선적이고 계급적인 냄새를 풍긴다. 자신의 노동 시간을 빠짐없이 계산하여 거래해도 생계가 어려운 사람들에게 사적 이해로부터 거리를 두는 것(dis-interest-)이 배운 자의 교양 있는 태도라는 말은 가슴 시리다. 무관심성은 삶의 모든 조건이 충족된 상태에서 떠올려 볼 수 있는, 혹은 '완전한 인간'이라는 이상에 적합한 이야기이다. 또한 대상에 관심을 두지 않는 태도를 아름다운 인간의 모습이라 교육하고 각인시킴으로써 사람들을 기득권의 지배 시스템에 쉽게 순응하도록 길들인다.

현대 철학자인 랑시에르(Jacques Rancière), 아렌트(Hannah Arendt) 등은 무관심성을 공동체적 삶을 위한 전적인 평등과 공통감의 근본 원리로 지적하기도 한다. 개인주의와 서열화된 가치관에서 벗어나 새로운 공통의 삶을 위한 존재론적 근거를 마련하고자 하는 이들의 의도에는 충분히 공감한다. 그러나 대상에 무관심한 태도를 취하는 것만으로 평등하고 공동체적인 삶을 향한 의지가 저절로 생기는지는 의문이다. 무관심성이 공동체적 삶의 조건이라면, 여기에는 자기 영역과 소유의 욕망을 잠시 접는 일에 더하여 함께 사는 삶을 향한 깊은 '관심'과 그것을 기꺼이 지향하겠다는 내적인 결단이 필요하다.

무관심한 미학은 당대 발명된 순수예술 개념의 주요 원리이기도 했다. 진-선-미의 고전적 결합이 분해되고 이제 아름다움과 예술은 자율적인 원리에 따라 독립적인 영역을 구축한다. 도덕이나 윤리, 참된 것, 신(神) 등에 무관심한 예술은 오로지 인간의 '즐거움'을 위한 형식을 생산하는 일에 바쳐진다. 이에 따라 삶과 예술 사이에 분리가 일어나는 것은 자연스러웠다. 예술가는 생계에 허덕이면서도 세상의 이해관계로부터 벗어난 순수한 예술 세계를 건설하는 일에 때로는 기꺼이, 때로는 자기 삶을 저주하며 몰두해 갔다. 인간사의 희로애락과 각종 사회 문제에 깨어있지 않은 바는 아니었으나, 그러한 의식 활동의 예술적 터전 자체는 사회 구성을 위한 하나의 독립적인 영역으로, 그것도 하는 말에 비해 그리 큰 영향력은 주지 못하는 정도로 안정화되었다.

낭만주의 이후 예술의 내면화와 관념화는 이러한 경향을 더욱 가속화했다. 헤겔(Georg Wilhelm Friedrich Hegel)의 '예술의 종말' 이후, 시대에 맞는 새로운 예술 형식의 등장을 기대하기도 했으나, 신매체의 등장과 기술 변이 속에서도 예술은 자기중심적, 자기 반영적 관념 운동을 지속한다. 자기만을 생산할 뿐 다른 세계와 연결되길 거부한 예술의 정신은 20세기 이후 자본의 추상 운동에 가볍이 올라탄다. 이 과정은 생각보다 쉬웠는데, 이는 자본이 현대적 삶의 기본 조건으로 자리하게 된 탓도 크지만, 예술 스스로 기꺼이 '개념'의 형태를 취했기 때문이기도 하다. 관념 운동과 자본 운동은 모든 것을 끝내 '자기' 안으로 끌어들여 '자기'를 증대시킨다는 점

working together in order to resist the violence of distorted relationships.

Elitism is not unique to Adorno; it is found as an undertone all across modern Western aesthetics. The field of modern aesthetics emerged from an emphasis on the emotional realm holding an independent role in the pursuit of truth. At the time, reason was seen as holding a position of predominance. The critique of the dogmatic application of reason, and the attitude that human wholeness and the truth of the world cannot be fathomed through reason alone, helped to open up new horizons in academia at the time. But despite creating an opportunity to newly consider emotion (and the body as its proper setting), the field of aesthetics makes compromises in a way that subordinates its own role and identity to the philosophy of reason. Within the plan of the Enlightenment and the central role that it assigned to reason, aesthetics used emotion as a basis for understanding humans, though the process was focused on using this as a way to produce individuals who were "cultivated" along Enlightenment lines. In particular, the disinterestedness of modern aesthetics was presented as an optimal principle for achieving the cultivation ideal.

Disinterestedness is a basic attitude of the judge of beauty. In moments of judgments of taste, people exist (or are supposed to exist) in an aloof and disinterested internal state, distancing themselves from any personal stake or interest. But in an era of increasingly acute sensitivity to private property and possession, the aesthetic stance based on disinterestedness evokes a hypocritical, classist sense. To people who struggle to make ends meet even as they calculate and trade their labor time down to the second, it is painful to hear people speak of "disinterest"—distance from personal interests—as the cultivated attitude of the learned person. Disinterestedness is something we can imagine happening in a state where all the needs of life are met; it is suited to the ideal of the "consummate human." In education, we instill people with the idea that an attitude of disinterest in objects is a form of human beauty, and in the process, we push them to submit readily to a system of control by established interests.

In modern philosophy, figures like Jacques Rancière and Hannah Arendt have referred to disinterestedness as a basic principle of utter equality and common sense for the sake of community living. One can certainly sympathize with their aim to provide an existential basis for a new shared life that would exist beyond individualism and the ranking of values. The question is whether the desire for an equitable, communitarian life simply arises of its own accord from our adoption of a disinterested attitude toward an object. If disinterestedness is a prerequisite for a communitarian life, then this entails on our part an inner determination not only to temporarily let go

에서 하나의 가족이다.

생명을 맞이하는 일에서 현대 예술이 수줍어하거나 소극적인 태도를 보이는 것은 자기 영역을 형성하는 관념 외에 다른 운동을 일으킬 힘을 망각했기 때문으로 보인다. 관념 생산을 통한 자기 증대 운동은 아무리 맹렬하다고 해도 역시 같은 운동을 낳을 뿐이다. 이성-무관심성-순수성은 자기만의 배타적 영역을 구축한다는 점에서 공통적이다. 자본의 존재 목적 역시 무한한 자기 증대이다. 자기 안을 맴돌며 자기만을 키우는 운동은 지루할 뿐만 아니라 폭력적이다. 자기에게만 관심 있는 냉담하고 딱딱한 운동이 아닌 생명과 만나려는 새로운 운동이 일어나길 기대하는 것은 무리일까? 지금 우리의 사는 모습이 그리 나쁘지 않고 그런대로 괜찮다면 특별히 무엇인가를 하기 위해 시간을 쓸 필요는 없을 것이다. 그러나 이대로는 힘들어 '도저히 견딜 수 없는' 어떤 것이 목구멍까지 차오른다면 우리는 변화를 위한 행동을 해야 한다. 말은 뼈와 근육, 피가 펄떡이는 심장을 입고 다시 태어나야 한다. 예술은 자아와 자기라는 순수한 이성의 한계에서 벗어나 복수의 주체성으로 거듭나야 한다.

너에게 들리다

근대 미학과 순수예술의 자율적 작동 원리 중 하나는 '쾌' 감정이다. 이 기조는 현대 예술에서도 유지되는 모습이다. '복잡하게 생각하지 말고 즐겁게 놀다 가'라는 말이 작품 소개에 습관적으로 따라붙는다. 그런데 오로지 즐겁게 노는 것을 생각하면 오락실이나 유원지에 가는 것이 손쉽다. 미디어의 화려한 색채와 이미지, 유혹적인 말들이 우리 일상을 채우고, 흥미를 유발하는 내러티브가 하루에도 셀 수 없을 정도로 쏟아져 나온다. 자본과 과학기술이 삶의 주류가 된 현실에서 '단지 즐거움'이란 감정은 관성적이고, 표피적이고, 순종적이다.

쾌 감정은 앞에서도 지적한 '앎'의 활동과 직접적으로 연결되어 있기도 하다. 공포영화를 볼 때 우리는 정체를 분명하게 '알 수 없는' 대상이나 상황 앞에서 두려움을 느낀다. 무지는 인간의 앎의 욕구를 불러일으키고, 근원적 무지 상태에서 벗어나고자 하는 인간의 노력은 지금과 같은 고도로 발전한 문명의 모습을 이룩했다. 지식의 추구는 즐거움의 추구이며, 같은 맥락에서 지금 우리는 역사상 가장 즐거운 시대를 살고 있(어야 한)다.

표피적 쾌 감정은 생태 감수성과 생명 가치로의 전환을 이야기할 때도 등장한다. 위험 인자를 확인했을 때 드는 순간적인 앎의 쾌감이나, 생태 친화적 삶을 살(고 있다고 생각할) 때 드는 윤리적인 쾌감 등으로 말이다. 그러나 이러한 쾌감은 근대의 지식 생산 방식과 그로 인한 현대의 자본 운동을 그대로 반복하는 모습에 그치기 쉽다. 인과에 대한 선형적 인식과 자본주의 속에서 '힐링' 차원의 소비 활동 외에 마땅한 일을 찾지 못하는 한, 기존 굴레를 벗어나지 못한

of our own realm and desires for possession, but also to adopt and willingly pursue a profound *interest* in a life lived together.

"Disinterested aesthetics" also represent a core principle in the concept of fine art, which is a modern invention of the Enlightenment. The classical trinity of truth, goodness, and beauty has broken down; today, beauty and art form and occupy their own independent realms according to their own independent principles. Art that is disinterested in morality/ethics, truth, or the divine ends up devoted to the creation of form purely for the sake of human enjoyment. It is only natural that this would lead to a separation between life and art. Even amid financial hardship, artists at the time devoted themselves to building realms of fine art remote from worldly interests—sometimes willingly, other times cursing their own fates. This is not to say that they were unaware of the highs and lows of human affairs or the various problems afflicting society. The very artistic base in which such activities of consciousness arose had established itself as an independent realm for the formation of society—and one with little influence compared with what it had to say.

In the wake of Romanticism, the internalization and ideation of art further fueled this tendency. After Hegel's thesis on "the end of art," some awaited the emergence of a new form of art suited to the times. But even with the arrival of new media and technological transformations, self-centered and self-reflective conceptual art movements have persisted. The spirit of art, with its production of the self and repudiation of any connection with other worlds, has ridden lightly on the back of abstract movements of capital since the 20th century. This happened more easily than one might have imagined, and though it is largely due to capital having established itself as one of the main conditions of modern life, another reason lies in art itself having willingly taken on "conceptual" forms. Conceptual movements and capital movements share kinship in the way they amplify themselves by absorbing everything.

The timidity or reluctance of modern art to confront life seems to be a consequence of it having forgotten its power to awaken other movements besides the concepts that shape its realm. Self-enlargement that is based on the production of ideas, no matter how intense, only gives rise to the same kind of movement. Reason, disinterestedness, and purity share a common trait in the way they construct their own exclusive domains. Capital's raison d'être is endless self-amplification. And movements that remain confined within themselves, focusing only on growth, aren't merely tedious—they are violent. Is a new movement that tries to connect with life (rather than a hard and callous movement whose only interest is itself) too much to hope for? If our lives today are not that bad—fine in their way—we may not have any particular

다. 우리의 인식 범위는 한정적이며, '힐링' 비즈니스는 이러한 한계에 따른 공포를 부드러운 감촉으로 포장한다. 삶이 공포스러울수록 지식의 양은 계속 증가하고, 쾌적한 형태로 포장되어 불티나게 팔린다. 자본의 운동에 매몰된 교육과 종교가 이의 선봉에 서는 모습은 이제 일상 풍경이 되었다.

생명 가치로의 전환을 위해 무엇보다 필요한 것은 길들지 않은 원초적 생명력의 회복일 것이다. 앎과 즐거움 역시 인류가 현재까지의 모습으로 문명과 문화를 일구기 위해 일시적으로 고안한 방법이자 감정일 뿐이다. 앎은 이성만의 몫이 아니다. 기계적이고 도구적인 이성 사용 외에도 우리가 취할 수 있는 방법은 이미 우리 안에 존재한다. 이성만의 앎을 넘어설 때 우리는 생명 차원의 관계 맺기를 실현할 수 있다. 즐거움은 우리 삶의 귀한 감정이지만, 쾌감 일변도의 문화만으로는 생명 가치의 심도를 만들어 내지 못한다. 감정 역시 인간이 만들어 낸 관념의 일종이며, 사회 구성을 위한 약속에 의해 늘 새롭게 발명되고 조직된다. 그간 존재하지 않는 줄만 알았던 개체가 사회 구성의 주체로 거듭 발견되고 등장한다면 인간 감정의 형태 역시 달라질 수밖에 없고 또한 마땅히 달라져야만 한다.

콜린 세로(Coline Serreau)가 각본·연출·음악·주연을 맡은 영화 〈뷰티풀 그린(Beautiful Green/La Belle Verte)〉(1996)에는 흥미로운 장면이 등장한다. '뷰티풀 그린' 별의 사람들이 사는 모습은 이성 원리에 따라 작동하는 현대 문명과 대조적인 삶의 양식을 보여 준다. 산수 시간에 아이들은 선생님의 손바닥 위에서 장난스레 움직이는 자갈의 개수를 '계산하지' 않고 '직관적으로' 알아맞힌다. 사람들은 언덕 위에서 바람을 감상하며 때때로 함께 웃음을 터뜨린다. 엄마를 찾으러 도착한 지구별에서 주인공은 사람들이 전화를 사용하는 모습에 '이들은 텔레파시를 쓸 줄 모르는가'라며 의아해한다. 대도시 현대인들의 삶을 생태적 관점에서 성찰하도록 하는 이 영화는 어쩌면 우리가 가지고 있었지만 그간 망각해 온 자연스러운 삶의 모습을 상기시킨다. 우리는 꼭 계산이나 분석이 아니더라도 사물의 드러난 모습을 전체적으로 헤아릴 줄 안다. 바람결을 타고 온 그리운 이의 향기를 맡기도 하고, 원거리의 상대와 직접 대화를 나눌 수도 있다. 사물과 세상에 대한 이성적 이해, 우리가 길든 이 사유 패턴에서 약간만 벗어나더라도 잠자고 있던 감각은 깨어날 것이며, 더 넓고 풍요로운 세상과 만날 수 있을 것이다.

코막 컬리넌(Cormac Cullinan)의 책 『야생의 법』은 원초적 생명력을 일깨우는 시적인 정신만이 아니라 포스트휴먼 시대에 인간과 비인간 개체가 평등하게 공존할 수 있도록 하는 현실적 방법을 고민하고 있다는 점에서 인상적이다. 그는 난개발로 인한 자연 훼손, 동물 등 비인간 개체를 과도한 인간 욕망을 충족시킬 수단으로만 보는 오랜 관습에서 벗어나, 우주 전체의 기능을 관장하고 규율하는 '위대한 법학(Great Jurisprudence)'을 제안한다. 그에 따르

need to invest time in moving toward something else. But when things are as difficult as they are, when we feel something intolerably rising up in our throats, we find ourselves obliged to take action toward making a change. Words must be reborn, clad in muscle and bone and a heart pulsing with blood. Art must escape the bounds of pure reason—"ego" and "self"—and emerge anew as plural subjectivities.

Possessed by you

One of the independent operating principles in fine art and the modern aesthetic is the emotion of "pleasure." The emphasis on pleasure has continued into contemporary art; it has become customary for introductions to artwork to include messages that urge viewers not to "overthink" it, but to simply enjoy it and move on. But if it were only about enjoying ourselves, it would be simpler to go to an arcade or an amusement park. The dazzling colors and images and seductive words of the media fill our daily lives; each day brings countless narratives that arouse interest. In a reality where capital and technology represent life's mainstream, the emotion of "mere pleasure" seems inert, superficial, and submissive.

Pleasure also has direct ties to the aforementioned act of "knowing." When watching a horror movie, we feel terror at the things and situations whose identities we cannot clearly understand. Ignorance awakens the human desire for knowledge, and it is our human efforts to escape our fundamental ignorance that have made us the highly advanced civilization we are today. The pursuit of knowledge is the pursuit of enjoyment; in the same context, we are (or should be) living in the most enjoyable time in history.

Superficial feelings of pleasure also come up when we talk about ecological sensitivity and the transition toward life-centered values. These include the momentary pleasure of knowledge that we get when we identify a risk factor, or the moral pleasure we experience when we lead (or believe ourselves to lead) eco-friendly lives. Yet such pleasures simply repeat the same modern methods of knowledge production and the resulting movements of modern capital. We will never escape our current chains unless we find something suitable beyond the linear perception of cause-and-effect and "self-care" consumption activities within the capitalist system. Our scope of awareness is limited, and "self-cafe" industries use soft textures to package the terror we feel when confronted with those limits. The more terrifying life is, the more our knowledge proliferates in volume, packaged into pleasurable forms that sell like hotcakes. Education and religion, subsumed as they are within capital movements, stand at the vanguard of this as a matter of routine.

For us to make the shift toward the values of life, we first and foremost need to restore an untamed, primitive vitality.

면 위대한 법학은 행성들의 정렬과 식물의 성장, 낮과 밤의 순환 속에서 작동하고 있다. 오늘날 사회 구성체 일반의 헌법 체계는 근대 이성의 원리에 따라 정립되었으나, 컬리넌은 이성적 사유만으로는 우리가 사는 세상의 실상을 다 파악할 수 없으며, 새로운 시대의 법 체계는 이 위대한 법학에 기초한 '지구법학'의 모습으로 다시 작성되어야 한다고 역설한다. 우주의 일부로서 인간은 자기 신체의 뼈와 근육, 힘줄, 사고 패턴 안에 기록된 위대한 법학의 원칙을 파악해야만 한다. 그것은 이성만이 아니라 전일성(holism) 차원에서 일어나는 공감과 자기 성찰, 우주와의 유대감 속에서 드러난다. 딱딱한 법학 영역에서 '생명을 주는 영혼', '어머니 대지' 등의 언사를 듣는 것은 한편 낯설기도 하지만 이성 원리에서 벗어난 새로운 사회 구성 원리를 고안하고자 할 때 풍부한 영감을 준다.

이성 우월과 인간 중심의 독단적 권력 사용으로 발전시켜 온 인류의 역사는 이제 다른 페이지를 써야만 한다. 지구의 역사는 인간만의 역사가 아니다. "그 절반의 증인들은 텍스트나 언어가 아닌 침묵으로, 펌프들, 돌들, 조각상들과 같은 적나라한 잔류물로 이루어져 있다."[1] 우글거리는 이 무언의 증인들을 사회 구성의 주체로 등장시키기 위해 우리는 그 높다고 하는 이성의 권좌에서 기꺼이 내려오는 연습을 해야만 한다. 아래로 내려온 정신은 순수성을 부르짖지도, 또 그것을 기준으로 서로를 차별하지도 않을 것이다. 그는 자기가 소유하고 있다고 생각하던 자리를 기꺼이 타자에게 내어줄 줄 안다. 자기를 내어주는 일은 그 자체로 관심과 사랑의 행위이며, 그것의 본질은 그에게 '들리는' 일과도 같다. 나는 '너에게 들린다.' 우리는 나무에, 산에, 바다에, 바람에, 새에 들린다. '자기'라는 확고하고 우월적인 관념에서 내려와 타자에게 들려 그와 하나가 된 정신은 순수하기보다는 잡스럽다. 우리가 춤을 출 수 있는 것은 우리의 이 잡스러움에 기뻐하기 때문이리라. 생명의 춤에 들린 기쁨은 단순한 쾌감이라고 표현할 수만은 없는, 우주의 기나긴 역사를 관통하면서 겪었을 온갖 존재의 애환과 비극적 지혜를 그 뿌리로 지니고 있을 것이다.

1.   브뤼노 라투르, 『우리는 결코 근대인이었던 적이 없다』 홍철기 옮김(갈무리, 2009), 211.

"Knowledge" and "pleasure" are merely emotions, expedients devised by humans to develop culture and civilization into what they are today. Knowledge does not belong to reason alone. The methods that we can turn to—beyond the mechanical and instrumental use of reason—already exist inside of us. Once we have transcended knowledge that is based on reason alone, we can achieve relationships at the level of "life." Pleasure is an invaluable emotion in our lives, but we cannot achieve great depths in our life-centered values when our culture is focused solely on enjoyment. "Emotion" is another concept that humans have created, and it is constantly being reinvented and reorganized by our contract to create society. When the kinds of individuals we once imagined did not exist are rediscovered and emerge as agents in shaping society, the forms of human emotion will inevitably change—and indeed they should.

The film *La Belle Verte* (*Beautiful Green*, 1996), which stars and is directed, scripted, and scored by Coline Serreau, features a fascinating scene. The people who live on a planet known as the Beautiful Green demonstrate a way of life that contrasts with our contemporary civilization, which functions according to the principles of reason. In math class on the Beautiful Green, the children don't "count" the playfully shifting pebbles in the teacher's palm—they "intuit" them. People enjoy the wind on the hills, sometimes bursting into laughter together. The protagonist, a woman who travels to earth to find her mother, sees people using their phones and wonders, "Don't they know how to use telepathy?" Encouraging the viewer to reflect on modern big-city life from an ecological perspective, the film evokes a natural image of life that we may have once possessed but have lost sight of. Even if it's not a matter of calculation or analysis, we know how to fathom the visible aspects of objects in their totality. We can detect the scent of someone we long for as it is carried on the wind, and we can speak directly to people over long distances. There is a dormant sense that awakens when we deviate even a little bit from these ingrained thought patterns, this rational understanding of objects and the world—and when this occurs, we are able to encounter a broader and richer world.

The book *Wild Law* by Cormac Cullinan is striking in the way it does not simply express a poetic spirit to awaken a primitive life force, but also ponders realistic ways of allowing human and non-human beings to coexist equally in the post-human era. Cullinan urges us to let go of our old habits of destroying nature through untrammeled development and viewing animals and other non-human life forms as a means of satisfying our excessive human desires; as an alternative, he posits a "Great Jurisprudence" that governs and regulates the workings of the universe as a whole. He describes the Great Jurisprudence as something that operates in the arrangements of the planets, the growth of plants, and the cycle of night and day. The constitutional system that applies to members of society today is based on the principles of modern reason, but Cullinan insists that we cannot fully grasp the truth of our world through rational thinking alone, calling instead for the legal system of our new era to be rewritten in the form of "Earth jurisprudence" based on the Great Jurisprudence. As part of the universe, humans must grasp the principles of the Great Jurisprudence that are recorded in our bones, muscles, tendons, and thought patterns. This is manifested not through pure reason, but within sympathy at the holistic level, self-reflection, and a sense of connection with the cosmos. It is strange to hear talk of the "life-giving soul" or "Mother Earth" in the dry context of law, but this book offers a rich source of inspiration for our attempts to devise new principles for societal creation beyond the principles of reason.

It's time to write a new page in human history, which has hitherto developed through the use of dogmatic power centered on humans and the supremacy of reason. The history of the earth is not that of humans alone: "The witnesses to this second half of history are constituted not by texts or languages but by silent, brute remainders such as pumps, stones, and statues". To introduce these mute, swarming witnesses as actors in establishing society, we must practice willingly stepping down from the throne of reason that we see as so high. The spirit that comes when we descend does not cry of purity, nor does it discriminate on its basis. It knows how to yield the places it once believed that it owned to others. Yielding oneself is an act of care and of love in itself, similar in essence to being "possessed." I am possessed by you. We are possessed by the trees, by the mountains, by the sea and wind and birds. Coming down from our rigid and supreme concept of the "self," we are possessed by others to become one with them—a spirit that is more secular than pure. Perhaps what allows us to dance is our joy at this vulgarity within us. The joy of being possessed by the dance of life may come from something that cannot be described as mere "pleasure," as it instead contains the roots of the joys, sorrows, and tragic wisdom that all the different beings have experienced over the universe's long history.

1.   Bruno Latour, *We Have Never Been Modern*, trans. Catherine Porter (Cambridge: Harvard University Press, 1993), 82.

지구를 망쳐가는 인간의 시대, 인류세

최평순
EBS 프로듀서

The Anthropocene: The Epoch of Humanity's Destruction of the Earth

Choi Pyeong-soon
Producer of EBS

여섯 번째 대멸종

호주는 6개월 동안 불탔다. 국가비상사태가 선포될 정도로 초유의 대규모 들불(bushfire)이었다. 화재는 호주 산림의 14퍼센트를 태우고서야 끝이 났고 이는 영국 전체 면적과 맞먹는다. 호주 전역에 많아야 10만여 마리 산다는 코알라의 3분의 1이 2019년 9월부터 2020년 2월까지의 화재로 숨을 거뒀다. 개체 수가 많아서 걱정하던 동물의 멸종 위기 등급 조정을 검토할 정도로 기후위기는 수많은 생명을 앗아갔다.

"들불이 많은 호주의 특성상 소방관들은 화재 경험이 풍부하죠. 이제 많은 경우 그들은 불을 끄다가 멈추고 돌아서서 이렇게 말해요. '이 화재는 진압할 수 없습니다. 너무 큽니다.' 그들은 이런 것을 한 번도 본 적이 없어요. 인류세를 살아가면서 우리는 자연적인 현상에 스테로이드를 퍼붓고 있죠. 더 크게, 강하게, 심각하게, 통제가 어렵게 되도록 말이에요."

지구 시스템 과학자이자 호주국립대학교 명예 교수인 윌 스테픈(Will Steffen)은 이것이 인류세의 징후라고 말한다. 들불은 자연적인 현상이지만, 기후위기로 인해 '화재 체계'가 악화하며 화재의 강도, 빈도, 피해 규모가 비정상적으로 증가했다. 지난 20-30년간 호주 대륙의 강수량은 점차 줄었고, 특히 화재 발생 전 3년간의 강수량 수치는 처참했다. 여름에 섭씨 30도, 때때로 40도를 넘는 날이 늘어나면서 대형 들불이 발생할 모든 조건이 갖춰졌다. 윌 스테픈이 말한 스테로이드는 바로 화석 연료다. 석탄, 석유, 천연가스 등 화석 연료를 쓰는 한 기후위기로 인한 자연재해는 더 잦아진다. 서울, 샌프란시스코, 상파울루, 모스크바 등 지구 전역에서 에너지를 사용하며 땐 불이 올해 아마존, 시베리아, 미국과 캐나다 서부의 숲에 옮겨붙었다.

다큐멘터리 프로듀서이자 디렉터로서 〈여섯 번째 대멸종〉이라는 시리즈를 제작하며 호주 대규모 들불 사태를 취재하기 위해 캥거루 아일랜드를 찾았다. 녹색이어야 할 숲은 검은 잿더미였고, 나무 위에 있어야 할 코알라는 주검이 된 상태로 땅에 널브러져 있었다. 살아남은 야생동물도 만날 수 있었는데, 화상을 입어 거동이 불편한 경우가 부지기수였고 운 좋게 멀쩡하더라도 섬의 초목 절반 정도가 사라져 먹을 것을 찾기 힘든 상황이었다. 매일 아침 숙소를 나서면 전날 먹이 활동을 하지 못해 굶어 죽은 캥거루의 눈을 마주했다. '호주의 갈라파고스'라 불리던 섬은 그렇게 죽음의 땅이 되어 있었다.

The sixth mass extinction

Australia burned for six months. A state of emergency was declared as bushfires spread on an unprecedented scale. The fires destroyed 14 percent of Australia's forests, an area that is almost as large as the UK. Between September 2019 and February 2020, one-third of the approximately 100,000 koalas in Australia died in the fires. The climate crisis has annihilated countless lives, causing even highly populous animals to be classified as endangered species.

"Australian firefighters are experienced because bushfires are common in Australia. But now, in many cases, they stop fighting the fires, saying that they are too great to be extinguished. They've never seen anything like this. Living in the Anthropocene, we are pouring steroids into natural phenomena, making them greater, stronger, more serious, and harder to control."

Will Steffen, an earth system scientist and an emeritus professor at the Australian National University, says that this is a sign of the Anthropocene. Bushfires are a natural phenomenon, but the planet's "fire system" has weakened due to the climate crisis, causing abnormally intense, frequent, and destructive fires. Precipitation on the Australian continent has declined steadily over the past 20 to 30 years, and rainfall figures plummeted in the three years before the devastating fire. With an increasing number of days exceeding temperatures of 30°C and sometimes even 40°C in the summer, the climate conditions are just right for large bushfires. The "steroids" that Will Steffen mentions are none other than fossil fuels, so continuing to use coal, oil, and natural gas will only result in more frequent natural disasters triggered by the climate crisis. This year, fires used to generate power in Seoul, San Francisco, Sao Paulo, Moscow, and other parts of the world spread to the Amazon and forests in Siberia, the US, and western Canada.

As the producer and director of the documentary series Anthropocene, I visited Kangaroo Island cover Australia's large-scale bushfires. There, green forests had been reduced to ashes, and koalas were lying dead beneath the trees they used to climb. Many of the wild animals that had survived were wounded and unable to move freely, and those that were lucky enough to escape unscathed still struggled to find food because half of the forests on the island had been decimated. Every morning, I would meet the empty eyes of kangaroos that, unable to find

과학자들이 지질 시대를 나누는 기준 중 하나가 대멸종이다. 소행성 충돌로 공룡이 멸종하며 중생대에서 신생대로 지질 시대가 바뀌었다. 지구 역사 46억 년 중 다섯 번의 대멸종이 있었다. 첫 번째 대멸종은 고생대 오르도비스기 말, 4억 5,000만 년 전에서 4억 4,000만 년 전의 일이다. 오소세라스 같은 앵무조개류와 삼엽충이 번성했는데, 해양 생물 50퍼센트와 해양 무척추동물의 100여 과가 멸종했다. 전 지구적 기후 한랭화와 남반구의 빙하기가 멸종의 원인인 것으로 추정한다. 두 번째 대멸종은 고생대 데본기 말로, 원시 어류가 살던 시기이다. 3억 7,000만 년 전에서 3억 6,000만 년 전에 발생해 생물종 70퍼센트가 사라졌다. 세 번째 대멸종은 고생대 페름기 말, 2억 5,100만 년 전인데 해양 생물종 약 96퍼센트와 육상 척추동물 70퍼센트 이상이 절멸했다. 역대 대멸종 중 가장 큰 규모였다. 네 번째 대멸종은 중생대 트라이아스기 말로, 2억 500만 년 전에 일어났다. 공룡이 출현해 번성하던 시기였고, 공룡, 익룡, 악어를 제외한 대부분의 파충류가 사라졌다. 대규모 화산 폭발을 그 원인으로 본다. 마지막 대멸종은 중생대 백악기 말인 6,600만 전으로 가장 최근이다. 이 사건으로 공룡이 멸종했고, 소행성 충돌이 그 원인이었을 것으로 추정한다.

지금 그와 비견될 규모와 속도로 여섯 번째 대멸종이 이뤄지고 있다. 앞선 다섯 번은 소행성 충돌, 화산 폭발, 빙하기 도래 등이 원인이었는데, 현재진행형 대멸종은 인간의 활동이 그 원인이다. 한 생물종에 의해 지구 시스템 전체가 위협받는 상황. 과학자들은 진지하게 지질 시대의 이름을 바꾸는 것을 검토 중이다. 그 이름에는 행성적 위기를 초래한 인류가 포함된다. 그래서 인류세(人類世, anthropocene)다. 우리는 인간의 시대를 살고 있다.

인간이란 무엇일까

인류세란 용어는 우리를 생각에 잠기게 한다. 지질 시대에 우리 이름을 박아 넣는다는 건 무엇을 의미할까? 지질학은 46억 년 지구 역사

any food, had died of starvation. The "Galapagos of Australia" had become an island of death.

One of the criteria that scientists use to divide periods of geologic time is mass extinction. For example, the asteroid impact event that wiped out the dinosaurs marks the change in geologic time from the Mesozoic era to the Cenozoic era. There have been five mass extinctions in the 4.6 billion years of the earth's history, the first being at the end of the Ordovician period, between 450 and 440 million years ago. The chambered nautilus, such as *Orthoceras*, and trilobites thrived in this period, but 50 percent of all marine creatures and around 100 species of marine invertebrates disappeared in the mass extinction. The event is thought to have been caused by the cooling of the earth and glaciation in the southern hemisphere. The second mass extinction happened at the end of the Devonian period, the age of ancient fish. It occurred 370 to 360 million years ago and wiped out 70 percent of all species that existed at the time. The third mass extinction was at the end of the Permian period, 251 million years ago. The largest of the mass extinctions, it wiped out 96 percent of marine life and more than 70 percent of land vertebrates. The fourth mass extinction occurred at the end of the Triassic period, 250 million years ago. The earth became populated by dinosaurs during this period, and almost all reptiles excluding dinosaurs, pterosaurs, and crocodilians died in the event, which is thought to have been caused by massive volcanic eruptions. Finally, the fifth and most recent mass extinction occurred at the end of the Cretaceous period, 66 million years ago. Attributed to an asteroid striking the earth, this was the event that wiped out the dinosaurs.

Currently, the earth's sixth mass extinction is underway at a comparable speed and scale. While the previous extinctions were caused by an asteroid, volcanic eruptions, and glaciation, the current event is being driven by human activities. In short, one species is jeopardizing the

잿더미가 된 호주 캥거루 아일랜드 화재 현장.　　Kangaroo Island burned to ashes.

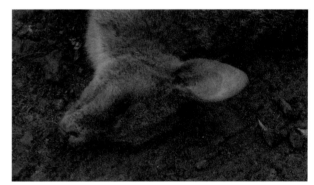

먹이를 구하지 못해 굶어 죽은 캥거루.　　A kangaroo that has died of starvation.

를 누대(累代, eon)-대(代, era)-기(紀, period)-세(世, epoch, cene)라는 시대 단위별로 분류하는데, 인류세(anthropocene)는 이 중 하위 단위인 '세(cene)'와 그리스어로 인류를 뜻하는 접두사 'anthropos'를 결합한 용어다. 100만 년, 1,000만 년의 시간을 다루는 지질 시대 단위인 '세' 앞에 '인류'가 놓인다는 건 무엇을 의미할까?

20만 년 전에 등장한 인류가 46억 년을 버텨온 지구를 파괴했다. 인간의 수명은 길어야 100년인데, 자본주의가 가속 페달을 밟은 최근 70년 동안 본격적으로 행성을 망치고 있다. 하나의 생물종에 불과한 인류에게 그만한 힘이 있다는 것은 놀라운 사실이지만, 막상 그 현장을 돌아다니면 암담하고 슬프다. 껑충껑충 뛰어다녀야 할 캥거루는 이미 불타 죽었거나, 화상을 입은 채로 힘겹게 걷고 있거나, 굶어 죽는다. 호주의 소방관들은 불을 끄지 못한 채 무기력했다 (결국 호주 대규모 들불은 비가 와서 꺼졌다). 인류세의 과거와 현재를 마주한다는 건 인류 문명을 객관적으로 바라보고 인간이란 존재의 본질을 들여다본다는 의미이다. 인류세를 취재하며 만난 석학에게 인간이란 어떤 존재인지 물었다.

"우리는 오랜 시간 동안 자연을 파괴하면서 번영해 온 종일지도 몰라요. 오늘날 우리는 인류세를 살고 있고, 계속해서 자연을 파괴할 거예요. 하지만 우리는 변할 수 있어요."

개미 연구와 '통섭' 개념으로 유명한 에드워드 윌슨(Edward Wilson) 하버드대학교 명예교수는 93년을 살아오면서 인간이 개미를 비롯해 얼마나 많은 생물을 멸종시키는지 지켜본 생물학자다. 그는 동료들과 척추동물의 방대한 자료를 분석해 인류 출현 이전의 멸종 속도보다 최소 100배 이상 빨리 멸종이 진행되고 있다고 결론 내린 바 있다. 그런데도 그는 인류의 미래에 대해 부정적이지만은 않다. 그간 세계야생동물기금[World Wildlife Fund, WWF; 현 세계자연기금(World Wide Fund For Nature, WWF)] 등 국제적 환경보호 단체가 창설되고, 국립공원이 탄생하고 확산하는 등 인류가 지구에서 성공시켜 온 몇몇 프로젝트들 또한 경험했기 때문이다. 그 활동들이 없었다면 지금보다 육상 척추동물의 멸종률이 약 20퍼센트 높았을 것이라고 한다. 지금도 그는 지구의 절반을 자연보호 구역으로 지정하면 모든 생물종의 85퍼센트를 살릴 수 있다며 '지구의 절반 프로젝트(Half-Earth Project)'를 주창하고 있다.

에드워드 윌슨이 평생 개미를 관찰했다면, 캘리포니아주립대학교 지리학과 교수인 재레드 다이아몬드(Jared Diamond)는 57년 동안 한 곳을 지켜본 사람이다. 그는 1964년 자신이 미지의 땅 뉴기니를 처음 찾았을 당시 석기시대를 살던 뉴기니 원시 부족이 문명을 접한 뒤 벌목과 광산 사업에 노출되며 어떻게 바뀌었는지, 뉴기니의 자연은 얼마만큼 파괴됐는지 잘 알고 있다. 물론 뉴기니는 인류세의 전 지구적 현장 중 한 군데일 뿐이다.

entire earth system. Scientists are seriously considering changing the name of the current geologic era to acknowledge humankind and its role in bringing about a planetary crisis. The name of this era is the Anthropocene. We are living in the age of humans.

What are humans?

The term "Anthropocene" gives us much to think about. What does it mean to engrave our name into geologic time? In geology, the 4.6 billion years of the earth's history is divided into eons, eras, periods, and epochs. The Anthropocene is an epoch (typically denoted using the suffix "-cene") named using *anthropos*, the Greek word for "human." What does it mean, then, to name a geologic time interval that covers millions or tens of millions of years with the word "human?"

Although the earth has survived 4.6 billion years, it is now being destroyed by *Homo sapiens*, which first appeared 200,000 years ago. A life span of 100 years is long for humans, but the past 70 years of rampant capitalism have been dismantling the planet. It is mind-blowing that a single species can possess so much power, but to witness actual scenes of human destruction is a dismal, sad experience. I saw kangaroos, scathed and limping, dying of hunger, or lying dead instead of leaping around. Firefighters were helpless before the ravaging flames. (The bushfires were eventually extinguished by rain.) To face the past and present of the Anthropocene means looking objectively at human civilization and examining the essence of human existence. In my research on the Anthropocene, I asked esteemed scholar Edward Wilson about the meaning of human existence.

"It is possible that we are a species that has prospered by destroying nature over a long period of time. We are living in the Anthropocene and will continue to destroy nature. However, we can change."

Wilson, a Harvard University emeritus professor famous for his research on ants and his theory of "consilience," is a biologist who has witnessed how humans have pushed ants and countless other species into extinction over the 93 years of his life. With his colleagues, he analyzed an extensive amount of research material on vertebrates and concluded that species were going extinct at least 100 times faster than the typical progression of extinction before humans appeared. However, he is not wholly pessimistic about the future of humanity. He has witnessed the success of various projects, including the establishment of the World Wide Fund for Nature (formerly the World Wildlife Fund) and other international environmental groups and the creation of national parks. He says that without these projects, the extinction rate of land vertebrates would be about 20 percent higher than it is today. He is currently leading the Half-Earth Project, which aims to protect 50 percent of the planet to save 85

"현재 세계에는 지속 불가능한 일들이 벌어지고 있어요. 우리가 자원을 써 버리는 속도를 보면 수십 년 이내에 많은 자원이 고갈될 거예요. 그리고 절벽 같은 상황에 놓이게 되겠죠."

재레드 다이아몬드는 앞으로 남은 시간을 50년으로 꼽는다. 50년 안에 세계 경제를 지속 가능한 형태로 바꾸지 않으면 문명의 붕괴가 찾아온다는 것이다. 2021년 한 해 동안 지구촌 전역은 코로나19라는 신종 전염병을 겪으며 고장 난 시스템의 폐부를 여실히 드러냈다. 배달용 포장 용기와 일회용 마스크 사용까지 늘자 갈 곳을 잃은 쓰레기는 육지에서 쓰레기 산으로 솟아났고 바다에 떠다니는 거대 쓰레기 지대는 커졌으며, 플라스틱은 미세 플라스틱으로 잘게 쪼개져 해양 생물과 육상 동물을 가리지 않고 인간을 포함한 많은 생명체의 몸속으로 들어갔다.

애당초 78억 개체 수를 가진 하나의 종이 마음껏 자원을 소비하며 살아가도 무탈한 행성은 (우리가 아는 한) 우주에 없다. 게다가 인류는 소행성 충돌에 비견될 정도의 파괴력을 가진 지구의 정복자가 아닌가.

"인간은 힘입니다. 역사상 존재했던 그 어떤 종보다 강력한 종입니다."

《총, 균, 쇠》로 인간 문명을 통찰한 재레드 다이아몬드는 인간을 소행성 충돌 같은 힘으로 정의한다. 그리고 그 정의에서 해답을 찾는다. 소행성 충돌은 우리가 어쩌지 못하는 문제이지만, 지금 우리가 마주한 문제는 우리 스스로가 만든 문제라는 것이다. 이제 '인간이란 무엇일까'에 대한 질문은 우리 자신을 향한다.

인류세의 미래

기후변화를 해결하는 방법은 간단하다. 화석 연료를 덜 쓰면 된다. 개인은 석유를 태우는 차량을 타지 않고 전기 사용량을 줄여야 한다. 국가는 석탄 화력 발전소를 없애고 재생 에너지의 비율을 높여야 한다. 국제 사회는 2015년에 채택한 파리기후변화협약에 제시된 온실가스 감축 목표가 지켜지도록 해야 한다. 다른 말로 풀면, 시민은 불편함을 감수하고 국가는 지속 가능성을 적극적으로 고려하며 국제 사회는 이를 잘 감시해야 한다.

안타깝게도 현실은 아직은 이렇다. 현대인은 풍요로운 문명 생활에 중독돼 있고, 정부는 경제를 살려야 장기 집권이 가능하며, 국제 사회는 힘을 모으지 못한다. 편리함과 경제, 개별 국가의 이익이 우선시되는 상황에서 문제는 방치됐고 결국 인류세 시대가 열렸다. 과연 우리는 무언가를 포기할 수 있을까?

지구가 신음하는 이때, 인류세 개념을 창안한 파울 크뤼천(Paul Crutzen) 교수가 2021년 1월 28일 타계했다. 어릴 때부터 눈 쌓인 산을 좋아했던 네덜란드의 소년은 눈을 연구하고 싶어서 기상학과에 진학했고, 에어컨, 냉장고, 헤어스프레이 등에 쓰이는 프레온 가스가 오존층 파괴의 주범임을 과학적으로 증명해 동료들과 함께 1995년 노벨 화학상을 받았다. 그로 인해 1987년 프레온 가스의 생산

percent of all species.

As Edward Wilson has observed ants all his life, Jared Diamond, a professor of geography at the University of California, Los Angeles (UCLA), has studied one place for 57 years. He first visited the distant land of New Guinea in 1964. Since then, he has witnessed how the island's indigenous people, whose lifestyle was once similar to that of people in the Stone Age, were forced to change after being exposed to contemporary society and development. Particularly, the logging and mining industries have led to the sheer destruction of New Guinea's natural environment. However, New Guinea is merely one of the places on earth where the Anthropocene can be witnessed.

"Things are happening in the world that cannot continue. We are using up resources at a rate that will leave them exhausted in a couple of decades. Then, we will find ourselves on something like the edge of a cliff."

Diamond believes that we have 50 years left. If we do not transform the world economy into a sustainable form within 50 years, civilization will collapse. In 2021, the entire world suffered from the contagious COVID-19 virus, which revealed the heart of our broken system. As the use of takeout containers and disposable masks increased, garbage mountains on land and trash islands in the ocean grew bigger, and microplastics indiscriminately entered the bodies of marine and terrestrial creatures, including humans.

There is no planet in the universe (to our knowledge) on which a single species with 7.8 billion individuals can greedily consume all the planet's resources and get away with it. Besides, aren't humans conquerors? Our destructive power compares with the force of an asteroid hitting the earth.

"Humans are power. We are the most powerful species that has existed in world history."

Diamond, whose book *Guns, Germs, and Steel* explores human civilization, defines humans as a form of power, much like the impact of an asteroid. He also finds a solution in this definition. Asteroid impact events are beyond our control, but the problem that we face today is our doing. It is time to ask ourselves the question, "What are humans?"

The future of the Anthropocene

There is a simple solution to climate change: reduce the consumption of fossil fuels. Individuals should steer away from combustion engine cars and save electricity. States should scrap coal-fired power plants and raise the percentage of renewable energy being used. The international community must work toward achieving the carbon emission goals stated by the 2015 Paris Agreement. In other words, individuals must accept daily inconveniences, states must actively pursue sustainability, and

을 금지하는 국제 협약이 체결됐지만, 이미 대기에 떠돌고 있는 프레온 가스를 없앨 수는 없었다. 인간의 활동이 지구에 미치는 영향에 대한 그의 문제의식은 결국 2000년에 인류세 개념의 탄생으로 이어졌고, 그는 말년까지 세상에 헌신하며 삶을 마쳤다.

"그의 업적은 사후에도 과학과 사회의 진보를 이끌고, 국제 공동체에 계속 영감을 줄 것이다."

막스플랑크연구소 홈페이지에 올라온 파울 크뤼천에 대한 추도사 중 한 구절이다. 한 사람의 노력이 시발점이 된 인류세 담론으로 우리는 인류의 힘이 얼마나 강력하며 어떻게 지구에 작용하고 있는지 직관적으로 알게 됐다. 2000년에 제시된 '인류세'라는 세 글자는 21년의 시간 동안 학계와 국경의 장벽을 넘어 계속 확산했고, 우리를 계속 생각하게 만든다. 인류세에서 영감을 받아 끊임없이 함께, 동시에 스스로 질문해야만 한다. 우리는 정말 변할 수 있을까. 시간은 얼마 남지 않았다.

the international community must keep a close eye on the progress.

Unfortunately, reality is different from the ideal. Contemporary people are addicted to comfortable lifestyles, the government must protect the economy to retain its power, and the international community cannot reach a consensus. The problem has taken a back seat to personal convenience, the economy, and the interests of various countries, ultimately opening the door to the Anthropocene. Will we be able to give any of it up?

As the Earth cried out in pain, Paul Crutzen, who originated the concept of the Anthropocene, passed away on January 28, 2021. Growing up in the Netherlands, Crutzen loved snow-covered mountains, and he later became a professor of meteorology to research snow. In 1995, he and his colleagues won the Nobel Prize in Chemistry for scientifically proving that chlorofluorocarbons (CFCs) used in air conditioners, fridges, and hair sprays have an active role in the destruction of the ozone layer. These results led to the adoption of an international agreement to ban the production of CFCs in 1987, but nothing could be done to remove the CFCs that were already in the atmosphere. Crutzen's research on the impact of human activities on the earth led to the conceptualization of the Anthropocene in 2000. Even in his later years, he remained committed to making a better world.

"Paul and his great scientific work will continue to guide scientific and societal progress and serve as a unique source of inspiration."

The above is an excerpt from a memorial tribute to Crutzen posted on the Max Planck Society homepage. Conceived from the efforts of one person, the Anthropocene theory has shown us the power of humans and how it is affecting our planet. Over the past 21 years, the term "Anthropocene" has been spreading across academia and the world, inspiring us and forcing us to think. We must not stop asking ourselves, together and individually, the question, "Can we really change?" There isn't much time left.

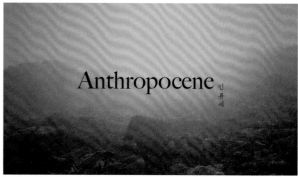

우리는 인류세, 인간의 시대를 살고 있다.

We are living in the Anthropocene, the age of humans.

바다와 우리의 시간

박현선
시셰퍼드 코리아 대표

한 달에 한 번, 바다에 뛰어든다. 무거운 공기통과 몸을 옥죄는 슈트를
입고 바다 깊은 곳으로 잠긴다. 수면에서 멀어질수록 햇빛은 점차
흐려진다. 보이는 것은 뿌연 부유물과 밧줄 하나. 겁도 없이, 우리
는 해저를 향해 가라앉는다. 목표 지점에 도달해 왼손에 쥔 랜턴을
켠다. 앙상한 불빛 끝에 시커먼 유령들이 정체를 드러낸다. 수심
약 30미터, 주어진 시간은 20분 남짓. 머뭇거릴 틈이 없다. 우리는
돌진한다. 같은 장소, 같은 어둠 속에서 '유령'과의 싸움이 시작된다.

상상의 바다, 실재의 바다
해양환경운동을 시작한 뒤 바다에서 처음 행한 직접행동은 해변의 쓰
레기를 치우는 일이었다. 태평양 한가운데에 남한 면적의 15배에
이르는 쓰레기섬이 있다는 것은 이미 흔한 이야기다. 하지만 막상
그 실체를 직접 마주한 사람은 많지 않다. 인간은 육지 동물이고
바다는 너무 넓기 때문이다. 나 역시 그러했다. '바다'를 좋아했지
만 관광지에서 본 겉면이 전부였고, 나머지는 머나먼 풍문에 불과
했다.
바다에 그렇게 많은 쓰레기가 있다는 사실을 피부로 실감한 것은 해변
청소를 시작하면서부터였다. 사람들의 발길이 닿지 않는 해변으
로 들어가자 쓰레기로 뒤덮인 모래사장이 나타났다. 어디서부터
치워야 할지 엄두도 나지 않는 쓰레기더미가 긴 해안선을 따라 끝
없이 이어졌다. 내 몸집보다 커다란 양식용 페스티로폼들을 치우
면서 나는 충격에 빠졌다. '그동안 내가 바다라고 믿어왔던 공간은
무엇이었지?'
곧 내가 믿어왔던 그 공간이 거짓이란 걸 알게 됐다. 우리가 보는 바다
는 대부분 관광지이기 때문에 어촌계나 지자체에서 청소를 하고
있는 것이었다. 그 좁은 '보이는' 영역을 벗어나면 바다는 온통 쓰
레기로 가득했다. 치워도 치워도 오물이 밀려왔다. 한나절을 청소
하고 해변에 앉아 쉬고 있으면 새로운 쓰레기가 파도에 실려 오는
것이 보였다.
둥둥 떠밀려오는 해양 쓰레기를 보며, 허무하기보다 무서웠다. 이 많은
쓰레기를 만든 것은 분명 인간인데, 인간의 손으로 다 치울 수 있
을 것 같지가 않았다. 당장 행동해도 부족한데 매 순간 버려지는
양이 수거되는 양에 비해 절대적으로 많다는 사실이 절망스러웠
다. 썩어 가는 바닷새의 내장에서 발견한 플라스틱 조각이 얼마나
홀로 선명했는지 떠올릴 때마다 소름이 끼치곤 한다. 부서지고 삼

The Ocean and Our Time

Park Hyeon-seon
President of Sea Shepherd Korea

Once a month, dressed in tight wetsuits and carrying heavy
diving cylinders, Sea Shepherd volunteers plunge into
the deep ocean. The sunlight fades as we swim further
from the surface until only blurry dust particles and a single rope are visible. Fearless, we sink toward the ocean
floor. At our destination, I switch on the flashlight in my
left hand, and the feeble spotlight falls on black ghosts.
At about 30 meters underwater, we only have 20 minutes.
We charge forward with no time to waste. At this place
and in this darkness, our fight with the "ghosts" begins.

The ocean in imagination and reality
After starting my ocean conservation movement, my first direct action was picking up trash on the beach. There is a
well-known story about a patch of garbage 15 times the
size of Korea floating in the middle of the Pacific Ocean,
but not many people have seen it with their own eyes. After all, humans live on land and the ocean is far too vast. I
was no different. I loved the "ocean," although only what
I had seen of it at tourist destinations; everything else
about it was nothing but a distant rumor.
The sheer amount of garbage in the ocean hit me only after I
began picking up litter on the beach. I entered a remote
part of the shore and immediately encountered a sandy
beach covered with garbage. The long coast was lined
with piles of trash so large I did not know where to begin.
Picking up pieces of industrial polystyrene foam that
were larger than my body, I was shocked and speechless.
What was the place that I had believed to be the ocean?
I soon realized that everything I had known about the ocean
was a lie. The areas of sea that we are familiar with are
mostly tourist sites, kept clean by fishing villages or local
governments. I discovered that the ocean was full of garbage beyond these small "for show" areas. No matter
how much litter I collected, more would wash ashore. After half a day of scouring the beach, I sat down to take a
break only to see the waves bringing in a new load of garbage.
Watching the marine debris float toward the shore, I was
struck not by a sense of futility, but by fear. It seemed impossible that all this human-made waste could be removed by human hands. Taking immediate action would
never be enough—the grim reality was that more waste
was being made than removed. The memory of a bright
plastic fragment that I saw in the gut of a decomposing
seabird still chills me. The shard refused to rot even as it
was shattered, swollen, and digested. The reality of the

해변 청소를 하는 모습. 산을 넘어가야 나오는 해변이라 정화 활동이 잘 이루어지지 않는다. 모은 쓰레기는 일일이 지고 산을 건너야 지자체에서 수거할 수 있다.

A beach cleanup in progress. This area of the shore is hidden behind a mountain, so it has a poor cleaning infrastructure. We had to carry loads of garbage over the mountain one by one to deliver them to an area accessed by municipal garbage collecting services.

켜지고 소화되는 동안에도 결코 썩지 않은 그것. 바닷새를 죽이고도 그대로 혼자 남아 다시 바다로 흘러갈 '그것'의 무한한 반복이 바다가 처한 현실이기 때문이다.

고작 몇 걸음뿐이다. 상상의 바다의 깨고 실제 바다를 마주하는 데 필요한 것 말이다. 예뻐 '보이는' 해변에서 조금 더 걸어 들어가면 누구나 사진 속에서 보던 쓰레기 해변을 한국 앞바다에서 쉽게 발견할 수 있다. 놀라기엔 아직 이르다. 해변을 뒤덮은 쓰레기는 바닷속에 있는 쓰레기에 비하면 새 발의 피니까.

ocean is the endless cycle of this thing—plastic—killing birds and returning alone to the water.

A few steps along the shore were all it took to shatter the image of the ocean in my imagination and replace it with reality. Starting from a "pretty" beach, take a short walk along the coast—you soon will come across one of those littered beaches often seen in photos. But even this sight should not shock you. The garbage covering the beach is nothing compared to the garbage in the ocean.

From the city to the beach, from the beach to the ocean

It was only natural that my ocean cleanup activities that began on that beach continued in the actual ocean. After recruiting a scuba diving instructor, the Sea Shepherd volunteers formed a team to engage in ocean cleanup activities in earnest. Even those of us who could not even swim learned to dive and obtained certificates, including me.

In the beginning, I simply thought that it would be fun; since I liked water, I figured I would enjoy diving as well. But the diving was neither fun nor enjoyable. It was much more difficult and physically tiring (not to mention expensive) than I had imagined. Every time I went to the pool, all I could think about was quitting. I wondered whether it was really necessary for me to actually enter the ocean when there was so much to do outside the water as well. It was only after my first real ocean cleanup endeavor that I made my final decision.

I will never forget the shock I felt when I first took the plunge into the ocean. If there is a heaven, it looks like the sea. I felt as if I were flying in the blue sky or swimming in the vast universe. Emotions engulfed me. I was immediately enraptured by the ocean's beauty, though it was not the kind of splendor often shown in the media. Colorful coral reefs, countless species of fish, and algal blooms were nowhere to be seen. The East Sea was barren, its scenery consisting of nothing but an endless sandy seafloor dotted with rusted artificial reefs. I had never before encountered such strange silence.

Even so, I was infinitely moved by the ocean. It was only in the embrace of the water—the source of life that first enabled human existence and continues to keep us alive today—that it finally became clear to me: the ocean is not just a vast body of saltwater, but a habitat for countless creatures and an immense world that breathes and lives on its own. I understood it with my whole body.

It was also there, in the depths of the ocean where humans cannot breathe without a device that weighs 10 kilograms or more, that I saw heaps of human-made waste. All my hesitation disappeared before the mountains of marine debris that were so large that I did not know where to begin. I had to do something immediately, no matter how small.

The ocean that had lapped at my feet became an entire world,

물속에서 올려다 본 시셰퍼드 다이버들. 수면에 구름이 비쳐 마치 하늘에 있는 것처럼 보인다. (아래) 인공 어초에 얽혀 있는 그물과 밧줄.

Sea Shepherd divers seen from below. The reflection of the clouds makes the divers appear as if they are floating in the sky. (on bottom) Nets and rope tangled around artificial coral reefs.

도심에서 해변으로, 해변에서 해저로

해변에서 시작한 해양 쓰레기 정화 활동이 바닷속으로 이어진 것은 어찌 보면 숙명적인 흐름이었다. 현직 스쿠버 다이빙 강사가 멤버로 합류하면서 우리는 본격적으로 수중 청소팀을 꾸렸다. 수영조차 할 줄 모르던 활동가들도 하나둘 다이빙을 배우고 자격증을 땄다. 나도 그중 하나였다.

초반에는 막연히 재미있겠다는 생각으로 시작했다. 물을 좋아하니 다이빙도 즐거울 것이라 짐작했다. 그런데 직접 배운 다이빙은 전혀 즐겁거나 재미있지 않았다. 생각보다 훨씬 어렵고 육체적으로 힘들었다. 돈도 많이 들었다. 훈련을 위해 수영장에 갈 때마다 그만둔다고 말할까 몇 번이나 고민했다. 물 밖에서 할 수 있는 일도 많은데 꼭 바다에 들어가야 할까. 고민이 말끔히 사라진 건 첫 번째 수중 청소를 시작하면서부터였다.

바닷속에 처음 들어갔을 때의 충격은 잊을 수가 없다. 천국이 있다면

engulfing me. I could no longer be lazy. When I finally learned to control my body in the water, I was ready with a knife in my hand to remove what we call "ghost gear," abandoned fishing gear that floats like ghosts and kills countless marine creatures.

Finally facing the ghosts

Ghost gear includes all fishing gear that has been discarded in the ocean, intentionally or accidentally, such as abandoned nets, traps, and fishing-related waste. Many people think that marine debris is made up of the waste we generate daily on land, but 48-60 percent of all marine debris is produced at sea by the fishing industry. According to statistics by the Ministry of Oceans and Fisheries, about 40,000 tons of waste from the fishing industry enters Korean waters every year.[1] But how is this waste, not even visible at the water's surface, such a dangerous threat to the marine ecosystem?

For a start, one problem with abandoned fishing gear is "ghost fishing," a phenomenon that occurs when abandoned fishing gear continues to catch fish and other sea creatures. According to statistics released by the Korea Coast Guard in 2021, the amount of fish "caught" through ghost fishing equals 10 percent of all fish caught per year in Korea.[2] This is a colossal amount. It implies that the death of one in every 10 fish killed by humans is due to marine debris.

Neither rescued nor removed, sea creatures caught in abandoned traps starve to death in the depths of the ocean. Many turtles or whales entangled in ghost nets must have body parts amputated in order to be saved. It is no longer surprising to see fish pierced by nets and hooks, wounded and dying. Freedom, the most basic right for all living creatures, is not guaranteed in the ocean.

Whenever Sea Shepherd volunteers go diving, we rescue sea creatures that are trapped in abandoned fishing gear. The fact that we come across them even though we only survey a very specific area of the ocean once a month proves that ghost fishing is not coincidental. How many creatures are dying out there in the unreachable ocean? This immeasurable vice weighs heavily on my mind.

The second problem with abandoned fishing gear is that it is mainly plastic waste. Nets, traps, and other fishing devices are mostly made of plastic, which does not decompose, so not only do these items have the potential to contribute to ghost fishing, but they also introduce microplastics to the marine ecosystem as they are eroded and broken down. So small that they are barely visible,

1. Ministry of Oceans and Fisheries, The 5th Comprehensive Plan for Marine Environment (2021–2030) (January, 2021), 16.
2. Related Ministries Joint (Ministry of Oceans and Fisheries, Ministry of Environment, Ministry of Foreign Affairs, and Ministry of Food and Drug Safety), Comprehensive Plan for Marine Plastics Reduction (May 30, 2019), 1.

이런 모습일 것 같았다. 푸른 하늘을 나는 것도 같고, 광활한 우주를 유영하는 것 같기도 했다. 이루 말할 수 없는 벅찬 감정이 밀려왔다. 바다의 아름다움이 순식간에 나를 압도했다. 하지만 흔히 매스컴에서 볼 수 있는 화려한 모습의 바다를 마주해서 그런 것은 아니다. 형형색색의 산호초나 수많은 종류의 어류, 무성한 해초 같은 풍경은 조금도 볼 수 없었다. 내가 마주한 동해 바다는 척박하기 그지없었다. 끝없이 펼쳐진 황망한 모래밭과 인간이 떨어뜨려 놓은 녹슨 인공 어초가 풍경이라고 할 만한 것의 전부였다. 그토록 기이한 적막을 느낀 것은 생애 처음이었다.

그런데도 바다는 그 자체로 무궁한 감동으로 다가왔다. 태초에 우리를 있게 했고 지금도 우리를 살아가게 하는 생명의 근원으로서의 바다가, 그 품속에서야 비로소 더할 나위 없이 명료해지는 느낌이었다. 그냥 짠맛 나는 물이 아니라 수많은 생명의 보금자리이자 스스로 숨을 쉬며 살아가는 거대한 세계라는 사실을 온몸으로 체감했다.

그리고 바로 그곳에, 10여 킬로그램의 장비를 차지 않고는 감히 인간이 잠시 숨을 쉴 수조차 없는 그곳에, 인간이 버린 쓰레기가 무덤처럼 쌓여 있었다. 무엇을 먼저 끌어올려야 할지 알 수 없을 정도로 방대한 해저 쓰레기 산 앞에서 망설임은 온데간데없이 사라졌다. 아무리 작은 일이라도 당장 해야 했다.

발끝을 적시던 바다는 어느새 내 몸을 흠뻑 적셔 온 세상이 되었다. 나는 더 이상 게으름을 부리지 않았다. 물속에서 겨우 몸을 가누게 되었을 즈음, 내 손에는 칼이 들려 있었다. 해저를 유령처럼 떠돌며 수많은 해양 생물을 죽이는 폐어구, 일명 '유령어구(ghostnet)'를 제거하기 위해서였다.

드디어 마주한 유령의 정체

유령어구는 자의나 타의로 어부의 통제를 벗어나 바다에 버려진 폐그물, 폐통발, 낚시 쓰레기 등의 모든 어업 도구를 뜻한다. 보통 해양 쓰레기라고 하면 육지에서 흘러들어 간 생활 쓰레기를 주로 떠올리는데, 실제로는 전체 해양 쓰레기의 48-60퍼센트가 해상에서 기인한 어업 쓰레기이다. 2018년 해양수산부 집계에 따르면 매년 4만 톤의 어업 쓰레기가 국내 바다로 유입되고 있다고 추산된다.[1] 그렇다면 눈에 띄지도 않는 곳에 가라앉아 있는 어업 쓰레기가 해양 생태계를 위협하는 심각한 요인인 이유는 무엇일까?

우선 폐어구의 첫 번째 문제점은 바닷속에서 '유령어업'을 반복한다는 점이다. 유령어업은 주인 없는 유령어구에 의해 일어나는 어획으로, 2021년 해양경찰청에서 발표한 바에 따르면 유령어업의 어획량은 국내 연간 어획량의 10퍼센트에 달한다.[2] 실로 어마어마한 수치다. 포획되는 어류 10마리 중 1마리가 쓰레기 때문에 희생된다는 뜻이니까.

폐통발에 잡힌 해양 생물은 구조되지도 수거되지도 못한 채 깊은 바다 아래서 굶어 죽을 날만 기다린다. 폐그물에 감긴 거북이나 고래가

microplastics destroy the marine ecosystem by entering the food chain. Ultimately, the effect reaches the predators at the top: humans.

In 2019, many people were stunned by a study released by the World Wide Fund For Nature (WWF) and the University of Newcastle in Australia whose results showed that people ingest a credit card's worth of plastic every day.[3] But looking back, what is so shocking about these results? The reality of the earth is that microplastics have already entered the water cycle. Seawater evaporates to create precipitation, so microplastics can now be detected in rain. We can no longer run away or ignore it. The consequences of exploiting the ocean and treating it as a landfill become clearer by the day.

What must be done?

By now, those who are environmentally conscious might be wondering what actions they should take to protect the ocean. My answer to this question is always the same: adopt a vegetarian diet. It might sound irrelevant, but vegetarianism has a great impact on ocean conservation. Waste is not the only threat to the marine ecosystem. In fact, marine debris is only the tip of the iceberg. Countless sea creatures have become extinct or are endangered due to large-scale commercial fishing, particularly its practices of overfishing and bycatch.

Today's fishing industry employs methods that are nothing short of destructive. Bottom trawling involves sweeping the seabed with a massive weighted net up to 1.5 soccer fields in length—that's enough to cover a Boeing 747. Longline fishing clears an area of fish by using thousands of bait hooks attached to a rope that can measure up to 170 kilometers long. The industry is guilty not only of

폐통발에 끼어 죽어 있는 물살이의 모습.　　A fish that has died in an abandoned trap.

신체 일부를 절단당하는 일은 부지기수로 일어난다. 낚싯줄과 낚싯바늘에 상처 입고 죽어 가는 물살이를 마주치는 것은 더는 놀랍지 않다. 생명체가 가질 최소한의 권리인 '자유'가 바닷속에서는 보장되지 않는다.

우리는 다이빙을 할 때마다 폐어구에 갇힌 해양 생물을 구조하고 있는데, 한 달에 한 번 아주 국지적인 장소밖에 살피지 못하는데도 항상 이런 경우를 목격한다는 것은 유령어업이 절대 우연히 일어나는 일이 아니라는 사실을 보여 준다. 그럼 미처 닿을 수 없는 저 드넓은 바다에서는 대체 얼마나 많은 생명이 쉴 새 없이 죽어 가고 있단 말인가. 가늠하기 힘든 죄악에 절로 마음이 무거워진다.

폐어구의 두 번째 문제는 그것이 대부분 플라스틱 쓰레기라는 점이다. 그물이나 통발 등 어업 도구는 대부분 플라스틱 재질로 이루어져 있는데, 썩지 않기 때문에 끊임없이 유령어업을 일으킬 수 있는 것은 물론이고, 파도 등에 깎이고 부서지면서 계속 해양 생태계로 미세 플라스틱을 유입시킨다. 눈에 보이지 않을 정도로 잘게 쪼개진 미세 플라스틱은 그대로 먹이사슬로 들어가 해양 생태계를 파괴하고, 나아가 최상위 포식자인 인간에게도 고스란히 화살이 되어 돌아온다.

2019년 세계자연기금(World Wide Fund For Nature, WWF)이 호주의 뉴캐슬대학과 함께 발표한 "현대인은 매주 신용카드 한 장만큼의 미세 플라스틱을 섭취하고 있다"[3]라는 연구 결과는 많은 사람을 놀라게 했다. 그러나 돌이켜 보면 그게 과연 놀라운 일일까? 바닷물이 증발해 비가 되는 대기 순환계에도 미세 플라스틱이 포함되어 이제 빗물에서도 미세 플라스틱이 검출되고 있다. 지구가 처한 현실이다. 더 이상 도망칠 수도 외면할 수도 없다. 바다를 쓰레기통 취급하고 함부로 착취한 결과는 날이 갈수록 선명하게 드러날 것이다.

무엇을 해야 하는가

이제 생태 감수성이 예민한 누군가는 바다를 지키기 위해 어떤 행동을 할 수 있는지 궁금해졌을지도 모르겠다. 나는 이 질문에 항상 같은 답을 한다. 채식을 하라고 말이다. 생뚱맞게 들릴지도 모르겠지만 채식의 비중을 높이는 것은 해양 환경을 보호하는 데 중대한 영향을 미친다. 해양 생태계를 위협하는 것은 쓰레기뿐만이 아니다. 쓰레기는 본질의 부스러기에 불과하다. 수많은 해양 생물이 멸종하

overfishing to the point where target species are completely depleted, but also of the bycatch of unwanted species.

Between 1950 and 2014, marine biomass (the amount of living matter) decreased around the world, except in the North Pacific Ocean, where it increased due to climate change and the development of new fishing grounds. The Pacific, Atlantic, and Indian Oceans each lost more than 50 percent of their biomass. At 65.8 percent of all fishing grounds, more sea creatures are caught than bred. In 2020, a team of researchers from Canada, Germany, and Australia discovered that only 18 percent of the world's marine zones had sufficient biomass.[4] In short, 82 percent of the ocean is seeing a rapid decline in biomass.

Bycatch also causes serious harm. According to Greenpeace, about 300,000 whales, 160,000 seabirds, and millions of sharks are killed as bycatch every year.[5] Unintentionally caught creatures are typically thrown back into the sea. If 300,000 whales, 160,000 seabirds, and millions of sharks had to die so that we could purchase a single can of tuna, how could that be ethical consumption? Additionally, four out of the eight main species of tuna are classified as endangered species. From an eco-ethical point of view, should we approve of the act of eating if it contributes to the extinction of a species?

As an environmental activist, my answer is, of course, "No." Today's fishing industry, designed to generate maximum profits, completely neglects the sustainability of the marine ecosystem—a fact that is both tragic and nonsensical because if the marine ecosystem disappeared, the first sector to collapse would be the fishing industry itself.

We must restore the dying ocean before it is too late. To do so, we must reduce our consumption of products from the fishing industry, which damages the ecosystem, while expanding marine protected areas to help the ocean maintain the minimum life force it needs. We will never be able to save the ocean after the world's fishing grounds have all been depleted. When the ocean dies, so do we.

The ocean's green belt: Expanding marine protected areas

If vegetarianism is an effective and powerful eco-friendly individual practice to protect the ocean, then the expansion of marine protected areas (MPAs) is an essential

1. 해양수산부, 「제5차 해양환경 종합계획(2021-2030년)」(2021. 1.), 16.
2. 관계부처 합동(해양수산부, 환경부, 외교부, 식약처), 「해양 플라스틱 저감 종합대책」(2019. 5. 30.), 1.
3. Dalberg Advisors, Wijnand de Wit, Nathan Bigaud, *No Plastic in Nature: Assessing Plastic Ingestion from Nature to People* (WWF, 2019), 7.

3. Dalberg Advisors, Wijnand de Wit, Nathan Bigaud, *No Plastic in Nature: Assessing Plastic Ingestion from Nature to People* (WWF, 2019), 7.
4. M. L. D. Palomares et. al., "Fishery biomass trends of exploited fish populations in marine ecoregions, climatic zones and ocean basins," *Estuarine, Coastal and Shelf Science* 243 (2020), 106896.
5. Park Doohyun, Youngran Lee, *A Journey Towards Sustainable Seafood* (WWF-Korea, 2018), 10.

거나 멸종 위기에 처한 본질적 이유는 남획과 혼획을 일삼는 '대규모 상업 어업'이다.

축구장 1.5개 길이에 보잉747 비행기가 들어갈 정도로 큰 어망에 무거운 추를 달아 바닥을 쓸면서 이루어지는 저인망어업, 최대 170킬로미터에 이르는 긴 밧줄에 수천 개의 낚싯바늘을 매달아 싹쓸이하는 연승어업 등 현대 상업 어업은 어느 방법이라고 할 것 없이 모두 파괴적이다. 목표 종을 씨가 마를 때까지 무분별하게 남획할 뿐더러 원치 않는 어종까지 모조리 혼획한다.

1950-2014년에 세계 바다의 생물량 변화를 보면 기후변화와 새로운 어장 개척으로 생물량이 증가한 북태평양을 빼고는 전부 생물량이 줄어들고 있다. 태평양, 대서양, 인도양에서 각각 50퍼센트 이상 생물량이 감소했고 세계 어장의 65.8퍼센트에서 해양 생물이 번식량보다 많이 잡히고 있다. 2020년 캐나다와 독일, 호주의 공동 연구팀이 조사한 바에 따르면 생물량이 '충분히 많은' 지역은 18퍼센트밖에 되지 않는다.[4] 즉, 82퍼센트의 바다에서 생물량이 급감하고 있다는 뜻이다.

혼획의 피해도 심각하다. 그린피스(Greenpeace)에 따르면 매년 약 30만 마리의 고래와 16만 마리의 바닷새, 수백만 마리의 상어가 혼획으로 목숨을 잃는다.[5] 혼획된 해양 생물은 그냥 바다에 버려진다. 내가 참치 한 캔을 먹기 위해 고래 30만 마리, 바닷새 16만 마리, 상어 수백만 마리가 필연적으로 죽을 수밖에 없다면 그것은 과연 정당한 소비일까? 게다가 참치는 8종 가운데 4종이 국제 멸종 위기종으로 지정되어 있다. 이처럼 먹는 것 자체가 한 생물종의 멸종에 대단히 큰 영향을 미치는 행위라면 그것은 생태 윤리적인 관점에서 용납될 수 있을까?

환경운동가로서 내가 가진 답은 당연히 "아니오"이다. 현대 상업 어업은 최대의 이윤만을 고려한 나머지 해양 생태계의 지속 가능성은 철저하게 배제하고 있다. 이것은 참담하고 우스운 일이다. 해양 생태계가 사라지면 어업이야말로 가장 먼저 사라질 산업일 테니 말이다.

더 늦기 전에 죽어 가는 바다를 되살려야 한다. 그러기 위해서는 반(反)생태적 수산물 소비를 줄이고 해양보호구역을 늘려 바다가 최소한의 생명력을 보전할 수 있도록 해야 한다. 전 세계 어장이 다 빈 다음에는 절대로 바다를 살릴 수 없다. 그리고, 바다가 죽으면 우리도 죽는다.

바다의 그린벨트, 해양보호구역 확대

개인이 바다를 위해 할 수 있는 효과적이면서 강력한 생태적 실천이 채식이라면, 범국가적 차원에서 바다를 지키기 위해 꼭 필요한 장치는 엄격히 관리되는 해양보호구역(Marine Protected Area, MPA)의 확대다. 해양보호구역은 '해양 생태계 및 해양 경관 등 특별히 보전할 필요가 있어 국가 또는 지자체가 보호구역으로 지정하여

strategy at the national level. An MPA is an area designated and protected by a state or local government for the special conservation of the marine ecosystem and scenery. Establishing MPAs is effective for protecting biodiversity, recovering fishery resources, and combating the effects of climate change.

Studies show that marine biodiversity in MPAs increased by 19 percent, total biomass by 251 percent, and the total catch in the surrounding waters more than doubled.[6] This is called the spillover effect, in which protecting one area has a positive impact on neighboring areas. Oceanographers claim that at least 30 percent of the world's ocean must be safeguarded as through the establishment of MPAs to protect the marine ecosystem. Based on this claim, a campaign called 30x30 is underway to protect 30 percent of the world's ocean by 2030.

Korea's MPAs account for only 2.16 percent of the total area of Korean waters by the standards of the International Union for the Conservation of Nature (IUCN). "No-take zones," where fishing is prohibited, do not even exist. At the Partnering for Green Growth and the Global Goals 2030 (P4G) Summit held this year, President Moon Jae-in declared that Korea would partake in the 30x30 campaign, but did not reveal any specific plans, raising concerns that this declaration will not be backed up by specific action. With 2030 less than 10 years away, it is high time that we act. We must raise our voices and call for more MPAs to ensure the president sticks to his promise.

The ocean, which much of humanity has believed would give itself to us unconditionally, has reached its limit. Its ability to absorb carbon dioxide is decreasing every year, resulting in more carbon emissions into the atmosphere. At

지속 가능한 바다를 염원하는 시셰퍼드 코리아 활동가들의 목소리.

Sea Shepherd Korea activists calling for a sustainable marine ecosystem.

관리하는 구역'으로, 생물 다양성 보전, 어획 자원 회복, 기후변화 완화 등의 영향을 미치는 것으로 알려져 있다.

한 연구에 따르면 해양보호구역으로 지정된 바다에서는 생물 다양성이 19퍼센트, 전체 생물량은 251퍼센트, 주변 바다의 어획량은 2배 이상 증가한 것으로 나타났다.[6] 이를 스필오버 효과(spillover effect)라고 하는데, 한 해역을 보호함으로써 주변 해역에도 선순환이 일어나는 현상을 뜻한다. 세계 해양학자들은 해양 생태계를 지키기 위해 전체 해양 면적의 최소 30퍼센트 이상을 해양보호구역으로 지정해야 한다고 밝히고 있으며, 이를 근거로 국제 사회에서는 2030년까지 전 세계 바다의 30퍼센트를 해양보호구역으로 지정하자는 '30×30' 운동이 전개되고 있다.

그런데 현재 한국의 해양보호구역은 세계자연보전연맹(International Union for the Conservation of Nature, IUCN) 기준으로 2.16퍼센트에 불과하다. 이 가운데 조업금지구역인 '노테이크존'은 0퍼센트로 아예 존재하지도 않는다. 2021년 열린 'P4G(녹색성장 및 2030 글로벌 목표를 위한 연대)'에서 문재인 대통령이 한국도 '30×30' 협약국으로 가입하겠다고 선언했으나 구체적인 계획이나 진행 사항이 전혀 없어 말뿐인 선언이 될 우려가 깊다. 목표 연도가 10년도 채 남지 않은 만큼 적극적인 행동이 필요한 시점이다. 해양보호구역을 요구하는 목소리를 높여 대통령의 약속이 실현될 수 있도록 힘을 모으자.

언제까지고 아낌없이 줄 것이라 생각했던 바다가 지금 한계치에 다다라 있다. 매년 이산화탄소 포집 능력이 떨어져 점점 더 많은 탄소를 대기로 뿜어내고 있다. 지금의 추세대로면 2040년에는 탄소 배출량이 여섯 번째 대멸종을 일으키는 필요조건을 만족할 것이다. 20년 남짓 남은 인류와 바다의 시간을 어떻게 쓸 것인가. 게걸스럽게 소모할 것인가, 아니면 20년을 40년으로, 40년을 60년으로 바꾸는 행동을 취할 것인가. 선택은 우리에게 달려 있다. 바다는 아무 말이 없다.

this rate, carbon emissions will reach a level that could cause the sixth mass extinction in 2040. How shall we spend the 20 or so years remaining for humanity and the ocean? Will we consume everything greedily, or will we take action to transform those 20 years into 40 years and then 60 years? The choice is ours to make. As for the ocean, it says nothing, simply maintaining its silence.

4.   M. L. D. Palomares et. al., "Fishery biomass trends of exploited fish populations in marine ecoregions, climatic zones and ocean basins," *Estuarine, Coastal and Shelf Science* 243 (2020), 106896.
5.   박두현, 이영란, 『지속가능한 수산물을 위한 WWF의 제안』(WWF-Korea, 2018), 10.
6.   Partnership for Interdisciplinary Studies of Coastal Oceans, *The Science of Marine Reserves*, 2nd ed. Europe (PISCO, 2011), 4, www.piscoweb.org.

6.   Partnership for Interdisciplinary Studies of Coastal Oceans, *The Science of Marine Reserves*, 2nd ed. Europe (PISCO, 2011), 4, www.piscoweb.org.

식물에서 얻은 가르침에 대하여!:
어느 생태학자이자 박물관 직원의 이야기

장즈산(張至善)
국립대만선사문화박물관(國立臺灣史前文化博物館) 보조 연구위원

나는 대학에서 산림학을 전공하고 지금은 국립대만선사문화박물관에서 일하고 있다. 오랜 기간 식물을 공부한 사람에게, 식물은 언제나 놀라움을 선사하며 때로는 충격과 감동을 주기도 한다. 그간 업무와 현장 연구에서 식물을 다루며 얻은 세 가지 흥미로운 경험을 통해, 식별, 분류, 생태 조사를 넘어 식물이 가르쳐 준 것들을 공유하고자 한다.

식물은 어머니의 축복을 전한다: 식물 문양 아기띠
첫번 째는 아기띠에 관한 이야기다. '슬링' 또는 '포대기'라고도 불리는 아기띠는 아기를 감싸고 끈으로 고정해 안고 다니기 위해 사용한다. 어린 아이를 돌볼 때 쓰는 퀼트 천이나 넓은 밴드가 아기띠로 쓰이는 경우도 있다. 아기띠는 중국 남서부의 많은 소수 민족 지역에서 여성들의 직조나 자수 솜씨를 보여 주는 것이자, 농장일이나 육체 노동을 하는 동안에도 아기를 안고 있을 수 있도록 하는 도구다. 이러한 실용적 기능에 더해, 아기띠에는 특별한 의미를 담고 있는 많은 장식 문양이 있다. 중국 남서부 소수 민족 지역을 예로 들어 보자. 이 곳에서 발견되는 아기띠 장식 문양들은 풍나무, 철

Things That Plants Have Taught Me!: An Ecologist and Museum Staff Say...

Dr. Chang, Chi-Shan
Assistant Research Fellow of National Museum of Prehistory

I studied in the forestry department when I was in college, and I work in the National Museum of Prehistory, Taiwan, now. For a person who has studied plants a long time, I find that plants will always give me a sense of surprise, even shock and feeling touched. I will talk about three interesting examples from my work and field research, and share what plants have taught me, beyond identification, classification, and ecological investigation.

Plant decoration on the baby carrier: Plants carry the mother's blessings
The first example is the story about the baby carrier. The baby carrier, also known as a child's "sling" or "swaddling," is used to carry, tie, and wrap the baby. Sometimes it is a broad band or quilt used to carry young children. In many ethnic minority areas in southwest China, the baby carrier reflects the craftsmanship of women's weaving and embroidery skills, and it is also for carrying children during farmwork and labor. In addition to practical functions, there are many decorative patterns on these baby carriers, which have special meanings. Take the ethnic minority areas in southwest China as an example. Many of the patterns on the baby carriers in this area are based on depicting plants, such as liquidambar (Liq-

그림 1. 이족의 아기띠에 그려진 철쭉 모티프.

Figure 1. Rhododendron motif on the baby carrier of the Yi people.

그림 2. 동족의 아기띠에 그려진 반얀나무 모티프.

Figure 2. Banyan tree motif on the baby carrier of the Dong people.

쭉, 석류, 반얀나무와 같은 식물에 바탕을 두고 있다. 풍나무는 묘족(苗族)의 어미나무이며, 철쭉은 이족(彝族)의 조상신이다(그림 1). 석류는 자식과 손주를 많이 갖는 다산을 상징한다. 또 다른 소수민족인 동족(侗族)은 반얀나무가 아이들을 보호해 준다고 믿는다(그림 2). 아기띠의 식물 문양은 부적과 같은 의미를 지닌다. 그 안에는 모성애와 애착이 가득한 기념물이자, 출산, 축복, 보호라는 깊은 뜻이 담겨 있다.[1] '식물은 어머니의 축복을 전한다'라고 말할 수 있다.

식물은 인간 이주의 역사를 전한다: 꾸지나무와 오스트로네시아족

또 다른 예는 꾸지나무(그림 3)에 대한 필자의 연구에서 찾아볼 수 있다. 꾸지나무는 수피포(樹皮布)를 만드는 주재료 중 하나로, 꾸지나무 속껍질로 만든 수피포를 쓰는 것은 오스트로네시아족의 독특한 소재 문화 중 하나다. 꾸지나무는 뽕나무과의 자웅이주(암수딴그루) 식물로, 동아시아 토종 식물이다. 문헌 기록상 꾸지나무는 동남아시아나 오세아니아의 섬에서는 열매를 맺지 않으므로, 이 지역의 꾸지나무 개체군은 자연적으로 자라난 것이 아니다. 따라서 꾸지나무의 분포에 관해 연구하는 것은 곧 수피포 문화를 따라가는 것과 같다(그림 4). 오스트로네시아족이 동아시아에서 오세아니아로 이주했으므로, 꾸지나무의 전파 역사를 연구하다 보면 오스트로네시아어의 이동에 관한 중요한 단서를 얻을 수 있다.[2]

연구팀은 중국 남부, 베트남, 대만, 일본, 인도네시아, 필리핀, 하와이의 여러 지역에서 꾸지나무 표본을 수집했다. 또한, 칠레팀 구성원들은 태평양 여러 지역의 꾸지나무 표본을 제공해 주었다. 영국 국립자연사박물관, 뉴욕식물원, 미주리식물원, 스미소니언박물관을 포함한 여러 식물 표본실에서도 꾸지나무 표본을 제공해 주었고, 그 엽록체 'ndhF-rpl32'의 DNA 염기 서열을 분석해 꾸지나무 개체군의 유전적 전파 역사를 재구성했다. 그 결과, 꾸지나무의 유전적 다양성이 가장 풍부한 지역으로 중국 남부, 그 다음으로 대만이 꼽혔고, 이는 동아시아가 꾸지나무의 발생지라는 예상과도 맥이 통한다. 대만 동부와 남부 지역에 꾸지나무의 원래 유전자인 하플로타입(haplotype)이 분포해 있고, 이는 인도네시아 술라웨시, 인근 오세아니아(Near Oceania)와 오지 오세아니아(Remote Oceania) 지역에서도 나타났다. 이러한 사실들은 대만이 오세아니아 꾸지나무의 고향이라는 주장에 힘을 싣는다. 연구 결과, 꾸지

uidambar formosana), rhododendron, pomegranate, and banyan. Liquidambar is the mother tree of the Miao people, and rhododendron is the ancestral god of the Yi people (fig.1). The pomegranate symbolizes having many children and many grandchildren, and the banyan tree is the protector of children for the Dong people (fig.2). The decorative pattern of plants on the baby carrier has the meaning of amulets. It is a memorial full of maternal love and affection and conveys the deep meaning of fertility, blessing, and protection.[1] We can say that "plants carry the blessings of mothers."

Paper mulberry and Austronesian: Plants carry the message of people's migration

Another example from my studies is the paper mulberry (fig.3). Paper mulberry is one of the main materials for making bark cloth. The bark cloth made from the inner layer of the bark of the *Broussonetia papyrifera* is one of the distinctive material cultures of the Austronesian people. *B. papyrifera* is a dioecious plant of the Moraceae family, native to East Asia. As the literature records that the *B. papyrifera* does not bear fruit in the islands of Southeast Asia or Oceania, the *B. papyrifera* population in this area should be non-naturally distributed, and it is more likely to follow the bark cloth culture (fig.4). Austronesian people migrated from East Asia to Oceania, so studying the history of the spread of *B. papyrifera* can provide important clues for the migration of Austronesian.[2]

We collected *B. papyrifera* samples from various provinces in southern China, Vietnam, Taiwan, Japan, Indonesia, the Philippines, and Hawaii. In addition, members of the Chilean team provide samples of *B. papyrifera* from various parts of the Pacific Ocean. Many herbariums, including the British Museum of Natural History, the New York Botanical Garden, the Missouri Botanical Garden, and the Smithsonian Institution, provided samples from paper mulberry specimens, analyzed its chloroplast *ndhF-rpl32* DNA sequence fragments, and reconstructed the history of genetic transmission of the population. The results show that southern China and Taiwan are the regions with the highest and the second highest genetic diversity of *B. papyrifera*, which is in line with the expectation that East Asia is the origin site of *B. papyrifera*. An original gene haplotype, distributed in eastern

1. Chang, Chi-Shan, "An analysis of the decorative biological patterns on baby carriers of the ethnic minorities of southwest China: Base on examples from the collections in the National Museum of Prehistory," in *Fertility, blessings and protection: The Cultures of Asia baby carriers*, ed. Lin, Chih-Hsing (Taitung: National Museum of Prehistory, 2012), 49-63.
2. Chang, C. S. et al., "A holistic picture of Austronesian migrations revealed by phylogeography of Pacific paper mulberry," *Proceedings of the National Academy of Sciences of the United States of America* 112, no. 44 (2015): 13537-13542.

1. Chang, Chi-Shan, "An analysis of the decorative biological patterns on baby carriers of the ethnic minorities of southwest China: Base on examples from the collections in the National Museum of Prehistory." in *Fertility, blessings and protection: The Cultures of Asia baby carriers*, ed. Lin, Chih-Hsing (Taitung: National Museum of Prehistory, 2012), 49-63.
2. Chang, C. S. et al., "A holistic picture of Austronesian migrations revealed by phylogeography of Pacific paper mulberry," *Proceedings of the National Academy of Sciences of the United States of America* 112, no. 44 (2015): 13537-13542.

나무의 전파 경로가 오스트로네시아족의 이동에 관한 가설 중 '대만 기원설'과 일치한다는 것이 밝혀졌고, 이는 오스트로네시아족의 이주 역사에 있어 대만이 매우 중요한 위치를 차지한다는 것을 말한다.[3] 이것이 바로, 식물이 인간 이주의 역사를 보여 주는 예이다.

작은 에피소드가 하나 있다. 2016년 11월 2일 인도네시아 자카르타섬 유박물관에서 열린 전시 《두드린 나무껍질: 숨겨진 보물—푸야, 타파, 다루앙(Beaten Bark: Hidden Treasure—Fuya, Tapa, Daluang)》의 개막식에 참석했을 때였다. 주최 측에서 개막식을 위해 두 가지 특별 이벤트를 기획했는데, 하나는 내빈에게 꾸지나무 묘목을 선물로 주는 것이고, 다른 하나는 VIP 행사로 박물관 정원에 꾸지나무를 심는 것이었다. 꾸지나무는 대만에서는 어디서나 볼 수 있지만 인도네시아에서는 보기 드문, 귀한 수종이다. 꾸지나무와 수피포의 가치를 인정하고 널리 알리기 위해, 주최 측에서는 미리 꾸지나무 묘목을 길러 개막식 행사 중 하나로 '나무 심기'를 기획한 것이다. 주최 측은 전시품을 대여해 준 지역 박물관 여덟 곳에 묘목을 보낸 뒤, 그들이 박물관에 올 때 그것들을 심을

그림 3. 꾸지나무, 암그루(학명: Broussonetia papyrifera).

Figure 3. Paper mulberry, female (Broussonetia papyrifera).

그림 4. 수피포(樹皮布).

Figure 4. Bark cloth.

and southern Taiwan, also appeared in Sulawesi, Indonesia, Near Oceania, and Far Oceania. These results support that Taiwan is the homeland of B. papyrifera in Oceania. The results of this study found that the propagation path of B. papyrifera is consistent with the "out of Taiwan" hypothesis in the Austronesian migration, showing that Taiwan occupies an extremely important position in the history of the Austronesian migration.[3] In this case, the plant carries the message of people's migration.

There is a small episode. I participated in the opening of the exhibition named "Beaten Bark—Hidden Treasure: Fuya, Tapa, Daluang" held by the Jakarta Textile Museum on November 2, 2016. During the period, the organizer also planned two special events for the opening: one was to give guests the saplings of B. papyrifera as a gift, and another was "planting the paper mulberry" in the garden of the museum for VIPs. B. papyrifera can be seen everywhere in Taiwan, but it is a rare and precious tree species in Indonesia. In order to recognize and promote the value of "paper mulberry" and "bark cloth," the organizer cultivated paper mulberry seedlings in advance, arranged the "planting activities" during the opening ceremony, and gave saplings to the eight local museums that loaned the artifacts for the exhibition, hoping that they could take the paper mulberry seedlings back to their museum for planting. A small plant carries the future and hope of culture. It also points out the connection between human cultural heritage and natural resources, showing special value and significance.[4]

Having a covenant with ancestral spirits, stopping the movement of evil spirits: Plants communicate with spirits

The third example is the plants used in rituals by Taiwan's indigenous people, such as the Paiwan ethnic group. We take the Tjuwabar tribe in Taitung County in eastern Taiwan as an example. The tribe has a ritual called "maljeveq," held every five years. One of the key points of the ritual is "stabbing the ball." The ritual is an agreement between people and ancestral spirits. The smoke from burning millet stems is used as a signal to summon ancestral spirits (fig.5). In addition, before the ceremony is held, a ritual will be carried out to block evil spirits from the tribe. The vine of yellow rotang palm (Calamus jenkinsianus), which is covered with thorns, will be used in the "pakigecen" ritual to block and defeat the evil spirits (fig.6). This concept is also applied to contemporary epidemics. For example, during SARS in 2003 and COVID-19 in 2020, tribal wizards ("pulingau") performed blocking rituals on tribal borders. The community manages and

3.   As footnote 2.
4.   Chang, Chi-Shan, "Using 'Bark' as a Cultural Carrier: an Introduction to Bark Painting, Bark Cloth and Bark Paper," Taiwan Natural Science 38, no. 3 (2019): 36-41.

수 있도록 다시 가지고 오기를 바랐다. 작은 나무 한 그루가 문화의 미래와 희망을 전달하는 것이다. 또한 이것은 인류의 문화유산과 천연 자원 사이의 연결고리를 보여 주며, 그 특별한 가치와 의미를 일깨워 준다.[4]

식물은 영혼과 소통한다: 조상신과의 약속, 악령 차단

세 번째 예는 식물이 의식에 사용되는 경우로, 대만 원주민인 파이완족의 예이다. 대만 동부 타이둥 현의 투와바(Tjuwabar) 부족은 5년마다 '오년제(maljeveq)'라는 축제를 여는데, 이 축제 의식의 핵심 중 하나는 '공 찌르기'이다. 이 의식을 통해 조상의 영(靈)과 사람 사이에 만남과 약속이 이루어진다. 수수 줄기를 태운 연기는 조상의 영을 소환하기 위한 신호로 사용된다(그림 5). 또한, 본 의식에 앞서 악령이 오는 것을 막기 위한 의식도 거행된다. 가시로 뒤덮인 노란 로딴 야자(Calamus jenkinsianus)의 덩굴을 사용해 악령을 막고 싸워 이기는 '파키제센(pakigecen)' 의식을 행한다 (그림 6). 이러한 개념은 현대 전염병에도 똑같이 적용된다. 예를 들어, 2003년 사스(SARS)와 2020년 코로나바이러스감염증-19(COVID-19) 유행에 맞서 부족의 주술사 '푸린가우(pulingau)'는 부족 거류지 간 경계를 차단하는 의식을 행했다. 공동체가 자체적으로 부족 간 경계를 관리하고 통제하며 자기 부족의 건강을 보살피기 위한 의식을 실시한 것으로, 외부인의 접근을 막고 부족 구성원들을 위로하는 데 중점을 두었다.[5] 현대 공중 보건의 위기 속에서, 전통 의식은 투와바 부족이나 다른 원주민 공동체가 능동적으로 대응하는 방법 중 하나로 작용한다. 요약하자면, 이 사례에서 식물은 조상신과 소통하고 악령을 차단하며 부족을 보호하기 위해 쓰였다고 할 수 있다.

요약

'어머니의 축복이 담긴 식물', '인간 이주의 역사를 보여 주는 식물', '영혼과 소통하는 식물'이라는 세 가지 예를 통해 식물과 인간 사이의 특별한 관계를 살펴보았다. 앞서 이족의 철쭉 무늬가 있는 아기띠를 예로 들었는데, 연구자들은 그 외에도 여러 지역에서 이족이 숭배하는 20종의 식물이 있음을 발견했다. 윈난성 추슝에 거주하는 이족의 전통적인 식물 문화는 풍부한 문화적 함의를 담고 있을 뿐만 아니라 생물학적 다양성도 표현하고 있다.[6] 생물다양성 보존과

그림 5. 수수 줄기를 태운 연기는 조상신을 소환하기 위한 신호로 사용된다.

Figure 5. The smoke from burning millet stems is used as a signal to summon ancestral spirits.

그림 6. 악령을 막기 위해 투와바 부족 마을 출입구에서 벌어지는 '파티제센' 의식.

Figure 6. "Pakigecen" ritual at the entrance of Tjuwabar tribe to stop the movement of evil spirits.

controls borders autonomously, and practices the ritual to care for the people's health and prevent outsiders from entering the tribe. In addition, they attach importance to comforting tribesmen.[5] In the face of contemporary public health crises, traditional rituals serve as one way that Tjuwabar and other indigenous communities

3. 주석 2 참조.
4. Chang, Chi-Shan, "Using 'Bark' as a Cultural Carrier: an Introduction to Bark Painting, Bark Cloth and Bark Paper," *Taiwan Natural Science* 38, no. 3 (2019): 36-41.
5. Mamauwan, "Pakingecen (Shield): The Ritual Practice and Tribal Identity of Contemporary Tjuwabar Tribal Wizards," *Anthropology Vision* 27 (2020): 26-38.
6. Liu, Ai-Zhong, Pei Sheng-Ji, and Chen San-Yang, "Plant Worship of the Yi People in Chuxiong of Yunnan, China" *Ethnobotany* 11, no. 1 (1999): 1-8.

5. Mamauwan, "Pakingecen (Shield): The Ritual Practice and Tribal Identity of Contemporary Tjuwabar Tribal Wizards," *Anthropology Vision* 27 (2020): 26-38.

문화다양성 보존은 서로 밀접하게 연관되어 있는 듯하다. 꾸지나무는 수피포라는 문화 유산을 전하고 이어가는 역할을 하며, 꾸지나무와 인간 이주의 관계에 대해 밝혀낸 이 연구는 과학 연구의 측면에서 중요한 발견이자 고무적인 결과이다. 대만 동부 파이완 소수민족의 투와바 부족의 경우, 식물은 소중한 전통 문화를 행하는 데 있어 중요한 매체로 역할한다. 또한, 현대의 위기 상황에 대처할 수 있도록 전통 문화로부터 양분을 흡수해 나아가는 모습을 세상에 보여 주기도 한다.

앞선 예시에서, 식물은 음식이나 어떤 것의 재료로 쓰이는 데 국한되지 않는다. 과학적인 깨달음, 형이상학적 발견, 심지어는 현대 사회와 상호 작용 등 여러 중요한 의미를 지닐 수 있는 것이 식물이다. 생각해 보자. 우리 삶에서 의식주와 식물은 불가분의 관계이다. 예술, 영적 신념, 철학적 사고에서도 식물의 영향은 어디서든 찾아볼 수 있다. 지구에 살고 있는 인간으로서, 어떻게 식물을 사랑하지 않을 수 있을까?

make an active response. In this case, plants are used to communicate with the ancestral spirits, and plants are also used to block evil spirits and protect the tribe.

Summary

We used the examples of "plants carry the mother's blessings," "plants carry the message of people's migration," and "plants communicate with spirits" to review some special relationships between plants and us. In addition to the case of baby carriers of the Yi people's rhododendron flowers, researchers have found that there are twenty kinds of plants worshipped by the local Yi people in different areas. The traditional plant culture of the Yi people in Chuxiong, Yunnan, reflects the rich cultural connotation and expresses the rich biodiversity[6], and it seems that the conservation of biodiversity and the preservation of cultural diversity are closely related. In the paper mulberry case, paper mulberry can be used as the carrier of the cultural heritage of bark cloth, and the research is an important discovery and inspiration in a scientific research aspect. In the case of the Tjuwabar tribe of the Paiwan ethnic group in eastern Taiwan, the plants are important media in the practice of precious traditional culture, and they also show the world that the people can absorb nutrients from the traditional culture to face contemporary situations.

From the above examples, plants are not only used for food or their material applications. They also have other important meanings, such as scientific enlightenment and metaphysical symbols, and even contemporary societal interaction. Let's think about it: in our lives, food, clothing, and housing are inseparable from plants. In art, spiritual beliefs, and philosophical thinking, the influence of plants can be seen everywhere also. As a human being on earth, can we not love plants?

6.   Liu, Ai-Zhong, Pei Sheng-Ji, and Chen San-Yang, "Plant Worship of the Yi People in Chuxiong of Yunnan, China" *Ethnobotany* 11, no. 1 (1999): 1-8.

언제쯤 '흐린 눈'을 거둘 수 있을까

홍상지
중앙일보 기자

살다 보면 가끔은 '흐린 눈'이 편했다. 직시하는 순간 보이는 것들이 너무 많았다. 재활용 선별장에 산처럼 쌓인 플라스틱 쓰레기, 전 세계적인 이상 기후로 삶의 터전을 잃은 사람과 동물, 자신의 몸 크기만도 못한 축사에서 빛도 못 본 채 평생을 살아가는 가축들의 모습 등등……. 여러 콘텐츠의 형태로 현실을 접할 때는 아주 잠시 변화를 다짐했다. 그러다 하루가 지나고 또 하루가 지나면 다시 '흐린 눈'이 됐다.

일에 치이다 보니 '어쩔 수 없이' 배달 음식을 주문하는 날이 늘었다. 분리수거가 귀찮아 종량제 쓰레기봉투에 남은 쓰레기들을 쑤셔 넣었다. 유난히 더웠던 어느 여름에는 하루 종일 에어컨을 틀어 놓고 '생각보다 전기료가 덜 나왔다'며 현대 기술의 발달을 마음껏 즐겼다. 알면서도, 알고는 있지만 '당장 오늘 내가 피곤하니까' 어쩔 수 없었다. '흐린 눈'은 그런 내가 취할 수 있는 가장 쉬운 선택지였다.

코로나19로 찾은 길고도 깊은 연결 고리

코로나19(COVID-19)가 찾아왔다. 감염병은 당연했던 일상에 많은 제약을 만들어 냈다. 어쩌면 이전의 삶으로 다시는 돌아가지 못할 거라고 많은 전문가가 말했다. 일상의 소중함을 깨달아 갈 무렵, 나는 새삼 '인간과 동물'의 관계를 다시금 생각해 보게 됐다. 당시 내가 파고들었던 질문은 이것이었다. '코로나19의 숙주가 박쥐라는데, 박쥐는 어떻게 인간과 만나 감염병을 퍼뜨릴 수 있었을까?'

여러 자료를 찾아보다가 에볼라 출혈열, 메르스(MERS), 신종 인플루엔자, 에이치아이브이(HIV) 등 다른 바이러스 감염병 사례까지 넘어갔다. 각 바이러스 감염병에는 공통점이 있었다. 모두 동물에서 인간으로 바이러스가 옮겨 간 사례였고, 대체로 인간이 더 많은 생활 터전과 식량을 확보하기 위해 야생동물의 서식지를 침범하면서부터 시작됐다. 서식지를 빼앗긴 야생동물은 살아남기 위해 인간의 생활 영역에 더 자주 찾아오게 됐고 늘어나는 인간과 동물의 접점 속에서 바이러스는 퍼져 나갔다. 박쥐와 인간도 그렇게 만났다.

인간과 동물 사이의 길고도 깊은 연결 고리를 들여다보다가 '원헬스(One Health)'라는 용어도 알게 됐다. 원헬스란 인간과 동물, 생태계의 건강은 서로 연결되어 있으므로 새로운 질병을 이해하고 예방하기 위해서는 인간뿐 아니라 비인간 동물과 환경에 미치는 영향 또한 통합적으로 검토되어야 한다는 학술 용어.

When Will We Stop Turning a "Blurred Eye?"

Hong Sangji
Reporter of JoongAng Ilbo

It was easier for me to turn a "blurred eye" sometimes. The moment I looked squarely at the world, too many things would become too apparent: the mountains of plastic waste piled up in my building's recycling area, the people and animals around the world evicted from their habitats due to climate anomalies, and the livestock who live in pens that barely fit their body without ever seeing the light of day. Every time I encountered the truths through different media, I would vow to change, but my promises never lasted long. And as the days passed, my eyes would start to blur again.

Buried in work, I ordered more and more delivery food, even though I didn't have to. I would stuff all the leftovers in a standard plastic garbage bag because sorting out the recyclables was too bothersome. Through one exceptionally hot summer, I kept the air conditioning turned on 24/7 and binged on the privilege of modern technology, relieved when my electricity bill turned out to be lower than expected. Sure, I knew better. But I couldn't help myself because I was "too tired" at the moment, and turning a "blurred eye" was the easiest option.

An extensive and profound link uncovered by COVID-19

Then COVID-19 hit, and with it came numerous restrictions on daily life. Experts projected that we would never go back to life as we knew it. And as I began to feel renewed appreciation for mundane activities, I came to reinquire into the relationship between humans and animals. It all stemmed from the question, "They say bats were the original carriers of COVID-19, but how did bats come into contact with humans to transmit the disease?"

My inquiry began with various research on COVID-19 and eventually expanded to the cases of other viral infections such as Ebola, MERS, swine flu, and HIV. One factor connects these diseases: they were all transmitted from animals to humans due to the human invasion of wildlife habitats to secure living space and food. Wild animals deprived of their homes had no choice but to frequent human residential areas for survival, and as contact between humans and animals increased, viruses began to spread. This is also how bats and humans came into contact.

While delving into the extensive and profound link between humans and animals, I came across the term "One Health," a technical term for the concept that human health, animal health, and environmental health are interlinked and interdependent and therefore, to under-

이렇게 설명하면 좀 쉬울까? 인터뷰로 알게 된 천명선 서울대 수의학과 교수가 들려준 이야기다. 한 원헬스 포럼에서 의사와 수의사가 함께 모여 감염병에 대해 논의하는 시간이 마련됐다. 의사들은 '반려동물이 매개체가 돼 인간에 병을 옮길 수 있는 위험성'에 대해 이야기하자고 제안했다. 수의사들에게는 이 말이 와닿지 않았다. 수의사들에게 환자는 '동물'이니까. 수의사 입장에서 동물은 질병의 매개체라기보다는 질병에 고통 받는 또 다른 '환자'였던 것이다.

두 집단은 의견을 나눈 뒤 동물과 인간 모두에게 위험을 줄이는 방식으로 전략을 변경했다. 반려동물이 감염의 '매개체'라는 인간 중심적인 사고에서 벗어나 '인간도 반려동물을 만지기 전에는 손을 씻고, 감기에 걸렸을 때 반려동물과의 직접적인 접촉을 피해야 한다'라는 내용이 논의에 추가됐다.

기자이자 콘텐츠 제작자인 나는 '원헬스'라는 세 글자에 완전히 꽂혀버렸다. 현재 우리의 상황을 꿰뚫는 가장 시의적이면서도 직관적인 용어라고 느꼈다. 감염병과 질병에 국한해 생각하지 않더라도, 생태계를 구성하는 모든 개체가 서로 연결되어 영향을 주고받는다는 감각이 내겐 중요했다.

기후위기, 비거니즘, 동물권, 제로 웨이스트 등 각각의 이슈에 모두 적당히 관심을 갖고 있던 나는 '원헬스'라는 키워드로 이 이슈들을 엮어 2020년 5월 팟캐스트·유튜브 채널 '듣다 보면 똑똑해지는 라이프(듣똑라)'를 통해 '원헬스 프로젝트'라는 캠페인을 기획하기도 했다. 인간-동물-환경 간의 삼각 연결 고리를 바탕으로 동물권부터 비거니즘, 기후위기, 제로 웨이스트 활동까지 폭넓은 주제를 팟캐스트와 유튜브 콘텐츠로 만들었다. 각 분야의 전문가나 활동가를 만나 인터뷰를 할 때마다 정신이 번쩍 들었다. 더 이상 '흐린 눈'으로는 살기 어려울 것 같았다. 직시해야 할 때가 온 것이었다.

연결감을 믿는 사람들

"왜 어떤 사람은 비거니즘을 지향하고, 어떤 사람은 제로 웨이스트 운동을 하고, 어떤 사람은 기후위기가 우리의 문제라고 말할까요?" 이 질문에 대한 가장 간단한 답은 "지구에 살아가는 모든 개체가 서로 연결되어 있기 때문이에요"인 것 같다. 누군가는 자신이 쓰레기를 줄이는 것이, 육류를 먹지 않는 것이 그래도 조금이나마 세상을 나은 방향으로 변화시키는 길이라고 여긴다. 내가 하는 크고 작은 행동이 타인을 넘어 비인간 동물과 환경에 어떤 식으로든 영향을 미칠 것이라고 생각해서다. 그 '연결감'을 믿어서다.

비건인 친구 A는 비건을 지향하게 된 계기에 대해 이런 이야기를 들려줬다. "예전에는 내가 먹는 돼지고기, 소고기, 닭고기가 살아 있는 돼지·소·닭에서 나왔다는 생각을 애써 안 하려고 했던 것 같아. 생각을 하는 순간 너무 낯설고 불편한 거야. 근데 어느 날 차를 타고 가는데 옆 차선에 살아 있는 돼지들을 가득 실은 트럭이 보였어. 문득 내가 마트에서 산 600그램짜리 삼겹살의 출처가 궁금해지

stand and prevent novel diseases, we must integratively assess the impact one's health has on others.

It may be easier to explain this concept through a story. I met Chun Myungsun, professor of veterinary humanities at Seoul National University through an interview, and she told me about a One Health forum where doctors and veterinarians had gathered to discuss infectious diseases. The doctors proposed that they talk about "the risk of pets to humans as carriers of transmittable diseases," which baffled the veterinarians. After all, animals were their patients. From their perspective, a sick animal was just like any other human patient suffering from a disease, not a "carrier." The two groups exchanged opinions and modified their strategies to reduce the risk for both animal and human patients. Breaking away from human-oriented modes of thinking that see pets as potential carriers of infectious diseases, they decided to add to their agenda: "Humans should wash their hands before touching a pet and avoid direct contact with them when showing symptoms of a cold."

As a journalist and content creator, I became hooked on the term "One Health." I felt it was the most timely and intuitive term to penetrate our current situation. Even outside the frame of infectious diseases, the sense that every entity that makes up the ecosystem is connected to and affected by one another was important to me.

Having been moderately invested in climate change, veganism, animal rights, and zero waste, I wove these issues together under the keyword "One Health" to organize the campaign One Health Project, which I launched through my podcast *Listen for a Smart Life*. Whenever I interviewed an expert or an activist in those fields, I felt reawakened. It dawned on me that I would no longer be able to live with a "blurred eye"—it was time to face reality.

People who believe in the sense of connection

The most straightforward answer to the question, "Why do some people pursue veganism, partake in the zero waste movement, or argue that climate change is our problem?" would be, "Because all living things on earth are interconnected." Some believe that their efforts to reduce waste and exclude meat from their diet can change the world for the better, if only minutely. This is because they reckon that their actions, big or small, are bound to affect not only humans but also animals and the environment in one way or another. They trust that "sense of connection."

My vegan friend "A" once told me about the incident that motivated her to go vegan: "In the past, I think I tried very hard to avoid thinking about the fact that the pork, beef, and chicken I ate came from pigs, cows, and chickens because the idea immediately made me feel unsettled and uncomfortable. But then one day, while driving, I saw a truck loaded with live pigs in the next lane, and I sud-

더라고."

A는 이후 정말로 다큐멘터리나 책을 통해 돼지고기 등 육류의 생산 과정을 알아봤다. 상상했던 것보다 훨씬 열악한 환경에서 사육·도축되는 동물들의 상황을 본 뒤 "적어도 나는 이 체계에 일조하고 싶지 않아졌다"라고 했다. A는 만 3년째 비건으로 살고 있다.

자신이 버린 쓰레기의 최후를 직접 목격한 사람도 있다. 제로 웨이스트 카페 '보틀라운지'를 운영하는 정다운 대표다. 나는 2020년 6월 정다운 대표를 인터뷰했다. 그는 자신이 버린 테이크아웃용 플라스틱 컵이 끝내 어떻게 처리되는지 그 과정이 궁금했다고 한다. 그래서 환경미화원에게 양해를 구해 각 집의 쓰레기를 수거하는 쓰레기차에 동행했다.

골목 곳곳에는 치킨이나 족발의 뼛조각들이 담긴 배달 용기, 먹다 남은 음료가 들어 있는 페트병이 분리수거도 되지 않은 채 버려져 있었다. 쓰레기를 수거하던 노동자 한 분이 말했다. "포장 용기에 어떻게 버려야 하는지 정보를 넣어 주면 지금보다는 좀 더 나아질까요?" 누군가가 누린 편의는 다른 누군가의 노동으로 전가되고 있었다.

재활용 선별장으로 간 쓰레기 중에는 같은 플라스틱이어도 성분이 달라서, 색소가 들어가서, 음식물이 묻어서, 크기가 너무 작아서 재활용이 어려운 플라스틱 쓰레기가 넘쳐 났다. 다시 활용되지 못한 쓰레기들은 그대로 땅에 묻히거나 태워졌다(수백 년은 썩지 않을 이 쓰레기들은 브레이크가 고장 난 듯 지금 이 시간에도 계속 생산되고 있다). 정다운 대표는 이 경험을 통해 "서비스나 제품을 제공하는 기업에서 자신들이 생산한 제품의 마지막을 직접 봐야 한다고 절실히 느꼈다"라고 했다.

내가 쓰는 것의 '처음과 끝'을 고민하는 삶

이들의 이야기를 들으며 내가 먹고, 입고, 쓰는 모든 것들의 처음과 끝을 생각한다. 거기에 얼마간 마음의 빚을 두고 있다. 요즘 세계적인 시사 키워드 중 하나가 '탄소중립'이다. 개인이나 기업, 단체에서 배출하는 탄소를 최대한 줄이거나 다시 흡수할 대책을 마련해 실질적인 탄소 배출량을 '제로(0)'로 만들자는 거다. 눈앞에 닥친 기후변화에 전 세계 역시 인간이 먹고, 입고, 쓰느라 배출해 온 것들을 어떻게든 책임지기 위해 고군분투 중이다. (물론 이 흐름을 부정하는 이들도 존재하지만) 개개인을 넘어 전 세계가 비슷한 문제의식을 공유하고 있다는 걸 그나마 다행이라고 여겨야 할까. 늦은 감은 있지만 일단 그렇게 믿고 싶다.

나는 2년째 (완벽하진 않지만) 고기를 끊은 상태다. 무언가 늘리는 것보다는 줄이는 것을 더 많이 고민하고 있다. 가끔 '흐린 눈'이 될지라도 그 흐린 눈을 부끄러워하게 됐다. 주변에도 나와 비슷한 고민을 하는 지인들이 많아졌다. 우리는 맛있는 비건 레시피를 공유하고, 리필 스테이션에 함께 가 다회 용기에 세제나 오일 등을 받아

denly began to think about where the 600 grams of pork belly I bought at the supermarket came from."

"A" began watching documentaries and reading books on the production process of pork and other meat. After learning that the animals are raised and slaughtered in a much more brutal environment than she had imagined, she decided that she didn't want to contribute to the system. "A" has now been vegan for three years.

Dawoon Chung, an acquaintance of mine who owns the zero-waste café Bottle Lounge, witnessed what happens to her garbage in person. When I interviewed her last June, she told me that she had become curious about how the plastic takeout cups that she had thrown away had eventually been disposed of and that she once asked for permission to ride along on a garbage truck that was collecting waste around her neighborhood.

There in the alleys of the neighborhood, she saw delivery food containers filled with leftover bones from fried chicken and pig's feet and half-filled soda bottles discarded without having been emptied. She heard one of the waste collectors lament, "Would things get any better if we printed instructions on the food containers on how to dispose of them?" It was then that she realized that convenience is one person's labor transferred to another.

Among the plastic waste that ended up at the recycling site that day, literal tons were unfit for recycling because they were the wrong type of plastic, had been dyed or food-stained, or were too small in size. This unrecyclable waste was either buried in the ground or incinerated. (This type of waste, which takes hundreds of years to decompose, is being produced inexorably and unrelentingly even at this very moment.) Through this experience, Chung says she came to believe that "companies that provide services and products urgently need to see for themselves the end of their products' life cycles."

Living while conscious of the beginning and end of all products

Listening to these stories, I thought about the beginning and end of everything I eat, wear, and use and how much I am indebted in that regard. One of the keywords in today's world is "carbon neutrality," as we seek to achieve a state of net-zero carbon dioxide emissions by preparing measures to offset as much of the carbon emitted by individuals, companies, and organizations as possible. In the face of imminent climate change, the world is working to take responsibility for the human waste we produce by eating, wearing, and using. Though there are those who are still in denial, I take a little comfort in knowing that such awareness is at least shared at a global level and not just by a handful of individuals. It is still quite late, but it's a start.

I have been meat-free (though not ideally) for two years now,

오곤 한다. '원헬스 프로젝트' 이후 듣똑라 구독자들과도 환경과 생태에 대한 이야기를 종종 나눈다. 국립현대미술관의 《대지의 시간》 전시 소식을 들었을 때, 나는 반가움이 앞섰다. 동시대 예술가들과도 같은 고민을 간접적으로 나누고 공명하는 경험이 될 테니 말이다.

그럼에도 앞으로 우리의 일상이 쉽지만은 않을 것 같다. 지금보다 내려놔야 할 것이 훨씬 많아질 터다. 그건 무엇을 '할지'보다 '안 할지'를 선택하는 삶에 가깝다. 환경 담당 기자로 꽤 오래 일해 온 『중앙일보』의 김정연 기자는 이를 '등산'에 비유하곤 한다. 높은 산을 오를 때 등산객은 자기가 만든 쓰레기를 내려갈 때까지 지고 가야 한다. 산을 오르는 다른 등산객에게도, 그 산을 이루는 숲과 서식하는 동물들에게도 그것은 최소한의 예의다. 마찬가지로 내가 먹고 쓰는 모든 것들을 등산객의 짐이라고 생각한다면 딱 책임지고 하산할 수 있을 만큼만 써야 한다는 게 이 이야기의 결론이다. "삶에 제약이 많아지면 피곤하지 않아?"라고 누군가 묻는다면 일단 "그렇다"라고 해야겠다. 조금 피곤하긴 하다. 그래도 예전보다 앞을 보는 시야는 더 넓고 명료해졌다. 아마 애써 게슴츠레하게 떠 온 흐린 눈을 조금은 거둬서일 것이다.

and I concern myself more with reducing things than acquiring them. I have come to feel ashamed of the times I turned a "blurred eye," even though I still do sometimes, and I am surrounded by more people who share similar concerns. We exchange good vegan recipes and visit refill stations with our reusable bottles to stock up on detergent or oil together. Ever since I organized the One Health Project, I have regularly exchanged thoughts on the environment and ecology with my subscribers. When I heard about the MMCA exhibition *Time of the Earth*, I was elated by the fact that this would be an opportunity to indirectly share my thoughts with contemporary artists and resonate with them.

Nevertheless, it is likely that the road ahead will be challenging. We will have to give up many more things than we already have, and our lives will be more about deciding what not to do than what to do. Kim Jeongyeon, a reporter of *JoongAng Ilbo* and long-time journalist of environment-related news, often compares an ideal lifestyle to a hike. When climbing a high mountain, hikers must carry the garbage they produce to dispose of it away from the mountain—it is a minimum courtesy to the hikers after them and the flora and fauna whose habitat they are exploring. This means that everything they eat or use accounts for their luggage. The moral of the story is that we must be responsible and consume only as much as we can carry up and down a mountain. If someone were to ask me, "Isn't it tiring to have so many restrictions in your life?" I would have to say, "Yes." It is a bit tiring. But my perspective on the future has never been so broad and clear. Perhaps this is because I stopped purposefully blurring my vision with half-closed eyes.

작가 약력
참고 문헌

Biography
Bibliography

김보중

주요 개인전

2020 《투명의 역설: 투명하게 존재하라 II—김보중 개인전
인내지(人乃地)》, 스페이스몸미술관, 청주
2019 《2018년 전혁림미술상 수상기념전》, 전혁림미술관, 통영
2017 《흐르는 거주지—길》, 인디프레스 갤러리, 서울
2012 《김보중 개인전》, 서울문화재단 금호예술공장 PS333, 서울
2006 《흐르다 그리고 흐르다—눈(目)이 달린 발(足)》, 대안공간 풀,
서울
2005 《회화, 길을 묻다》, 갤러리 스케이프, 서울
2004 《다수의 부분들이 표류하는 장소 숲-그림》, 덕원 큐브갤러리, 서울
2001 《3개 방에 의한 풍경》, 성곡미술관, 서울
1999 《시인과 화가의 동행》, 녹색갤러리, 서울
1996 《김보중 개인전》, 금호미술관, 서울
1993 《Kim Bo Joong Solo Exhibition》, 버뱅크 크리에이티브 아트,
캘리포니아, 미국

주요 단체전

2019 《가족의 정원》, 양평군립미술관, 양평
2017 《성남의 얼굴—성남을 걷다》, 성남아트센터 큐브미술관, 성남
2016 《생생화화 2016—산책자의 시선》, 경기도미술관, 안산
2015 《경기팔경과 구곡》, 경기도미술관, 안산
《2015 GIAX 평창비엔날레》, 알펜시아, 평창
《1980년대와 한국미술》, 전북도립미술관, 완주
2007 《2007 찾아가는 경기도미술관》, 포천반월아트홀, 포천 외 13곳
순회전
《한·중 현대미술전—환영의 거인》, 세종문화회관 미술관, 서울
2006 《성남의 얼굴》, 성남아트센터, 성남
《바깥미술—자라섬》, 자라섬, 가평군
2002 《국제환경미술전—무당개구리의 울음》, 예술의전당 한가람미술관,
서울
《不二—저절로 자연되기》, 영은미술관, 경기도 광주
2001 《환경과 미술—새로운 아틀란티스의 꿈》, 부산시립미술관, 부산
《2001 오딧세이》, 성산아트홀, 창원
2000 《풍경과 장소—유토피아 & 아토피아》, 경기문화예술회관, 수원 외
2곳 순회전
1994 《민중미술 15년: 1980-1994》, 국립현대미술관, 과천
1984 《삶의 미술》, 관훈미술관, 서울
《거대한 뿌리》, 한강미술관, 서울
1983 《시대정신》, 제3미술관, 서울
1982 《한국현대미술 80년대 조망》, 대학로 미술회관, 서울

수상 및 레지던시

2018 전혁림미술상 수상, 전혁림미술관, 통영
서울문화재단 중견작가 자료집 발간 지원 선정, 서울
2017 경기문화재단 우수작가 지원 선정, 수원
2016 경기문화재단 전문예술 창작 지원 선정, 수원
2013 토지문화재단 레지던시, 원주
경기창작센터 기획 레지던시, 안산
2012 3기 금천예술공장 레지던시, 서울문화재단, 서울
서울문화재단 전문예술 창작 지원 선정, 서울
2011 2기 경기창작센터 레지던시, 안산

김주리

주요 개인전

2020 《모습 某濕 Wet Matter》, 송은 아트스페이스, 서울
2017 《일기(一期)생멸(生滅)》, SO.S(Sarubia Outreach & Support),
프로젝트 스페이스 사루비아다방, 서울
2012 《Scape_Collcetion》, 프로젝트 스페이스 모, 서울
2008 《조용한 침범》, 가 갤러리, 서울
2005 《Room#203》, YA Project 03, 가 갤러리, 서울

주요 단체전

2021 《현시적 전경》, 경기 시각예술 성과발표전 생생화화: 生生化化,
단원미술관, 안산
《대지의 시간》, 국립현대미술관, 과천
《KOREA. Gateway to a rich past》, 프린세스호프
국립도자박물관, 레이우아르던, 네덜란드
《보더리스 사이트》, 문화역서울284, 서울
《Fortune Telling: 운명상담소》, 일민미술관, 서울
2020 《Korean Eye 2020》, 사치갤러리, 런던, 영국
《창원조각비엔날레: 비조각-가볍거나 유연하거나》, 용지공원 /
성산아트홀, 창원
2018 《Indian Ceramics Triennale: Breaking Ground》, 자와르 칼라
켄드라, 자이푸르, 인도
2017 《Place and Practices》, 월드 오브 웨지우드, 스토크온트렌트,
영국
《British Ceramic Biennial》, 차이나 홀(옛 스포드 공장 터),
스토크온트렌트, 영국
《송은 수장고: Not your ordinary art storage》, 송은 수장고,
서울
《Contemporary Korean Ceramics》, 빅토리아 앤드 앨버트
미술관, 런던, 영국
《빈 페이지》, 금호미술관, 서울
2016 《1st Central China International Ceramics Biennale》,
허난박물관, 정저우, 중국
《홈그라운드》, 청주시립미술관, 청주
《Céramique Coréenne Contemporaine》, 베르나르도재단,
리모주, 프랑스
《Made in Seoul》, 메이막 현대아트센터, 메이막, 프랑스
《Decapod》, 에어스페이스 갤러리, 스토크온트렌트, 영국
2011 《아시아 현대미술 프로젝트 city_net ASIA 2011》,
서울시립미술관, 서울
《21세기 풍경: Emptiness》, 성곡미술관, 서울
《제10회 송은미술대상전》, 송은 아트스페이스, 서울
2009 《휘경: 揮景, 사라지는 풍경》, 통의동 보안여관, 서울

수상 및 레지던시

2022 서울문화재단 예술창작활동지원 선정, 서울
2021 경기문화재단 지금예술창작지원 선정, 수원
프린세스호프 국립도자박물관 레지던시, 레이우아르던, 네덜란드
인천아트플랫폼 레지던시, 인천
2020 서울문화재단 예술창작활동지원 선정, 서울
국립현대미술관 고양레지던시, 고양
2017 빅토리아 앤드 앨버트 미술관 레지던시, 런던, 영국(-2018)
2016 시테 인터내셔널 아트 레지던시, 파리, 프랑스
2012 소버린 아시안 아트 프라이즈 최종 30인, 소버린문화재단, 홍콩
2010 제10회 송은미술대상 대상 수상, 송은문화재단, 서울
2007 문예진흥기금 신진작가 성장프로그램 선정, 한국문화예술위원회,
서울

나현

주요 개인전

2021 《빅풋을 찾아서》, 문화비축기지, 서울
2018 《바벨-서로 다른 혀》, 대구미술관, 대구
2016 《PRO-JECT》, 초이 앤드 라거 갤러리, 쾰른, 독일
2014 《프로-젝트》, LIG아트스페이스, 서울
     《The Babel Tower》, 쿤스틀러하우스 베타니엔, 베를린, 독일
2012 《로렐라이의 노래》, 갤러리정미소, 서울
2011 《나현 보고서—민족에 관하여》, 성곡미술관, 서울
2010 《PILE》, 아틀리에 엠에크, 뒤셀도르프, 독일
2009 《실종》, 갤러리상상마당, 서울
2008 《Painting on the Water》, 시테 앵테르나시오날 데 자르, 파리,
     프랑스
2007 《Painting Landscapes project》, 패링던 로드, 런던, 영국 /
     청계천, 서울
2005 《White Cloud Minnow project》, 세인트 에드문드 홀 도서관,
     옥스퍼드, 영국 / 국립중앙도서관, 서울
2004 《Strange Event》, 돌핀갤러리, 옥스퍼드, 영국

주요 단체전

2021 《Spielraum × Phytology_식물의 방》, 뮤지엄산, 원주
     《컬렉션_오픈 해킹 채굴》, 서울시립미술관, 서울
2020 《낯선 전쟁》, 국립현대미술관, 서울
     《기억전달자 디 아키비스츠》, 부천아트벙커 B39, 부천
2019 《Tilted Scenes—What do you see》, 아스날레 해군장교클럽,
     베니스, 이탈리아
     《Wandering》, 가오슝미술관, 가오슝, 대만
2018 《균열 Ⅱ: 세상을 보는 눈 / 영원을 향한 시선》, 국립현대미술관,
     과천
     《Wandering Seeds》, 국립선사박물관, 타이둥, 대만
2017 《접경개화 Blooming at the Junction》, 홍콩한국문화원 개관전,
     홍콩
     《난지10년》, 서울시립미술관, 서울
2016 《동백꽃 밀회유》, 아르코미술관, 서울
     《Please Return to Busan Port》, 베스트포센 미술연구소,
     베스트포센, 노르웨이
2015 《올해의 작가상》, 국립현대미술관, 서울
     《제주 4·3 미술제》, 제주도립미술관, 제주
2014 《메디에이션 비엔날레 2014》, 포즈난, 폴란드 / 베를린, 독일
2013 《에르메스 재단 미술상》, 아뜰리에 에르메스, 서울
     《트란스페어 한국-엔에르베》, 아르코미술관, 서울 / 오스트하우스
     하겐, 하겐, 독일
2012 《세라믹스 코뮌》, 아트선재센터, 서울
2011 《Innerspacing the City》, 첼시미술관, 뉴욕, 미국
     《인터뷰》, 아르코미술관, 서울
2010 《이미지의 틈》, 서울시립미술관, 서울
     《과거로부터 온 선물 Present from the Past》, 주영한국문화원,
     런던, 영국
2009 《악동들 지금 / 여기》, 경기도미술관, 안산
2008 《젊은 모색 2008》, 국립현대미술관, 과천
2007 《유클리드의 산책》, 서울시립미술관, 서울

수상 및 레지던시

2017 금천예술공장 레지던시, 서울문화재단, 서울(-2018)
2013 쿤스틀러하우스 베타니엔 레지던시, 베를린, 독일(-2014)
2012 트란스페어 한국-엔에르베 레지던시, 오스트하우스 뮤지엄 하겐,
     독일
2011 호세 마르티 문화학회 레지던시, 하바나, 쿠바
2010 가스타텔리어 레지던시, 뒤셀도르프문화부, 뒤셀도르프, 독일
2007 시테 앵테르나시오날 데 자르 레지던시, 삼성문화재단, 파리,
     프랑스(-2008)

백정기

주요 개인전
2021 《물에 빠진 금》, 스페이스 윌링앤딜링, 서울
2020 《남단》, 갤러리ERD, 서울
2019 《접촉주술》, OCI미술관, 서울
2015 《Revelation》, 두산갤러리 뉴욕, 뉴욕, 미국
     《Mind Walk》, 두산갤러리, 서울
2012 《Is of》, 대안공간루프, 서울
2011 《The 20th Bridge Guard》, 브릿지 가드 아트 앤드 사이언스
     센터, 슈투로보, 슬로바키아
2010 《Sweet Rain》, 인사미술공간, 서울
     《Blue Pond》, 스톤앤워터, 안양
2009 《Wasser + Oleon》, 스페이스 15번지, 서울

주요 단체전
2021 《Herzog & de Meuron. Exploring Songeun Art Space.》,
     송은, 서울
2020 《이퀄리브리엄》, 국립아시아문화전당, 광주
     《Korean Eye 2020》, 사치갤러리, 런던, 영국
     《오늘의 질문들》, 부산현대미술관, 부산
2019 《The way a Hare transforming into a Tortoise》, 니콜라이
     쿤스탈, 코펜하겐, 덴마크
2018 《Power Play》, 델피나재단 / 주영한국문화원, 런던, 영국
     《Will you be there?》, 프로젝트 풀필 아트 스페이스, 타이베이,
     대만
     《Jimei × Arles International Photography Festival》, 샤먼,
     중국
     《날씨의 맛》, 서울시립 남서울미술관, 서울
2017 《Spirit from objects》, 크리에이티브 아트 스페이스
     오사카(CASO), 오사카, 일본
     《Ecology of Creation》, 후쿠오카아시아미술관, 후쿠오카, 일본
2016 《Nanjing International Art Festival》, 바이자후미술관, 난징,
     중국
     《아트스펙트럼》, 리움미술관, 서울
     《다중시간》, 백남준아트센터, 용인
2015 《Séoul, Vite, Vite !》, 릴3000, 트리포스탈, 릴, 프랑스
     《Singapore Open Media Festival 2015》, 길먼 배럭스,
     싱가포르
2014 《그만의 방》, 아트선재센터, 서울
     《Gate Opener》, 베이징 코뮌, 베이징, 중국
     《초자연》, 국립현대미술관, 서울
2013 《젊은 모색 2013》, 국립현대미술관, 과천

수상 및 레지던시
2019 김세중 청년 조각상 수상, 김세중미술관, 서울
2018 엑시트 레지던시, 인도한국문화원, 델리, 인도
2016 델피나재단 레지던시, 런던, 영국
2015 두산레지던시 뉴욕, 두산아트센터, 뉴욕, 미국
2014 노마딕 아티스트 레지던시, 한국문화예술위원회, 첸나이, 인도
2013 난지미술창작스튜디오, 서울시립미술관, 서울
2012 제12회 송은미술대상 수상, 송은문화재단, 서울
2011 아르코 영 아트 프론티어(AYAF) 지원 작가로 선정,
     한국문화예술위원회, 서울

서동주

주요 개인전
2020 《그림일기》, 탈영역우정국, 서울
2011 《Empty Space》, 닻프레스 갤러리, 서울

주요 단체전 및 프로젝트
2021 《제로원데이 '플레이그라운드'》, 온라인 전시
     《BTS × 100번째 광화문글판》, 온라인 전시 / 교보 강남사옥, 서울
     〈Chic, Le Sport!〉, 에르메스 스카프 디자인
     《친근하고도 신비한 아세안의 동물들》, 한국국제교류재단
     아세안문화원, 부산
     《DREAMERS》, SPACE U, 서울
2020 《제로원ZER01NE 오픈 스튜디오 with P:LAYERS》, 제로원 강남
     스튜디오, 서울
     《백야》, LG 시그니처 올레드 R, 서울
2019 《Because of You》, 세종 현대 모터갤러리, 세종문화회관, 서울
     《Deep Space 8K》, 아르스 일렉트로니카 센터, 린츠, 오스트리아
     《제로 ZERO》, 그래픽·전시 디자인, 포항시립미술관, 포항
     《세상의 끝과 부재 중 통화》, 평창남북영화제, 평창
     《아세안의 삶과 물》, 한국국제교류재단 아세안문화원, 부산
     《천 개의 수평선》, 현대자동차그룹 비전홀, 용인
2018 《설화문화전: 포춘랜드—금박》 전시 감독, 아모레퍼시픽그룹 본사,
     서울
     《올림픽 조각 프로젝트—포스트 88》, 소마미술관, 서울
     《아모레퍼시픽의 건축가들》, 아모레퍼시픽미술관, 서울
     《만화 기호 展: 소용돌이 눈》, 갤러리밈, 서울
2017 《밀월 密月; 가까운 달》, 갤러리 포트폴리오, 서울
2016 《MMCA-현대차 뮤지엄 페스티벌: 마당》, 국립현대미술관, 서울
2015 《설화문화전: 설화(說話)—백일홍 이야기》, 블루스퀘어
     복합문화공간 네모, 서울
2014 《apmap 2014 jeju: BETWEEN WAVES》, 서광다원/오설록,
     서울
2011 《One Another》, W 서울 워커힐, 서울
2010 《국제현대무용제: The Rest》, 아르코미술관, 서울
     《A4 용지》, 서교예술실험센터, 서울
2009 《블루닷 아시아 BlueDot Asia》, 예술의전당, 서울

수상 및 레지던시
2020 제로원ZER01NE 레지던시, 서울(-2021)
2020 탐페레 국제단편영화제 국제 경쟁 부문, 탐페레, 핀란드
2019 프로젝토 에이스 피랄 레지던시, 한국문화예술위원회,
     부에노스아이레스, 아르헨티나
     에르메스 국제 스카프디자인 공모전 파이널리스트, 파리, 프랑스
     롯데뮤지엄 영아티스트 어워즈 수상, 서울
     현대자동차그룹 VH 어워드 그랑프리 수상, 서울
2018 아르스 일렉트로니카 센터 레지던시, 현대자동차그룹, 린츠,
     오스트리아
2008 어도비 글로벌 디자인 공모전 대상 수상, 뉴욕, 미국

OAA(정규동)

올라퍼 엘리아손

주요 전시 및 프로젝트

191쪽 영문 약력 참고.

2019 《오로라, 색의 비밀》, 로봇암 디자인 제작, 우란문화재단, 서울
2018 《Emotion-scape》, 카입(Kayip)+OAA, 블루메미술관, 파주
《보이지 않는 경계》, 카입(Kayip)+OAA, 향촌문화관, 대구
2017 《apmap 2017 jeju: mystic birth》, 오설록 티뮤지엄, 제주
2016 《설화문화전: 견우직녀》, 도산공원, 서울
《직지파빌리온》, 론 아라드(Ron Arad)+OAA, 직지페스티발, 청주
《apmap 2016 yongsan: make link》, OAA+카입(Kayip),
용산가족공원, 서울
권지안(솔비) 《블랙스완》, 인피니트 미러 큐브 디자인,
안국약품갤러리, 서울
2011 《Lie sang bong Exhibition》, 전시 부스 디자인, 해러즈 백화점,
런던

이경호

주요 개인전

2018 《디지털 문 Digital Moon》 기획 초대전 1회, 미디어338, 광주
2007 《No Signal(?HELP)》, 갤러리 세줄, 서울 / 시티 갤러리 류블랴나, 류블랴나, 슬로베니아
2006 《Traveler》, 갤러리 세줄, 서울
2002 《꿈과 카오스의 이중주, 끝없는 긍정과 부정 Chaos under Dream》, 갤러리 세줄, 서울

주요 단체전

2021 《강원국제트리엔날레》, 홍천중앙시장, 홍천군
 《전남 국제수묵비엔날레─일즉다 다즉일 一卽多 多卽一》, 유달초등학교, 목포
2020 《금강자연미술비엔날레》, 연미산자연미술공원, 공주
 《달성 대구현대미술제》, 강정보 디아크 광장 일원, 대구
2019 《지리산국제환경예술제》, 지리산아트팜 일원, 하동군
 《대한민국환경생태미술대전》, 예술의전당 한가람미술관, 서울
 《세종 카운터 웨이브─내재된 힘》, 세종문화회관 미술관, 서울
2018 《Les autres langues》, 보리바나 미술관, 다카르, 세네갈
 《아트부산 2018─미디어 아트 특별전》, 벡스코, 부산
 《Tamarindo Art Wave Festival》, 타마린도 해변, 코스타리카
 《저항과 도전의 이단아들─2부: 한국행위미술 1967-2017》, 대구미술관, 대구
2017 《태화강국제설치미술제》, 태화강 지방정원, 울산
 《China International Gallery Exposition: Asia Special Section》, 국립농업전시센터, 베이징, 중국
 《한국국제아트페어 특별전─한국 행위예술 50주년 기념 자료전: 실험과 도전의 전사들》, 코엑스, 서울
2016 《창원조각비엔날레》, 용지호수공원, 창원
 《순천만국제자연환경미술제》, 순천만국제습지센터, 순천
2015 《2015바다미술제》, 다대포해수욕장, 부산
2014 《Korean Contemporary Art K-P.O.P.》, 타이베이현대미술관, 타이베이, 대만
 《디지털 트라이앵글─한중일 미디어 아트의 오늘》, 대안공간 루프, 서울
2012 《몽유_마술적 현실》, 국립현대미술관, 과천
2011 《Happy Window》, 아트센터 나비, 서울
 《신나는 미술관─라이트 아트의 신비로운 세계》, 경남도립미술관, 창원
 《테크놀로지의 명상─미디어의 정원》, 포항시립미술관, 포항
2010 《5·18 광주민주화운동 30주년 기념전─오월의 꽃》, 광주시립미술관, 광주
 《아니 라티·이경호 2인전─Image of September》, 갤러리 세줄, 서울
2008 《Sevilla Biennale》, 세비야, 스페인
2007 《Thermocline of Art: New Asian Waves》, 카를스루에 아트 앤드 미디어 센터(ZKM), 카를스루에, 독일
2006 《Shanghai Biennale》, 상하이미술관, 상하이, 중국
2005 《Shanghai COOL》, 상하이 뒤룬현대미술관, 상하이, 중국
2004 《광주비엔날레》, 광주비엔날레관, 광주
 《Digital Sublime: New Masters of Universe》, 타이베이현대미술관, 타이베이, 대만
2003 《신소장품》, 국립현대미술관, 과천
2002 《미디어시티서울 2002─달빛 흐름》, 서울시립미술관, 서울

1993 비디오 설치와 회화 전시, 에스파스 몽조아(Espace Montjoie), 파리, 프랑스
1989 오를랑(ORLAN)과 다수의 행위예술제 참가: 《Poliphonix 89》(퐁피두센터, 파리, 프랑스), 《L'Acte pour l'art》(타라스콩, 프랑스) 등

수상 및 레지던시

1999 《Salon de la Jeune Création》에서 Espace Paul Ricard 수상, 50주년 기념 《Salon de la Jeune Peinture》, 파리, 프랑스

임동식

주요 개인전
2021 《임동식—사유의 경치 Ⅲ》, 아트센터고마, 공주
      《제5회 박수근미술상 수상 작가전—임동식》,
      양구군립박수근미술관, 양구군 / DDP 갤러리문, 서울
      《임동식 개인전—풍경의 단위》, 스페이스몸미술관, 청주
2020 《일어나 올라가 임동식》, 서울시립미술관 서소문본관, 서울
2018 《임동식—1980년대 함부르크시절 드로잉부터 2018 오늘까지》,
      dtc갤러리, 대전
2016 《임동식—동방소년 탐문기》, 대전시립미술관, 대전
2010 《임동식—자연예술가와 화가》, 스페이스 공명, 서울
2008 《사유의 경치》, 이화익갤러리, 서울
2006 《친구가 권유한 풍경》, 롯데화랑, 부산 / 대전
2005 《안에서 밖으로 밖에서 안으로》, 아르코미술관, 서울

주요 단체전
2019 《색맹의 섬》, 아트선재센터, 서울
2018 《보태니카》, 부산시립미술관, 부산
2017 《삼라만상: 김환기에서 양푸둥까지》, 국립현대미술관, 서울
      《대전다큐멘타2016: 공동체감각》, dtc갤러리, 대전
      《갤러리 닷 개관 기념—달콤, 살벌한 미술:
      김홍주·임동식·최병소·홍명섭》, 갤러리 닷, 대구
2016 《아틀리에 STORY》, 예술의전당 한가람미술관, 서울
      《현대미술 리포트—백제의 재발견》, 전북도립미술관, 완주군
2015 《한국근현대미술특별전—세기의 동행》, 대전시립미술관, 대전
      《아시아현대미술전》, 전북도립미술관, 전주
2014 《경계의 회화》, 금호미술관, 서울
2013 《기억의 시간, 시간의 기억》, 아트센터 화이트블럭, 파주
      《역사 속에 살다—초상, 시대의 거울》, 전북도립미술관, 완주군
2012 《풍경》, 하이트컬렉션, 서울
      《광주비엔날레》, 광주비엔날레전시관, 광주
      《여기 사람이 있다》, 대전시립미술관, 대전
2009 《모든 경계에는 꽃이 핀다》, 대전시립미술관, 대전
      《대학로 100번지》, 아르코미술관, 서울
      《플랫폼 인 기무사》, 구 국군 기무사령부 터, 서울
2008 《제10차 람사르총회 기념 특별전—태초의 현장》, 경남도립미술관,
      창원
2006 《드로잉 에너지》, 아르코미술관, 서울
2003 《자연의 시간, 인간의 시간》, 대전시립미술관, 대전

수상 및 레지던시
2020 박수근미술상 수상, 박수근미술관, 양구
1985 알토나미술상 수상, 알토나시청, 함부르크, 독일

장뤽 밀렌

186쪽 영문 약력 참고.

장민승

주요 개인전

2021	《둥글고 둥글게》, 주영한국문화원, 런던, 영국
	《voiceless》, 쿤스트할 오르후스, 오르후스, 덴마크
2016	《立石附近 입석부근》, 플랫폼엘 컨템포러리 아트센터, 서울
2014	《家具八字—hiddentrack》, 스페이스 윌링앤딜링, 서울
2012	《the moments》, 원앤제이 갤러리, 서울
2011	《水聲十景 수성십경》, 조현 갤러리, 부산
2010	《A Multi-Culture》, 원앤제이 갤러리, 서울
	《水聲十景 수성십경》, 아트라운지 디방, 서울
2008	《Intermission》, 서미앤투스, 서울
2006	《Cut & Bend》, 갤러리 모듈, 서울

주요 단체전 및 프로젝트

2021	《보이지 않는 도시들》, 플랫폼엘 컨템포러리 아트센터, 서울
	영화 〈둥글고 둥글게〉 연출
2020	《푸른 종소리》, 부산현대미술관, 부산
	《부산 비엔날레—열 장의 이야기와 다섯 편의 시》, 원도심 일대, 부산
2019	《국립현대미술관 개관 50주년 전시, 광장》, 국립현대미술관 덕수궁, 서울
2018	《균열 II: 세상을 보는 눈 / 영원을 향한 시선》, 국립현대미술관, 과천
	《불안의 서》, 경남도립미술관, 창원
	《씨실과 날실로》, 서울시립미술관, 서울
	영화 〈오버데어〉 연출
2017	《덕수궁 야외프로젝트: 빛·소리·풍경》, 국립현대미술관 덕수궁, 서울
2016	《보이드》, 국립현대미술관, 서울
	《달은 차고 어지러진다》, 국립현대미술관, 과천
	《사월의 동행》, 경기도미술관, 안산
	필름 〈입석부근〉 제작
2015	《The Darkside of Nature》, 부쿠레슈티 국립현대미술관, 부쿠레슈티, 루마니아
2014	《上林 상림》, 공공미술 프로젝트, 상림, 함양
2011	《Spheres part I in Mullae-dong》, 공공미술 프로젝트, 문래예술공장, 서울

수상 및 레지던시

2018	가파도 아티스트 인 레지던스 2기, 현대카드, 가파도, 제주
2015	난지미술창작스튜디오 9기, 서울시립미술관, 서울
2014	창동창작스튜디오 하반기 프로젝트 레지던시, 국립현대미술관, 서울
	에르메스재단 미술상 수상, 서울
2006	코리아 디자인 어워드 제품 부문 올해의 영 디자이너, 서울

정소영

주요 개인전

2021	《해삼, 망간 그리고 귀》, 원앤제이 갤러리, 서울
2020	《유리해변》, 인스턴트 루프, 서울
2016	《밤과 낮》, 아트선재 오프사이트, 서울
2013	《움직이지 않고 여행하기》, 디 프로젝트 스페이스 구슬모아당구장, 서울
2011	《On the ground floor of Geology building》, OCI 미술관, 서울
2008	《Zero Construction》, 프로젝트 스페이스 사루비아다방, 서울
2007	《A different kind of tension》, 금호미술관, 서울
2006	《Innerscape》, Gallery Miss China Beauty, 파리, 프랑스

주요 단체전

2021	《2021 DMZ 아트 & 피스 플랫폼》, 남북출입사무소 / 제진역, 고성
	《Margins of Error》, Nirox Foundation, Krugersdorp, 남아프리카 공화국
	《보더리스 사이트》, 문화역서울284, 서울
2020	《Negotiating Borders》, 피멩코재단, 로망빌, 프랑스
	《CAMP2020》, 캠프롱(옛 미군 주둔지), 원주
2019	《14th International Curitiba Biennial》, 쿠리치바, 브라질
	《Power Play》, 델피나재단, 런던, 영국
2018	《확장된 메뉴얼》, 남서울시립미술관, 서울
	《장르 알레고리—조각적》, 토탈미술관, 서울
	《기적의 안뜰》, 두산갤러리, 서울
	《The Real DMZ》, 뉴 아트 익스체인지, 노팅험, 영국
2017	《Triangulating Particulars》, 힐베르트라운, 베를린, 독일
2016	《제16회 송은미술대상전》, 송은 아트스페이스, 서울
	《건축도자—Earth》, 클레이아크김해미술관 개관 10주년 기념전, 클레이아크김해미술관, 김해
2015	《리-플레이: 4개의 플랫폼 & 17번의 이벤트》, 서울시립미술관, 서울
	《Séoul, Vite, Vite !》, 릴3000, 트리포스탈, 릴, 프랑스
	《공명하는 삼각형》, 아라리오뮤지엄 동문모텔 II, 제주
2014	《How to survive in the forest》, 르시클로프, 밀리라포레, 프랑스
	《apmap 2014 jeju: BETWEEN WAVES》, 서광다원/오설록, 제주
2012	《갈라파고스》, 일민미술관, 서울
	《간헐적 위치선정》, 아라리오 갤러리, 천안

수상 및 레지던시

2021	국립현대미술관 창동레지던시, 서울
2020	금천예술공장 레지던시, 서울문화재단, 서울
2018	가파도 아티스트 인 레지던스, 현대카드, 가파도, 제주
2017	델피나재단 레지던시, 런던, 영국
	ZK/U 레지던시, 베를린, 독일
2016	리얼 디엠지 프로젝트 양지리 레지던시, 아트선재센터, 철원

정재철   주세페 페노네

184쪽 영문 약력 참고.

주요 개인전
2021 《정재철: 사랑과 평화》, 아르코미술관, 서울
2017 《분수령》, 금산갤러리, 서울
2016 《실크로드 프로젝트—기록 2016》, 봉산문화회관, 대구
2015 《2015 블루오션 프로젝트—간석지대》, JM갤러리, 파주
2011 《오늘의 작가—실크로드 프로젝트》, 김종영미술관, 서울   크리스티앙 볼탕스키
     《이스탄불에서 런던까지》, 갤러리쿤스트독, 서울
2010 《3차 실크로드 프로젝트》, 위드아티스트 갤러리, 파주   182쪽 영문 약력 참고.
2009 《여행자 TRAVELER》, 지노스페이스, 서울
2007 《나무조각 드로잉》, 듀플렉스 갤러리, 서울
2005 《실크로드 프로젝트》, 프로젝트 스페이스 집, 서울
2004 《실크로드 프로젝트—세탁·포장》, 국립고양미술스튜디오, 고양

                                                히로시 스기모토

주요 단체전
2020 《새벽의 검은 우유》, 김종영미술관, 서울   185쪽 영문 약력 참고.
2019 《국제생태미술전—오션 뉴메신저스》, 제주현대미술관, 제주
2018 《서울미디어시티비엔날레—좋은 삶》, 서울시립미술관, 서울
2017 《제주비엔날레》, 제주도립미술관, 제주
2016 《산책자의 시선》, 경기도미술관, 안산
2015 《한·러 국제교류전—한줌의 도덕》, 이르쿠츠크주립미술관
     수카체바, 이르쿠츠크, 러시아
2013 《만물상—사물에서 존재로》, 광주시립미술관, 광주 / 서울시립
     남서울생활미술관, 서울(2014)
2010 《한·몽골 예술교류축제—시간과 공간》, 제주현대미술관, 제주
2009 《Made in Korea—Magic Moment: Korean Express》,
     진레페르스 백화점, 하노버, 독일
2008 《Time & Space》, 남고비미술관, 달란자드가드, 몽골
2007 《재활용 주식회사》, 아르코미술관, 서울
2006 《부산비엔날레》, 온천천, 부산
2004 《평화선언 2004—세계 100인 미술가》, 국립현대미술관, 과천
2003 《조각의 환기-물성과 공간》, 대전시립미술관, 대전
1997 《From the Ground Up》, 소크라테스 조각공원, 뉴욕, 미국
1995 《DMZ 문화예술운동 작업전》, 공평아트센터, 서울
1990 《호랑이에서 돼지까지》, 소나무갤러리, 서울
1988 《Another New Sculpture》, 토탈미술관, 장흥
1987 《대한민국 미술대전》, 국립현대미술관, 과천

수상 및 레지던시
2014 아르코 노마딕 레지던스, 바이칼, 러시아
2011 오늘의 작가, 김종영미술관, 서울
2010 노마딕 아트 레지던스, 타임앤스페이스, 제주
2008 아르코 노마딕 레지던스, 몽골
2002 아트 오마이: 아티스트 레지던시, 뉴욕, 미국
1997 아시아 작가상 수상, 버몬트 스튜디오 센터 프리먼 재단, 버몬트,
     미국
1996 김세중 청년조각상 수상, 김세중미술관, 서울
     에스칼레 스튜디오 프로그램, 모리셔스
1988 중앙미술대전 대상 수상, 중앙일보 / 호암미술관, 서울
1987 중앙미술대전 장려상 수상, 중앙일보 / 호암미술관, 서울

Beak Jungki

Selected Solo Exhibitions
2021 *Wet Metal*, Space Willing N Dealing, Seoul, Korea
2020 *South Altar*, Gallery ERD, Seoul, Korea
2019 *Contagious magic*, OCI Museum, Seoul, Korea
2015 *Revelation*, Doosan Gallery New York, New York, USA
Mind Walk, Doosan Gallery, Seoul, Korea
2012 *Is of*, Alternative Space LOOP, Seoul, Korea
2011 *20th Bridge Guard*, Bridge Guard Art & Science Centre, Štúrovo, Slovakia
2010 *Sweet Rain*, Insa Art Space of Art Council Korea, Seoul, Korea
2010 *Blue Pond*, Supplement Space Stone & Water, Anyang, Korea
2009 *Wasser + Oleon*, Space 15th, Seoul, Korea

Selected Group Exhibitions and Projects
2021 *Herzog & de Meuron. Exploring SongEun Art Space.*, SONGEUN, Seoul, Korea
2020 *Equilibrium*, Asia Culture Center, Gwangju, Korea
Korean Eye 2020, Saatchi Gallery, London, UK
Confronting Today's Questions, Museum of Contemporary Art Busan, Korea
2019 *The way a Hare transforming into a Tortoise*, Nikolaj Kunsthal, Copenhagen, Denmark
2018 *Power Play*, Delfina Foundation / Korean Cultural Centre UK, London, UK
Will you be there? Project Fulfill Art Space, Taipei, Taiwan
Jimei × Arles International Photography Festival, Xiamen, China
Tastes of Weather, Seoul Museum of Art, Seoul, Korea
2017 *Spirit from objects*, Creative Art Space Osaka (CASO), Osaka, Japan
Ecology of Creation, Fukuoka Asian Art Museum, Fukuoka, Japan
2016 *Nanjing International Art Festival*, Baijia Lake Museum, Nanjing, China
Art Spectrum, Leeum Museum of Art, Seoul, Korea
Wrap around the time, Nam June Paik Art Center, Yongin, Korea
2015 *Séoul, Vite, Vite !*, Lille3000, Tripostal, Lille, France
Singapore Open Media Festival 2015, Gillman Barracks, Singapore
2014 *A room of his own*, Art Sonje Center, Seoul, Korea
Gate Opener, Beijing Commune, Beijing, China
Super Nature, National Museum of Contemporary Art Korea, Seoul, Korea
2013 *New Visions New Voices*, MMCA, Gwacheon, Korea

Awards and Residencies
2019 30th Kimsechoong Art Prize, Kimsechoong Art Museum, Seoul, Korea
2018 EXIT Residency, Korean Cultural Centre India, New Delhi, India
2016 Delfina Foundation Residency, London, UK
2015 Doosan Residency New York, DOOSAN Art Center, New York, USA
2014 Nomadic Artist Residency, Art Council Korea, Chennai, India
2013 Nanji Residency, Seoul Museum of Art, Seoul, Korea
2012 SongEun ArtAward, SONGEUN Art and Cultural Foundation, Seoul, Korea

Christian Boltanski

Selected Solo Exhibitions
2021 *Christian Boltanski: 4.4*, Busan Museum of Art, Busan, Korea
Christian Boltanski: Despu, Galeria Albarran Bourdais, Menorca, Spain
Christian Boltanski: Danach, Kewenig, Berlin, Germany
Christian Boltanski: Apr, Galerie Marian Goodman, Paris, France
2019 *Christian Boltanski: Faire son temps*, Centre Pompidou, Paris, France
Christian Boltanski: Lifetime, National Museum of Art, Osaka, Japan / National Art Center, Tokyo, Japan / Prefectural Art Museum, Nagasaki, Japan
2018 *Christian Boltanski: Storage Memory*, PSA Power Station of Art, Shanghai, China
Christian Boltanski: Lifetime, Israel Museum, Jerusalem, Israel
2017 *Christian Boltanski. Anime. Di Luogo in luogo*, Museo d'Arte Moderna di Bologna, Bologna, Italy
2011 *Christian Boltanski: Chance*, Venice Art Biennale, Venice, Italy
2010 *Christian Boltanski: No Man's Land*, Park Avenue Armory, New York, USA
Christian Boltanski: Personnes, Hangar Bicocca, Milan, Italy
Personnes, Monumenta, Paris, France
Christian Boltanski: Les Archives du Coeur, Permanent Installation at Teshima, Benesse Art Site Naoshima, Japan

Selected Group Exhibitions and Projects
2021 *Corpus Dominici*, Palazzo Reale, Milano, Italy
Diversity United, Berlin, Germany / Moscow, Russia / Paris, France
Art Triennale Echigo Tsumari, Nigata, Japan
2020 *Unexpected. Le hasard des choses*, Festival Images Vevey, Biennale des arts visuels, Vevey, Switzerland
2019 *The Dark Side*, Musja, Roma, Italy
Ombres, Fondation de l'Hermitage, Lausanne, Switzerland
La collection de la fondation Louis Vuitton, Musée Pouchkine, Moscow, Russia
2018 *Take me (I'm Yours)*, Villa Medicis, Rome, Italy
Fondation Cartier pour l'art contemporain. A Beautiful Elsewhere, PSA Power
Station of Art, Shanghai, China
Melancolia, Villa Empain, Fondation Boghossian, Bruxelles, Belgium
Au diapason du monde, Fondation Louis Vuitton, Paris, France
2017 *Ouvert la nuit, festival des lumies*, Académie de France à Rome, Villa Medicis, Rome, Italy
Etranger résident, La collection Marin Karmitz, La Maison Rouge, Paris, France
BIENALSUR (Bienal Internacional de Arte Contemporeo de América del Sur), Museo Nacional de Bellas Artes, Buenos Aires, Argentine
Manif d'art 8, la Biennale de Québec, Québec, Canada
2016 *De toi à la surface*, Le Plateau, Frac Ile-de-France, Paris, France
Carambolages, Grand Palais, Galeries nationales, Paris, France
Loss. In memory of Babi Yar, Pinchuk Art Centre, Kyiv, Ukraine
Refugees, Casula Powerhouse Art Centre, Liverpool, UK
Take Me (I'm Yours), The Jewish Museum, New York, USA
TANT DE TEMPS !: 50 artistes contemporains au musée Soulages, Musée Soulages, Rodez, France

Awards and Residencies
2014   Generalitat Valenciana's International Julio González
       Prize, IVAM Centre Julio Gonzalez, València, Spain
       (-2015)
2007   Créateurs sans frontières, award for visual arts by
       Cultures France (formerly AFAA), France
2006   Praemium Imperiale, Japan Art Association, Tokyo,
       Japan
2001   Kaiserring, Mönchehaus museum Goslar, Goslar,
       Germany
       Kunstpreis, Nord/LB, Braunschweig, Germany

Chung Soyoung

Selected Solo Exhibitions
2021   *Sea Cucumber*, Manganese and Ear, ONE AND J.
       Gallery, Seoul, Korea
2020   *Glass Beach*, Instant Roof, Seoul, Korea
2016   *Night and Day*, Offsite Art Sonje, Seoul, Korea
2013   *Traveling without moving*, D Project Space, Seoul,
       Korea
2011   *On the ground floor of Geology building*, OCI Museum of
       Art, Seoul, Korea
2008   *Zero Construction*, Project Space SARUBIA, Seoul,
       Korea
2007   *A different kind of tension*, Kumho Museum of Art,
       Seoul, Korea
2006   *Innerscape*, Gallery Miss China Beauty, Paris, France

Selected Group Exhibitions and Projects
2021   *2021 DMZ Art & Peace Platform*, Inter-Korean Transit
       Office / Jejin Station, Goseong, Korea
       Margins of Error, Nirox Foundation, Krugersdorp, South
       Africa
       Border-less.site, Culture Station Seoul 284, Seoul,
       Korea
2020   *Negotiating Borders*, Fondation Fiminco, Romainville,
       France
       CAMP2020, Camp Long (former US military base),
       Wonju, Korea
2019   *14th International Curitiba Biennial*, Curitiba, Brazil
       Power Play, Delfina Foundation, London, UK
2018   *Extended Manual*, Seoul Museum of Art, Seoul, Korea
       Genre Allegory—the Sculptural, Total Museum of
       Contemporary Art, Seoul, Korea
       Cour des Miracles, Doosan Gallery, Seoul, Korea
       The Real DMZ, New Art Exchange, Nottingham, UK
2017   *Triangulating Particulars*, Hilbert Raum, Berlin, Germany
2016   *16th SongEun ArtAward*, SongEun ArtSpace, Seoul,
       Korea
       Architectural Ceramics—Earth, Clayarch Gimhae
       Museum, Gimhae, Korea
2015   *Re-Play: 4 Platforms and 17 Events*, Seoul Museum of
       Art, Seoul, Korea
       Séoul, Vite, Vite !, Lille3000, Tripostal, Lille, France
       Resonating Triangle, Arario Museum, Jeju, Korea
2014   *How to survive in the forest*, Le Cyclop, Milly-la-Forêt,
       France
       apmap 2014 jeju: BETWEEN WAVES, Seogwang Tea
       Garden / OSULLOC, Jeju, Kora
2012   *Galapagos*, Ilmin Museum of Art, Seoul, Korea
       Sporadic Positioning, Arario Gallery, Cheonan, Korea

Awards and Residencies
2021   MMCA Residency Changdong, MMCA, Seoul, Korea
2020   Seoul Art Space Geumcheon Residency, Seoul
       Foundation for Arts and Culture, Seoul, Korea
2018   Gapado Artist in Residence, Hyundai Card, Gapado
       Island, Jeju, Korea
2017   Delfina Foundation Residency, Delfina Foundation,
       London, UK
       ZK/U Residency, ZK/U, Berlin, Germany
2016   Yangji-ri Residency, REAL DMZ PROJECT, Art Sonje
       Center, Cheorwon, Korea

Giuseppe Penone

Selected Solo Exhibitions
2021 *Giuseppe Penone. Alberi in versi*, The Uffizi Gallery, Florence, Italy
Giuseppe Penone. Sève et pensée, Bibliothèque nationale de France-François-Mitterrand, Paris, France
2016 *Giuseppe Penone in het Rijksmuseum*, Rijksmuseum, Amsterdam, Netherlands
2013 *Penone Versailles*, Château de Versailles, Versailles, France
2007 *Giuseppe Penone. Sculture di linfa*, Padiglione Italiano, 52. Esposizione Internazionale d'Arte, La Biennale di Venezia, Venice, Italy
2004 *Penone. Rétrospective*, Centre Georges Pompidou, Paris, France
1983 *Giuseppe Penone*, National Gallery of Canada, Ottawa, Canada / Fort Worth Art Museum, Fort Worth, USA / Museum of Contemporary Art, Chicago, USA (1984)
1977 *Giuseppe Penone. Bäume, Augen, Haare, Wände, Tongefäss*, Kunstmuseum Luzern, Luzern, Switzerland
1970 *Giuseppe Penone*, Aktionsraum 1, Munich, Germany
1969 *Giuseppe Penone*, Galleria Gian Enzo Sperone, Torino, Italy

Selected Group Exhibitions and Projects
2020 *Among the Trees*, Hayward Gallery, Southbank Centre, London, UK
2019 *Préhistoire, une énigme moderne*, Centre Pompidou - Mus national d'art moderne, Paris, France
2018 *Una fornace a Marsiglia: CIRVA*, Le stanze del vetro, Fondazione Giorgio Cini, Venice, Italy
2010 *documenta 13*, Karlsaue Park, Kassel, Germany / Museum Fridericianum, Kassel, Germany / Queen's Palace, Bagh-e Bagur Pavilion, Kabul, Afghanistan
2008 */Italics/ Arte italiana fra tradizione e rivoluzione 1968-2008*, Palazzo Grassi, Venice, Italy
/Italics/ Italian Art between Tradition and Revolution 1968-2008, MCA Museum of Contemporary Art, Chicago, USA
2007 *Drawing Connections: Baselitz, Kelly, Penone, Rockburne, and the Old Masters*, The Morgan Library & Museum, New York, USA
2001 *Zero to Infinity: Arte Povera 1962-1972*, Tate Modern, London, UK / Walker Art Center, Minneapolis, USA / MOCA Museum of Contemporary Art at The Geffen Contemporary, Los Angeles, USA / Hirshhorn Museum and Sculpture Garden, Washington, USA
2000 *La beauté in fabula*, Palais des Papes, Avignon, France
1997 *L'empreinte*, Musée national d'Art moderne Centre Georges Pompidou, Paris, France
1993 *Gravity & Grace. The changing condition of sculpture 1965-1975*, Hayward Gallery, London, UK
1987 *documenta 8*, Museum Fridericianum, Kassel, Germany
Skulptur Projekte in Münster 1987, Westfälischen Landesmuseum für Kunst und Kulturgeschichte, Münster, Germany
2nd Biennale, 4th Ushimado International Art Festival, Ushimado, Japan
1982 *Italian Art Now. An American Perspective. 1982 Exxon International Exhibition*, The Solomon R. Guggenheim Museum, New York, USA
1971 *7e Biennale de Paris*, Parc Floral, Bois de Vincennes, Paris, France
1970 *Between man and matter*, X Biennale, Tokyo Metropolitan Art Gallery, Tokyo, Japan
Processi di pensiero visualizzati: 15 italienische Künstler, Kunstmuseum Luzern, Luzern, Switzerland
Information, The Museum of Modern Art, New York, USA

1969 *Prospect 69: Internationale Vorschau auf die Kunst in den Galerien der Avantgarde*, Städtische Kunsthalle, Düsseldorf, Germany
Konzeption / Conception: Dokumentation einer heutiger Kunstrichtung, Städtisches Museum Schloss Morsbroich, Leverkusen, Germany

Awards and Residencies
2018 Grand Prix Artistique, Fondation Simone et Cino Del Duca, Institut de France, Paris, France
2017 McKim Medal, American Academy, Rome, Italy
2014 Praemium Imperiale, Japan Art Association, Tokyo, Japan
2009 Chevalier de la Légion d'Honneur, France
2001 Rolf Schock Prize for the Visual Arts, Royal Swedish Academy of Sciences, Stockholm, Sweden
1979 Mönchengladbach Residency, Städtisches Museum Abteiberg, Mönchengladbach, Germany (-1980)

Hiroshi Sugimoto

Selected Solo Exhibitions

2018 *Sugimoto Versailles: Surface of Revolution*, The Estate of Trianon / Palace of Versailles / Versailles, France
Hiroshi Sugimoto: Still Life, Royal Museum of Fine Arts of Belgium, Brussels, Belgium

2014 *Aujourd'hui, le monde est mort [Lost Human Genetic Archive]*, Palais de Tokyo, Paris, France

2013 *Hiroshi Sugimoto*, Leeum, Samsung Museum of Art, Seoul, Korea

2012 *From Naked to Clothed*, Hara Museum of Contemporary Art, Tokyo, Japan

2008 *History of History*, 21st Century Museum of Contemporary Art, Kanazawa, Japan

2007 *Hiroshi Sugimoto*, K20 Kunstsammlung Nordrhein-Westfalen, Düsseldorf, Germany

2006 *Mathematical Forms*, L'Atelier Brancusi, Centre Pompidou, Paris, France

2005 *Hiroshi Sugimoto: End of Time*, Mori Art Museum, Tokyo, Japan

2004 *Étant donné: Le Grand Verre*, Fondation Cartier pour l'art contemporain, Paris, France

1995 *Sugimoto*, Metropolitan Museum of Art, New York, USA

Selected Group Exhibitions and Projects

2020 *STARS: Six Contemporary Artists from Japan to the World*, Mori Art Museum, Tokyo, Japan

2017 *What Absence Is Made Of*, Hirshhorn Museum and Sculpture Garden, Washington D.C., USA

2014 *Simple Shapes*, Centre Pompidou-Metz, Metz, France

2012 *Phantoms of Asia*, Asian Art Museum, San Francisco, USA

2011 *Yokohama 2011 International Triennale of Contemporary Art*, Yokohama, Japan

2010 *17th Biennale of Sydney*, Sydney, Australia

2009 *Mapping the Studio*, Punta Della Dogana, Venice, Italy

2008 *Photography on Photography: Reflections on the Medium since 1960*, Metropolitan Museum of Art, New York, USA

2004 *Singular Forms (Sometimes Repeated): Art from 1951 to the Present*, Solomon R. Guggenheim Museum, New York, USA

2003 *The History of Japanese Photography*, The Museum of Fine Arts, Houston, USA

2002 *Moving Pictures*, Solomon R. Guggenheim Museum, New York, USA

2000 *Expanding Horizons: Landscape Photographs from the Whitney Museum of American Art*, Whitney Museum of American Art, New York, USA

1999 *The Museum as Muse: Artists Reflect*, Museum of Modern Art, New York, USA

1997 *In Visible Light: Photography and Classification in Art, Science and the Everyday*, Modern Art Oxford, Oxford, UK

1996 *By Night*, Fondation Cartier pour l'art contemporain, Paris, France

1995 *Art in Japan Today: 1985-1995*, Museum of Contemporary Art, Tokyo, Japan

1994 *Japanese Art after 1945: Scream Against the Sky*, Yokohama Museum of Art, Kanagawa, Japan / Guggenheim Museum Soho, New York, USA / San Francisco Museum of Modern Art, San Francisco, USA

1992 *Réflexions Voilées (Hidden Reflections)*, Israel Museum, Jerusalem, Israel

1991 *A Cabinet of Signs: Contemporary Art from Postmodern Japan*, Tate Gallery Liverpool, Liverpool, UK

1990 *The Past and the Present of Photography*, The National Museum of Modern Art, Tokyo, Japan

Awards and Residencies

2018 Medal of Honor in Photography, National Arts Club, New York, USA

2017 Person of Cultural Merit, Tokyo, Japan
Centenary Medal, The Royal Photographic Society, London, UK

2014 Isamu Noguchi Award, Isamu Noguchi Foundation and Garden Museum, New York, USA

2013 Officier de L'ordre des Arts et des Lettres, Paris, France

2010 The Medal of Honor with Purple Ribbon, Tokyo, Japan

2001 Hasselblad Foundation International Award in Photography, Göteborg, Sweden

1999 15th Annual Infinity Award for Art, International Center of Photography, New York, USA

1988 Mainichi Art Prize, Tokyo, Japan

1980 John Simon Guggenheim Memorial Foundation Fellowship, New York, USA

Jang Minseung

Selected Solo Exhibitions
2021   *ROUND AND AROUND*, Korea Cultural Centre UK,
       London, UK
       voiceless, Kunsthal Aarhus, Aarhus, Denmark
2016   *Ipsuk Bugeun*, Platform-L Contemporary Art Center,
       Seoul, Korea
2014   *hidden track*, Space Willing N Dealing, Seoul, Korea
2012   *the moments*, ONE AND J. Gallery, Seoul, Korea
2011   *In between times*, Johyun Gallery, Busan, Korea
2010   *A Multi-Culture*, ONE AND J. Gallery, Seoul, Korea
       In between times, Art+Lounge Dibang, Seoul, Korea
2008   *Intermission*, Seomi & Tuus, Seoul, Korea
2006   *Cut & Bend*, Gallery Modul, Seoul Korea

Selected Group Exhibitions and Projects
2021   *Invisible Cities*, Platform-L Contemporary Art Center,
       Seoul, Korea
       ROUND AND AROUND, film project, courtesy of Korea
       Film Archive Center, Seoul, Korea
2020   *Blue Peal of Bells*, Museum of Contemporary Art Busan,
       Busan, Korea
       *Words at an Exhibition: an exhibition in ten chapters
       and five poems*, Busan Biennale 2020, Busan, Korea
2019   *Fiftieth Anniversary Exhibition of MMCA Korea: The
       Square*, MMCA Deoksugung, Seoul, Korea
2018   *CRACKS in the Concrete II: A Glimpse into the World /
       Gazing into Eternity*, MMCA, Gwacheon, Korea
       Livro do Desassossego, Gyeongnam Art Museum,
       Changwon, Korea
       with weft, with warp, Seoul Museum of Art, Seoul,
       Korea
       over there, film project, courtesy of Amore Pacific
       Museum of Art, Seoul, Korea
2017   *Deoksugung Outdoor Project: Light, Sound, Landscape*,
       MMCA Deoksugung, Seoul, Korea
2016   *VOID*, MMCA, Seoul, Korea
       As the Moon waxes and wanes, MMCA, Gwacheon,
       Korea
       April the Eternal Voyage, Gyeonggi Museum of Modern
       Art, Ansan, Korea
       arcadia, film project, courtesy of MMCA, Korea
2015   *The Darkside of Nature*, National Museum of Art of
       Romania, Bucharest, Romania
2014   *sanglim*, public art project, Sanglim Forest, Hamyang,
       Korea
2011   *Spheres part I in Mullae-dong*, public art project, Mullae
       Art Space, Seoul, Korea

Awards and Residencies
2018   2nd Gapado Artist in Residence, Hyundai Card, Gapado
       Island, Jeju, Korea
2015   9th Nanji Residency, Seoul Museum of Art, Seoul, Korea
2014   MMCA Residency Changdong, MMCA, Seoul, Korea
       Winner, 15th Hermès Foundation Missulsang, Seoul,
       Korea
2006   Young Product Designer of the Year, Korea Design
       Award, Seoul, Korea

Jean-Luc Mylayne

Selected Solo Exhibitions
2020   *Autumn in Paradise*, Huis Marseille, Amsterdam,
       Netherlands
       Herbst im Paradies, Kestnergesellschaft, Hannover,
       Germany
2019   *Autumn in Paradise*, Long Museum, Shanghai, China
       Herbst im Paradies, Aargauer Kunsthaus, Aargau,
       Switzerland
       L'automne du Paradis, Fondation Vincent van Gogh,
       Arles, France
2015   *Mutual Regard*, The Arts Club of Chicago / The Art
       Institute of Chicago, Chicago, USA
2010   *Des signatures du ciel aux mains du temps*, Museo
       Nacional Centro de Arte Reina Sofia, Madrid, Spain
2010   *Jean-Luc Mylayne*, Lannan Foundation, Santa Fe, New
       Mexico, USA (2004, 2005)
2009   *Jean-Luc Mylayne: Tête d'or*, Musée d'Art contemporain
       de Lyon, Lyon, France
2007   *Jean-Luc Mylayne*, Parrish Art Museum, Southampton,
       New York, USA (-2009)
2004   *Jean-Luc Mylayne: les oies sauvages riaient et Dieu
       s'endormit tôt*, Musée des Arts
       Contemporains, Grand-Hornu, Belgium
1995   *Jean-Luc Mylayne*, ARC- Musée d'Art Moderne de la
       Ville de Paris, France

Selected Group Exhibitions and Projects
2020   *Among the Trees*, Hayward Gallery, Southbank Centre,
       London, UK
2017   *The Photographic Part 1*, S.M.A.K., Ghent, Belgium
2011   *ILLUMInations*, 54th Venice Biennale, Venice, Italy
1998   *Terra Incognita: Alighiero e Boetti, Vija Celmins, Neil
       Jenney, Jean-Luc Mylayne, Hiroshi Sugimito*, Neues
       Museum Weserburg, Bremen, Germany
1996   *Jurassic Technologies Revenant*, 10th Sydney Biennale,
       Sydney, Australia
1995   *Zeichen und Wunder (signs and wonder) Niko Pirosmani
       and Recent Art*, Kunsthaus Zürich,
       Zurich, Switzerland

Jeoung Jae Choul

Selected Solo Exhibitions

2021 *Jeoung Jae Choul: For Love and Peace*, Arko Art Center, Seoul, Korea
2017 *Watershed*, Keumsan Gallery, Seoul, Korea
2016 *Silkroad Project—Documentation 2016*, Bongsan Cultural Center, Daegu, Korea
2015 *Blueocean Project 2015—Tideland*, JM Gallery, Paju, Korea
2011 *Artist of Today—Silkroad Project*, Kim Chong Yung Museum, Seoul, Korea
     Istanbul to London, Kunstdoc Gallery, Seoul, Korea
2010 *3rd Silk Road Project*, With Artist Gallery, Paju, Korea
2009 *Traveller*, Zeeno space, Seoul, Korea
2007 *Wood Sculpture Drawing*, Duplex Gallery, Seoul, Korea
2005 *1st Silk Road Project*, Project Space Zip, Seoul, Korea
2004 *Silk Road Project—Washing & Packing*, Goyang National Art Studio, Goyang, Korea

Selected Group Exhibitions and Projects

2020 *Black Milk of Dawn*, Kim Chong Yung Museum, Seoul, Korea
2019 *International Ecological Art Exhibition: Ocean—New messengers*, Jeju Museum of Contemporary Art, Jeju, Korea
2018 *Seoul Mediacity Biennale 2018: Eu Zên*, Seoul Museum of Art, Seoul, Korea
2017 *Jeju Biennale*, Jeju Museum of Art, Jeju, Korea
2016 *In the Flaneur's Eyes*, Gyeonggi Museum of Modern Art, Ansan, Korea
2015 *Russia-Korea Exchange Exhibition: Minima Moralia*, Irkutsk Regional Art Museum Sukachov, Irkutsk, Russia
2013 *Multifarious Appearance of Ten Thousand Things— From Things to Beings*, Gwangju Museum of Art, Gwangju / Nam-Seoul Museum of Art, Seoul, Korea (-2014)
2010 *Mongolia-Korea Arts Festival: Time and Space*, Jeju Museum of Contemporary Art, Jeju, Korea
2009 *Made in Korea: Magic Moment—Korean Express*, Sinn-Leffers Department, Hannover, Germany
2008 *Time & Space*, South Gobi Museum, Dalanzadgad, Mongolia
2007 *Recycling, Inc.*, Arko Art Center, Seoul, Korea
2006 *Busan Biennale 2006*, Oncheon-Cheon, Busan, Korea
2004 *Declaration for Peace: 100 Artists from Korea and Overseas*, MMCA, Gwacheon, Korea
2003 *Rousing Sculpture: Material & Space*, Daejeon Museum of Art, Daejeon, Korea
1997 *From the Ground Up*, Socrates Sculpture Park, New York, USA
1995 *From DMZ*, Gongpyeong Gallery, Seoul, Korea
1990 *64 Artists Born in the Fifties*, Sonamoo Gallery, Seoul, Korea
1988 *Another New Sculpture*, Total Gallery, Seoul, Korea
1987 *Grand Art Exhibition of Korea*, MMCA, Gwacheon, Korea

Awards and Residencies

2014 ARKO Nomadic Artists Residency, Arts Council Korea, Baykal, Russia
2011 Artist of Today Award, Kim Chong Yung Museum, Seoul, Korea
2010 Nomadic Artists Residency, Time and Space, Jeju, Korea
2008 ARKO Nomadic Artists Residency, Arts Council Korea, Mongolia
2002 Art Omi: Artists Residency, Art Omi, New York, USA
1997 Asian Award, The Freeman Foundation, Vermont Studio Center, Vermont, USA
1996 Kim Se Joong Prize for Junior Sculptor, Kimsechoong Museum, Seoul, Korea
     Escale Studio Program, Mauritius
1988 Grand Prize, Grand-Prix Exhibition, *Jung-Ang Daily News* / Ho-Am Art Museum, Seoul, Korea
1987 Encouragement Prize, Grand-Prix Exhibition, *Jung-Ang Daily* / Ho-Am Art Museum, Seoul, Korea

Kim Bo Joong

Selected Solo Exhibitions

2020 *Kim Bo Joong Solo Exhibition: Land of Human(人乃地)*, Space Mom Museum of Art, Cheongju, Korea

2019 *Jeon Hyuk Lim Art Prize Exhibition*, Jeon Hyuk Lim Museum of Art, Tongyeong, Korea

2017 *Flowing Residency: Path*, Indipress Gallery, Seoul, Korea

2012 *Kim Bo Joong Solo Exhibition: Residence*, PS333, Seoul Art Space Geumcheon, Seoul, Korea

2006 *Flow and flow*, Art Space POOL, Seoul, Korea

2005 *Painting, Asking the Way*, Gallery Skape, Seoul, Korea

2004 *A Forest where many parts drift-Painting*, Dukwon Cube Gallery, Seoul, Korea

2001 *A Landscape*, Sungkok Art Museum, Seoul, Korea

1999 *Accompanying of a Poet and an Artist*, Rhok Saek gallery, Seoul, Korea

1996 *Kim Bo Joong Solo Exhibition*, Kumho Museum of Art, Seoul, Korea

1993 *Kim Bo Joong Solo Exhibition*, Burbank Creative Art gallery, California, USA

Selected Group Exhibitions and Projects

2019 *Family Garden*, Yangpyeong Art Museum, Yangpyeong, Korea

2017 *The Face of Seongnam*, Seongnam Cube Art Museum, Seongnam, Korea

2016 *In the Flâneur's Eyes*, Gyeonggi Museum of Modern Art, Ansan, Korea

2015 *Eight Views and Nine-Bend Streams of Gyeonggi*, Gyeonggi Museum of Modern Art, Ansan, Korea
PyeongChang Biennale GIAX, Alpensia, Pyeongchang, Korea
1980s and Korean Art, Jeonbuk Museum of Art, Wanju, Korea

2007 *Traveling Exhibition by Gyeonggido Museum of Art: New Landscape*, Pocheon Banweol Art Hall; touring: 13 other locations around Korea
Korea-China Contemporary Art Exhibition: Giants in Illusion, Sejong Museum of Art, Seoul, Korea

2006 *The face of Seongnam*, Seongnam Arts Center, Seongnam, Korea
Baggat Art—Jara Island, Jara Island, Gapyeong, Korea

2002 *International Eco-environmental Art Exhibition: The Call of the Toad*, Hangaram Art Museum, Seoul, Korea
To Become One with Nature, Youngeun Museum of Contemporary Art, Gwangju, Gyeonggi-do, Korea

2001 *Ecotopia: Dreaming of New Atlantis*, Busan Museum of Art, Busan, Korea
2001 Odyssey, Seongsan Art Hall, Changwon, Korea

2000 *The landscape and the place, Utopia & Atopia*, Gyeonggi Arts Center, Suwon; touring: 2 other locations in Gyeonggi-do, Korea

1994 *Fifteen Years of Minjung Art: 1980-1994*, MMCA, Gwacheon, Korea

1984 *The Art of the Life*, Kwanhoon Gallery, Seoul, Korea
The Great Roots Show, Han Gang Gallery, Seoul, Korea

1983 *Zeitgeist*, The 3rd Art Gallery, Seoul, Korea

1982 *The prospect of modern art in the 1980s'*, Misulhoegwan (Fine Art Center), Seoul, Korea

Awards and Residencies

2018 4th Jeon Hyuck Lim Art Prize, The Jeon Hyuck Lim Museum of Art, Tongyeong, Korea
Selected for Supporting the Publication of a Material Book for Established Artists, Seoul Foundation for Arts and Culture, Seoul, Korea

2017 Excellent Artist to Support, Gyeonggi Cultural Foundation, Suwon, Korea

2016 Professional Art Creation Support, Gyeonggi Cultural Foundation, Suwon, Korea

2013 Toji International Writers' and Artists' Residency, Toji Cultural Foundation, Wonju, Korea
Artist-In-Residence, Gyeonggi Creation Center, Ansan, Korea

2012 3rd Seoul Art Space Geumcheon Residency, Seoul Foundation for Arts and Culture, Seoul, Korea
Professional Art Creation Support, Seoul Foundation for Arts and Culture, Seoul, Korea

2011 2nd Artist-In-Residence, Gyeonggi Creation Center, Ansan, Korea

Kim Juree

Selected Solo Exhibitions
2020 *Wet Matter*, SongEun ArtSpace, Seoul, Korea
2017 *Impermanence*, SO.S (Sarubia Outreach & Support),
Project Space SARUBIA, Seoul, Korea
2012 *Scape_Collection*, Project Space Mo, Seoul, Korea
2008 *Silent Invasion*, Ga gallery, Seoul, Korea
2005 *Room#203*, Ya Project 03, Ga gallery, Seoul, Korea

Selected Group Exhibitions and Projects
2021 *KOREA. Gateway to a rich past*, Princessehof National
Museum of Ceramics, Leeuwarden, Netherlands
Time of the Earth, MMCA, Gwacheon, Korea
KOREA. Gateway to a rich past, Princessehof National
Museum of Ceramics, Leeuwarden, Netherlands
Border-less.site, Culture Station Seoul 284, Seoul,
Korea
Fortune Telling, Ilmin Museum of Art, Seoul, Korea
2020 *Korean Eye 2020*, Saatchi Gallery, London, UK
Non-Sculpture–Light or flexible, Changwon Sculpture
Biennale, Yongji Park / Seongsan Art Hall, Changwon,
Korea
2018 *Breaking Ground*, Indian Ceramics Triennale, Jawahar
Kala Kendra, Jaipur, India
2017 *Place and Practices–Terraced House*, World of
Wedgwood, Stoke-on-Trent, UK
British Ceramic Biennial, Korea Pavilion, China Hall
(former Spode factory site), Stoke-on-Trent, UK
Not your ordinary art storage, SongEun ArtStorage,
Seoul, Korea
Contemporary Korean Ceramics, Victoria and Albert
Museum, London, UK
Blank Page, Kumho Museum of Art, Seoul, Korea
2016 *First Central China International Ceramics Biennale*,
Henan Museum, Zhengzhou, China
Homeground, Cheongju Museum of Art, Cheongju,
Korea
Céramique Coréenne Contemporaine, Fondation
d'entreprise Bernardaud, Limoges, France
Made in Seoul, Centre d'art contemporain, Meymac,
France
Decapod, AirSpace Gallery, Stoke-on-Trent, UK
2011 *CITY-NET ASIA 2011*, Seoul Museum of Art, Seoul, Korea
Emptiness, Sungkok Art Museum, Seoul, Korea
10th SongEun ArtAward Exhibition, SongEun ArtSpace,
Seoul, Korea
2009 *Evanescent Scape*, Tongui-dong Boan Inn, Seoul, Korea

Awards and Residencies
2022 Creative Support, Seoul Foundation for Arts and
Culture, Seoul, Korea
2021 Now Art Creation Support, GyeongGi Cultural
Foundation, Suwon, Korea
Princessehof National Museum of Ceramics Residency,
Leeuwarden, Netherlands
Incheon Art Platform Residency, Incheon, Korea
2020 Creative Support, Seoul Foundation for Arts and
Culture, Seoul, Korea
MMCA Residency Goyang, MMCA, Goyang, Korea
2017 Victoria and Albert Museum Ceramics Residency,
London, UK (-2018)
2016 Cité internationale des Art Residency, Paris, France
2012 Sovereign Asian Art Prize, Sovereign Art Foundation,
Hong Kong
2010 Grand Prize, 10th SongEun ArtAward, Seoul, Korea
2007 Selected Artist for Young Artist Program, Arts Council
Korea, Seoul, Korea

Lee Kyung Ho

Selected Solo Exhibitions
2018 *Digital Moon*, Media 338 at Bitgoeul Art Space, Gwangju,
Korea
2007 *No Signal(?HELP)*, Gallery Sejul, Seoul, Korea / City
Gallery Ljubljana, Ljubljana, Slovenia
2006 *Traveler*, Gallery Sejul, Seoul, Korea
2002 *Chaos under Dream*, Gallery Sejul, Seoul, Korea

Selected Group Exhibitions and Projects
2021 *Warm Revitalization*, Gangwon Triennale 2021,
Hongcheon, Korea
Jeonnam International SUMUK Biennale, Yudal
Elementary School, Mokpo, Korea
2020 *Geumgang Nature Art Biennale*, Yeonmisan Nature Art
Park, Gongju, Korea
Dalseong Daegu Contemporary Art Festival, The ARC,
Daegu, Korea
2019 *Jirisan (Mt.) Arts Festa and Award (JIIAF)*, Jirisan Art
Farm, Hadong / Seoul Art Center, Seoul, Korea
Sejong Counter Wave: Immanent Power, Sejong
Museum of Art, Seoul, Korea
2018 *Les autres langues*, Musée Boribana, Dakar, Senegal
Media Art Exhibition, Art Busan, BEXCO, Busan, Korea
Tamarindo Art Wave Festival, Playa Tamarindo, Costa
Rica
*Renegades in Resistance and Challenge: Part2. 50-year
history of performance art of Korea: 1967-2017*, Daegu
Art Museum, Daegu, Korea
2017 *Taehwa Eco River Art Festival*, Taehwa river local
garden, Ulsan, Korea
*China International Gallery Exposition: Asia Special
Section*, National Agriculture Exhibition Center, Beijing,
China
*50 Years of Korean Performance Art and Archives:
Explorers of Experiment and Challenge*, KIAF special
exhibition, COEX, Seoul, Korea
2016 *3rd Changwon Sculpture Biennale*, Youngji Lake Park,
Changwon, Korea
*Suncheon Bay International Eco-Environmental Art
Festival*, Suncheon International Wetland Center,
Suncheon, Korea
2015 *Sea Art Festival 2015*, Dadaepo beach, Busan, Korea
2014 *Korean Contemporary Art K-P.O.P.*, Taipei MOCA, Taipei,
Taiwan
Digital Triangle: Media Art Today in Korea·China·Japan,
Alternative Space LOOP, Seoul, Korea
2012 *Dream, Walking in the Magical Reality*, MMCA,
Gwacheon, Korea
2011 *Happy Window*, Art Center Nabi, Seoul, Korea
Wonderful World of Light Art, Gyeongnam Art Museum,
Changwon, Korea
Meditation of Technology: Gardens of the Media,
Pohang Museum of Steel Art, Pohang, Korea
2010 *The Flower of May*, A Special Exhibition
Commemorating the 30th Anniversary of Gwangju
Uprising, Gwangju Museum of Art, Gwangju, Korea
Image of September with Annie Ratti, Gallery Sejul,
Seoul, Korea
2008 *Sevilla Biennale*, Sevilla, Spain
2007 *Thermocline of Art: New Asian Waves*, ZKM, Karlsruhe,
Germany
2006 *Shanghai Biennale*, Shanghai Art Museum, Shanghai,
China
2005 *Shanghai COOL*, Shanghai Duolun Museum of Modern
Art, Shanghai, China
2004 *5th Gwangju Biennale*, Gwangju Biennale Exhibition
Hall, Gwangju, Korea
Digital Sublime: New Masters of Universe, Taipei MOCA,
Taipei, Taiwan

2003 *New Collections*, MMCA, Gwacheon, Korea
2002 *Seoul Mediacity Biennale 2002: Luna's Flow*, Seoul Museum of Art, Seoul, Korea
1993 *Video Installation and Painting*, Espace Montjoie, Paris, France
1989 Participated in lots of performances with ORLAN including *Poliphonix 89*, Centre Pompidou, Paris, France; *L'acte pour l'art*, Tarascon, France.

Awards and Residencies
1999 Espace Paul Ricard Award, *Salon de la Jeune Création, 50s Salon de la Jeune Peinture*, Paris, France

Na Hyun

Selected Solo Exhibitions
2021 *Finding Bigfoot*, Culturetank, Seoul, Korea
2018 *BABEL—Different tongue*, Daegu Art Museum, Daegu, Korea
2016 *PRO-JECT*, Choi & Lager Gallery, Cologne, Germany
2014 *PRO-JECT*, LIG Art Space, Seoul, Korea
The Babel Tower, Kustlerhaus Bethanien, Berlin, Germany
2012 *A Song of Lorelei*, Art Space Jungmiso, Seoul, Korea
2011 *Na Hyun report—about the Ethnic*, Sungkok Art Museum, Seoul, Korea
2010 *PILE*, Atelier am Eck, Dusseldorf, Germany
2009 *Missing project*, Sangsang Madang Gallery, Seoul, Korea
2008 *Painting on the Water*, Cité Internationale des Arts, Paris, France
2007 *Painting Landscapes project*, Farringdon Road, London, UK / Cheonggyecheon Stream, Seoul, Korea
2005 *White Cloud Minnow project*, St Edmund Hall Library, Oxford, UK / National Library of Korea, Seoul, Korea
2004 *Strange Event*, Dolphin Gallery, Oxford, UK

Selected Group Exhibitions and Projects
2021 *Spielraum × Phytology*, Museum SAN, Wonju, Korea
Collection_Opening Hacking Mining, Seoul Museum of Art, Seoul, Korea
2020 *Unflattening*, MMCA, Seoul, Korea
The Archivists, Art Bunker B39, Bucheon, Korea
2019 *Tilted Scenes—What do you see*, Navy officer's club in Arsenale, Venice, Italy
Wandering, Kaohsiung Museum of Fine Art, Kaohsiung, Taiwan
2018 *CRACKS in the Concrete II*, MMCA, Gwacheon, Korea
Wandering Seeds, National Museum of Prehistory, Taitung, Taiwan
2017 *Blooming at the Junction*, Korean Cultural Center Hongkong, Hongkong
NANJI 10 Years, Seoul Museum of Art, Seoul, Korea
2016 *Mille-feuille de Camelia*, Arko Art Center, Seoul, Korea
Please Return to Busan Port, Vestfossen Kunstlaboratorium, Vestfossen, Norway
2015 *Korean Artist Prize*, MMCA, Seoul, Korea
Jeju 4·3 ART Festival, Jeju Museum of Art, Jeju, Korea
2014 *Mediation Biennale 2014*, Poznan, Poland / Berlin, German
2013 *Hermès Foundation Missulsang*, Atelier Hermès, Seoul, Korea
Transfer Korea-NRW, Osthaus Museum Hagen, Hagen, Germany / Arko Art Center, Seoul, Korea
2012 *Ceramics Commune*, Art Sonje Center, Seoul, Korea
2011 *Innerspacing the City*, Chelsea Art Museum, New York, USA
INTERVIEW, Arko Art Center, Seoul, Korea
2010 *Chasm in Image*, Seoul Museum of Art, Seoul, Korea
Present from the Past, Korean Cultural Centre UK, London, UK
2009 *Bad Boys Here and Now*, Gyeonggi Museum of Modern Art, Ansan, Korea
2008 *Young Korean Artists 2008*, MMCA, Gwacheon, Korea
2007 *Where Euclid Walked*, Seoul Museum of Art, Seoul, Korea

Awards and Residencies
2017 Seoul Art Space Geumcheon Residency, Seoul Foundation for Arts and Culture, Seoul, Korea (-2018)
2013 Künstlerhaus Bethanien Residency, Berlin, Germany (-2014)
2012 Transfer Korea-NRW Residency, Osthaus Museum Hagen, Hagen, Germany
2011 Sociedad Cultural José Martí Residency, Habana, Cuba
2010 Gastatelier Residency, Kulturamt Landeshauptstadt Düsseldorf, Düsseldorf, Germany
2007 Cité Internationale des Arts Residency, Samsung Foundation of Culture, Paris, France (-2008)

OAA (Jung Kyudong)

Selected Exhibitions and Projects
2019 *Aurora: The Secret of Color*, Robotic Arm design, Wooran Foundation, Seoul, Korea
2018 *Emotion-scape*, Kayip+OAA, Blume Museum of Contemporary Art, Paju, Korea
Invisible Border, Kayip+OAA, Hyangchon Cultural Center, Daegu, Korea
2017 *apmap 2017 jeju: mystic birth*, OSULLOC Tea Museum, Jeju, Korea
2016 *Sulwha Cultural Exhibition: Once upon a time*, Dosan Park, Seoul, Korea
Jikji Korea Pavillion, Ron Arad+OAA, Cheongju, Korea
apmap 2016 yongsan: make link, OAA+Kayip, Yongsan Family Park, Seoul, Korea
Black Swan by Kwon Jian a.k.a Solbi, Infinite Mirror Cube design, An-Guk Gallery, Seoul, Korea
2011 *Lie sang bong Exhibition*, Booth design, Harrods, London, UK

Olafur Eliasson

Selected Solo Exhibitions
2021 *Olafur Eliasson: Life*, Fondation Beyeler, Basel, Switzerland
2020 *Olafur Eliasson: Symbiotic seeing*, Kunsthaus Zurich, Zurich, Switzerland
Olafur Eliasson: Sometimes the river is the bridge, Museum of Contemporary Art, Tokyo, Japan
2019 *Olafur Eliasson: In real life*, Tate Modern, London, UK
2018 *The unspeakable openness of things*, Red Brick Art Museum, Beijing, China
2016 *Olafur Eliasson Versailles*, Palace of Versailles, Versailles, France
Olafur Eliasson: The parliament of possibilities, LEEUM, Samsung Museum of Art, Seoul, Korea
2015 *Olafur Eliasson: Verklighetsmaskiner*, Moderna Museet, Stockholm, Sweden
2010 *Olafur Eliasson: Innen Stadt Aussen*, Martin Gropius Bau, Berlin, Germany
2003 *The weather project*, Tate Modern, London, UK

Selected Group Exhibitions and Projects
2021 *Ecologies: A Song for Our Planet*, Montreal Museum of Fine Arts, Montreal, Canada
2020 *E Luce fu / And light was made*, Castello di Rivoli, Torino, Italy
2019 *The Nature Rules: Dreaming of Earth Project*, Hara Museum of Contemporary Art, Tokyo, Japan
Eco-visionaries, Royal Academy of Arts, London, UK
2018 *Into Nature: Out of Darkness*, Drenthe, Assen, The Netherlands
2017 *7th Moscow Biennale of Contemporary Art*, Moscow, Russia
2016 *Art Alive*, Louisiana Museum of Modern Art, Humlebæk, Denmark
2015 *Vidéodanse: Le corps en jeu [The Body at Play or The Body in Game]*, Centre Pompidou, Paris, France
2014 *The Space: Hack The Space event at Tate Modern*, Tate Modern, London, UK
Burning Down the House, Gwangju Biennale 2014, Gwangju, Korea
2013 *Re:emerge—Towards a New Cultural Cartography*, Sharjah Biennial 11, Sharjah Art Foundation, Sharjah, United Arab Emirates
2012 *Nam June Paik's 80th Anniversary: Nostalgia is an Extended Feedback*, Nam June Paik Art Center, Seoul, Korea
Common Ground, La Biennale di Venezia: 13th International Architecture Exhibition, Venice, Italy
2011 *A Sense of Perspective*, Tate Liverpool, Liverpool, UK
2010 *Still / Moving*, The Israel Museum, Jerusalem, Israel
People meet in architecture, La Biennale di Venezia: 12th International Architecture Exhibition, Venice, Italy
2009 *Shift—Field of Fluctuation*, Collection Exhibition, 21st Century Museum of Modern Art, Kanazawa, Japan
2008 *Revolutions—Forms that Turn*, 16th Biennale of Sydney, Sydney, Australia
YOUniverse, Third Biennial of Contemporary Art of Seville, Seville, Spain
2007 *Nature Design: Von Inspiration zu Innovation*, Museum für Gestaltung Zürich, Zurich, Switzerland

Rim Dong Sik

Seo Dongjoo

Selected Solo Exhibitions
2020 *A Picture Diary*, Post Territory Ujeongguk, Seoul, Korea
2011 *Empty Space*, Datz Press Gallery, Seoul, Korea

Selected Group Exhibitions and Projects
2021 *ZERO1NE DAY 2021: Playground*, Online exhibition
BTS × 100th Gwanghwamun billboard, Online exhibition
/ Kyobo Tower Gangnam, Seoul, Korea
Chic, Le Sport !, Hermès scarf design
ASEAN Animals, ASEAN Culture House, Busan, Korea
DREAMERS, SPACE U, Seoul, Korea
2020 *ZERO1NE OPEN STUDIO with P:LAYERS*, ZERO1NE
Gangnam studio, Seoul, Korea
White Night, LG SIGNATURE OLED R, Seoul, Korea
2019 *Because of You*, Sejong Hyundai Motor Gallery, Sejong
Art Center, Seoul, Korea
Deep Space 8K, Ars Electronica Center, Linz, Austria
ZERO, Graphic and exhibition designs, Pohang Museum
of Steel Art, Pohang, Korea
End of the World and Missed Calls, PyeongChang
International Peace Film Festival, Pyeongchang, Korea
Splash ASEAN! Water, a Celebration of Life, ASEAN
Culture House, The Korea Foundation, Busan, Korea
A Thousand Horizons, Vision Hall, Hyundai Motor Group,
Yongin, Korea
2018 *Sulwha Cultural Exhibition: Fortune Land–Gold Leaf*,
Exhibition Director, Amorepacific Headquarters, Seoul,
Korea
Olympic Sculpture Project: Post 88, Soma Museum of
Art, Seoul, Korea
Architects of Amorepacific, Amorepacific Museum of
Art, Seoul, Korea
Cartoon Symbols: SPIRAL EYES, Gallery Meme, Seoul,
Korea
2017 *Mil-Wol*, Portfolio Gallery, Seoul, Korea
2016 *MMCA-Hyundai Motor Museum Festival: Madang*,
MMCA, Seoul, Korea
2015 *Sulwha Cultural Exhibition: Sul-Wha–Once upon a time*,
Bluesquare Nemo Gallery, Seoul, Korea
2014 *apmap 2014 jeju: BETWEEN WAVES*, Seogwang Tea
Garden / OSULLOC, Jeju, Kora
2011 *One Another*, W Seoul Walkerhill, Seoul, Korea
2010 *MODAFE: The Rest*, Arco Art Center, Seoul, Korea
A4 Paper, Seokyo Experimental Art Center, Seoul,
Korea
2009 *BlueDot Asia 2009*, Seoul Arts Center, Seoul, Korea

Awards and Residencies
2020 ZERO1NE CREATOR Residency, Seoul, Korea (-2021)
2020 International Competition, Tampere International Short
Film Festival, Tampere, Finland
2019 Proyecto´ace Residency, Arts Council Korea, Buenos
Aires, Argentina
Finalist, Hermès International scarf design competition,
Paris, France
Winner, Lotte Museum of Art Young Artist Award, Seoul,
Korea
Grand Prix, Hyundai Motor Group VH Award, Seoul,
Korea
2018 Ars Electronica Center Residency, Hyundai Motor
Group, Linz, Austria
2008 Winner, Adobe Design Achievement Awards, New York,
USA

— 권혁인. 『에코사이언스』. 서울: 한경사, 2015.
— 김미수. 『생태 부엌』. 서울: 콤마, 2017.
— 김보중. 『흐르는 거주지』. 색다름, 2017.
— _____. 『추수 후, 콩밭에서 축제』. 색다름, 2018.
— 김성현. 『지구를 살리는 생명철학』. 서울: 지식과감성, 2018.
— 김익. 『에코액션』. 서울: 신광문화사, 2020.
— 남성현. 『위기의 지구, 물러설 곳 없는 인간』. 서울: 21세기북스, 2020.
— 너새니얼 리치. 『잃어버린 지구』. 김학영 옮김. 파주: 시공사, 2021.
— 다카기 진바부로. 『지금 자연을 어떻게 볼 것인가』. 김원식 옮김. 서울: 녹색평론사, 2006.
— 레이첼 카슨. 『우리를 둘러싼 바다』. 김홍옥 옮김. 서울: 에코리브르, 2018.
— _____. 『잃어버린 숲』. 김홍옥 옮김. 서울: 에코리브르, 2018.
— _____. 『침묵의 봄』. 김은령 옮김. 홍욱희 감수. 서울: 에코리브르, 2011.
— 로버트 콕스. 『환경 커뮤니케이션』. 김남수 옮김. 서울: 커뮤니케이션북스, 2013.
— 루이스 다트넬. 『오리진』. 이충호 옮김. 서울: 흐름출판, 2020.
— 마리아 미스 외. 『에코페미니즘』. 손덕수 외 옮김. 파주: 창비, 2020.
— 마이클 셸렌버거. 『지구를 위한다는 착각』. 노정태 옮김. 서울: 부키, 2021.
— 마크리더 편집부. 『쓰레기 문제 보고서』. 마크리더, 2019.
— 매슈 E. 칸. 『우리는 기후 변화에도 적응할 것이다』. 김홍옥 옮김. 서울: 에코리브르, 2021.
— 모리스 버먼. 『미국은 왜 실패했는가』. 김태언 외 옮김. 서울: 녹색평론사, 2015.
— 몸문화연구소 외. 『인류세와 에코바디』. 서울: 필로소픽, 2019.
— 미힐 로스캄 아빙. 『플라스틱 수프』. 김연옥 옮김. 서울: 양철북, 2020.
— 박경화. 『지구를 살리는 기발한 물건 10』. 서울: 한겨레출판사, 2019.
— 박길용. 『생태 자본과 공생 행복』. 서울: 커뮤니케이션북스, 2019.
— 박선순. 『우포 지독한 끌림』. 서울: 포토닷, 2017.
— 박은선. 『내성천 생태 도감』. 서울: 리슨투더시티, 2015.
— 박희병. 『한국의 생태사상』. 파주: 돌베개, 1999.
— 배리 카머너. 『원은 닫혀야 한다』. 고동욱 옮김. 서울: 이음, 2014.
— 배재대학교 북극연구단. 『북극의 눈물과 미소』. 서울: 학연문화사, 2016.
— 배종헌. 『배종헌 작업집서』. 파주: Monocle, 2015.
— 브뤼노 라투르. 『지구와 충돌하지 않고 착륙하는 방법』. 박범순 옮김. 서울: 이음, 2021.
— 신승철. 『펠릭스 가타리의 생태철학』. 홍성: 그물코, 2011.
— 신정근 외. 『생태미학과 동양철학』. 서울: 문사철, 2019.
— 신정근 외. 『유도(儒道)사상과 생태미학』. 서울: 문사철, 2020.
— 실비 드룰랭. 『쓰레기 제로 라이프』. 이나래 옮김. 서울: 북스힐, 2020.
— 씨더썬. 『Oven, We Bake Our Own Pie』. 서울: 씨더썬, 2021.
— 애니 레너드. 『너무 늦기 전에 알아야 할 물건 이야기』. 김승진 옮김. 파주: 김영사, 2011.
— 앤드류 슈왈츠 외. 『생태문명 선언』. 한윤정 옮김. 서울: 다른백년, 2020.
— 앤드류 파커. 『눈의 탄생』. 오은숙 옮김. 서울: 뿌리와이파리, 2007.

— 앨런 와이즈먼. 『인간 없는 세상』. 이한중 옮김. 최재천 감수. 서울: 알에이치코리아, 2020.
— 양해림. 『기후변화, 에코철학으로 응답하다』. 대전: 충남대학교 출판부, 2016.
— 얼 C. 엘리스. 『인류세』. 김용진 외 옮김. 파주: 교유서가, 2021.
— 에두아르도 콘. 『숲은 생각한다』. 차은정 옮김. 고양: 사월의 책, 2018.
— 에드워드 윌슨. 『지구의 절반』. 이한음 옮김. 서울: 사이언스북스, 2017.
— 에코포럼. 『생태적 상호의존성과 인간의 욕망』. 동국대학교출판부. 서울: 동국대학교 출판부, 2006.
— 요한 록스트룀 외. 『지구 한계의 경계에서』. 김홍옥 옮김. 서울: 에코리브르, 2017.
— 윌리엄 F. 러디먼. 『인류는 어떻게 기후에 영향을 미치게 되었는가』. 김홍옥 옮김. 서울: 에코리브르, 2017.
— 이반. 『DMZ의 과거·현재·미래』. 서울: 비무장지대 미술운동연구소, 1995.
— 이상헌. 『생태주의』. 서울: 책세상, 2011.
— 이-푸 투안. 『토포필리아 환경 지각 태도 가치의 연구』. 이옥진 옮김. 서울: 에코리브르, 2011.
— 이희선. 『에코토피아』. 서울: S&M미디어, 2018.
— 일본환경교육학회. 『환경 사전』, 자연의벗연구소 옮김. 정철 감수. 서울: 북센스, 2021.
— 전혜숙. 『인류세의 미술』. 서울: 선인, 2021.
— 정관용 외. 『코로나 사피엔스』. 서울: ㈜인플루엔셜, 2020.
— 정봉채. 『지독한 끌림, 정봉채 우포 사진 에세이』. 서울: 다비치, 2020.
— 정원. 『전지적 지구 시점』. 서울: 마음의숲, 2021.
— 존 벨러미 포스터 외. 『생태논의의 최전선』. 김철규 외 옮김. 고양: 필맥, 2009.
— 존 호턴. 『지구 온난화의 이해』. 정지영 외 옮김. 서울: 에코리브르, 2018.
— 주동주. 『70억의 별: 위기의 인류』. 파주: 한국학술정보, 2016.
— 주디스 콜 외. 『떡갈나무 바라보기』. 후박나무 옮김. 최재천 감수. 파주: 사계절출판사, 2002.
— 천옌 외. 『유·불·도, 환경과 예술을 말하다』. 김철 옮김. 파주: 경인문화사, 2017.
— 청강문화산업대학 에코라이프스쿨. 『에코라이프』. 파주: ITC, 2011.
— 최민자. 『생태정치학』. 서울: 모시는사람들, 2007.
— 최병두 외. 『녹색전환』. 파주: 한울아카데미, 2020.
— 최원형. 『착한 소비는 없다』. 서울: 자연과생태, 2020.
— 최재천. 『손잡지 않고 살아남은 생명은 없다』. 서울: 샘터, 2014.
— _____. 『생태적 전환, 슬기로운 지구 생활을 위하여』. 파주: 김영사, 2021.
— 최평순 외. 『인류세: 인간의 시대』. 서울: 해나무, 2020.
— 충남콘텐츠연구소. 『공주문화예술인 구술총서 01 - 임동식』. 공주: 공주문화재단, 2021.
— 카트린 하르트만. 『위장환경주의』. 이미옥 옮김. 서울: 에코리브르, 2018.
— 코샤 쥬베르트 외. 『세계 생태마을 네트워크』. 넥스트젠 코리아 에듀케이션 옮김. 순천: 열매하나, 2018.
— 콜린 베번. 『노 임팩트 맨』. 이은선 옮김. 서울: 북하우스, 2010.
— 클라이브 해밀턴. 『인류세』. 정서진 옮김. 서울: 이상북스, 2018.

— 타일러 라쉬. 『두 번째 지구는 없다』. 이영란 감수. 서울: 알에이치코리아, 2020.
— 탑이미지 편집부. 『자연과 예술의 조화있는 생태도시』. 탑이미지, 2021.
— _____. 『자연을 닮은 친환경, 생태에 휴머니즘을 접목하다』. 탑이미지, 2021.
— 폴 호컨. 『플랜 드로다운』. 이현수 옮김. 파주: 글항아리사이언스, 2019.
— 프랑수아 자리주. 『지구 오염의 역사』. 조미현 옮김. 서울: 에코리브르, 2021.
— 한삼희. 『위키드 프라블럼』. 서울: 궁리출판, 2016.
— 헤더 로저스. 『에코의 함정』. 추선영 옮김. 일산: 이후, 2011.
— 호프 자런. 『나는 풍요로웠고, 지구는 달라졌다』. 김은령 옮김. 파주: 김영사, 2020.
— 황대권 외. 『지구별 생태사상가』. 서울: 작은것이 아름답다, 2020.

— Beever, Erik et al.. *Ecological Consequences of Climate Change*. Boca Raton: CRC Press, 2011.
— Beisner, Beatrix et al.. *Nature All Around Us*. Chicago: University of Chicago Press, 2012.
— Cotgreave, Peter. *Introductory Ecology*. New Jersey: Blackwell, 2021.
— Ehlers, Eckart et al.. *Earth System Science in the Anthropocene*. Berlin: Springer, 2010.
— Feder, Helena. *Close Reading the Anthropocene*. London: Routledge, 2021.
— Fred D. Singer. *Ecology in Action*. Cambridge: Cambridge University Press, 2016.
— Gary G. Mittelbach et al.. *Community Ecology*. Oxford: Oxford University Press, 2019.
— Greipsson. *Restoration Ecology*. Burlington: Jones & Bartlett, 2010.
— John Berger. *Why Look at Animals?*. New York: Penguin Group USA, 2009.
— Jorgensen, Sven Erik. *Introduction to Systems Ecology*. Boca Raton: CRC Press, 2017.
— Linda Weintraub. *TO LIFE! ECO ART IN PURSUIT OF A SUSTAINABLE PLANET*. Berkeley: University of California Press, 2012.
— Lye, Irene Lin-Heng et al.. *Sustainability Matters*. Singapore: World Scientific Publishing Company, 2017.
— Merchant, Carolyn. *The Death of Nature*. San Francisco: HarperSanFrancisco, 1990.
— Peter Stiling. *Ecology*. New York: McGraw-Hill Education, 2016.
— Thomas M. Smith. *Elements of Ecology*. London: Pearson, 2015.
— Tony Juniper. *Ecology Book*. London: Dorling Kindersley, 2019.

— 경기문화재단. 『2006 공공전』. 수원: 경기문화재단, 2006.
— _____. 『2015 블루오션 프로젝트: 간석지대』. 수원: 경기문화재단, 2015.
— _____. 『실신 프로젝트 남·양·광·하』. 수원: 경기문화재단, 2016.
— 경기문화재단 외. 『블루오션 프로젝트 2016: 소용돌이』. 수원: 경기문화재단, 2016.
— 광주시립미술관. 『생태조감도』. 광주: 광주시립미술관, 2020.
— 금강현대미술제. 『예술과 마을』. 공주: 금강현대미술제2000 예술과 마을 위원회, 2000.
— _____. 『미술원, 우리와 우리 사이』. 청주: 국립현대미술관, 2021.
— 금강현대미술제연구회. 『금강현대미술제 창립야외현장전』. 공주: 금강현대미술제연구회, 1980.
— 김종영미술관. 『2011 오늘의 작가, 실크로드 프로젝트』. 서울: 김종영미술관, 2011.
— 김지수. 『울림: 그리면서 그려지는 생명의 그룹』. 대전: 문화예술공간 일리아, 2014.
— _____. 『김지수 개인전: 풀 풀 풀—향』. 파주: 아트스페이스 휴, 2019.
— _____. 『KIM Jee Soo』. 서울: 인사아트센터, 2010.
— 대구미술관. 『나현 바벨: 서로 다른 혀』. 대구: 대구미술관, 2019.
— 대안미술공간 소나무. 『2006 미술농장프로젝트: 미술로 자라는 식물, 식물로 자라는 미술』. 안성: 대안미술공간 소나무, 2006.
— _____. 『2008 미술농장프로젝트: 미술로 자라는 식물, 식물로 자라는 미술』. 안성: 대안미술공간 소나무, 2008.
— _____. 『2017 미술농장프로젝트: 녹색 게릴라』. 안성: 대안미술공간 소나무, 2017.
— _____. 『2018 녹색 호흡』. 안성: 대안미술공간 소나무, 2018.
— _____. 『2018 프로젝트 그린』. 안성: 대안미술공간 소나무, 2018.
— _____. 『격리해제 2020』. 안성: 대안미술공간 소나무, 2020.
— 대전시립미술관. 『임동식: 동방소년 탐문기』. 대전: 대전시립미술관, 2016.
— 마감뉴스. 『제2회 마감뉴스』. 마감뉴스, 1993.
— _____. 『제12회 마감뉴스 야외설치: 인간과 환경, 그 예술적 화해』. 마감뉴스, 1998.
— _____. 『제13회 마감뉴스 야외설치: 인간과 환경, 그 새로운 출발』. 마감뉴스, 1999.
— _____. 『제14회 마감뉴스 야외설치: 갯벌』. 마감뉴스, 1999.
— _____. 『제16회 마감뉴스 야외설치: 나무를 소재로 한 설치』. 마감뉴스, 2001.
— _____. 『제17회 마감뉴스 야외설치』. 마감뉴스, 2002.
— _____. 『제18회 마감뉴스 야외설치: 섬』. 마감뉴스, 2003.
— _____. 『제19회 마감뉴스 야외설치: 상상의 나무 차오름의 공간』. 마감뉴스, 2004.
— _____. 『제20회 마감뉴스 야외설치: 꿈을 찾아서』. 마감뉴스, 2005.
— _____. 『제21회 마감뉴스 야외설치: 나무공간』. 마감뉴스, 2006.
— _____. 『제22회 마감뉴스 야외설치: 바람—피우다』. 마감뉴스, 2007.
— _____. 『제23회 마감뉴스 야외설치: 시간으로부터의 여행』. 마감뉴스, 2008.

— _____.『제24회 마감뉴스 야외설치: 누구와 누구가 만나다』. 마감뉴스, 2009.

— _____.『제25회 마감뉴스 야외설치: STAY 72』. 마감뉴스, 2010.

— _____.『제26회 마감뉴스 야외설치: 자연을 읽다』. 마감뉴스, 2011.

— _____.『제28회 마감뉴스 야외설치: 유목민의 정원』. 마감뉴스, 2013.

— _____.『제29회 마감뉴스 야외설치: 섬놀이』. 마감뉴스, 2014.

— _____.『제30회 마감뉴스 야외설치: 雲 떠돈다는 것, 水 흐른다는 것』. 마감뉴스, 2015.

— _____.『제31회 마감뉴스 야외설치: 이야기 공장』. 마감뉴스, 2016.

— _____.『제32회 마감뉴스 야외설치: 소금꽃을 피우다』. 마감뉴스, 2017.

— _____.『제33회 마감뉴스 야외설치: 여기, 지금』. 마감뉴스, 2018.

— _____.『제34회 마감뉴스 야외설치: 보물 창고와 여행자』. 마감뉴스, 2019.

— 바깥미술회.『2000 바깥미술: 대성리전. 자생·생태·공동체』. 바깥미술회, 2000.

— _____.『공존하는 삶! 공명하는 예술!: 자생적 생태공동체를 향하여』. 바깥미술회, 2002.

— _____.『2011 자라섬 국제바깥미술전』. 바깥미술회, 2011.

— _____.『2015 바깥미술 서울대공원전: 울타리 새로운 경계』. 바깥미술회, 2015.

— _____.『2017 세미원: 두물경을 잇는 바깥미술. 두 강이 만나다』. 바깥미술회, 2017.

— _____.『2019 바깥미술 남한강전: 부유하는 섬』. 바깥미술회, 2019.

— _____.『2020 바깥미술 남한강전: 땅 밖의 땅—섬』. 바깥미술회, 2020.

— _____.『2020 바깥미술 두물머리전: 순환의 땅, 대지를 상상하다』. 바깥미술회, 2020.

— 부산비엔날레조직위원회.『2015 바다미술제: 보다—바다와 씨앗』. 부산: 부산비엔날레조직위원회, 2015.

— 부산현대미술관.『자연·생명·인간』. 부산: 부산현대미술관, 2019.

— 삼성미술관 Leeum.『HIROSHI SUGIMOTO, 히로시 스기모토』. 서울: 삼성미술관, 2013.

— _____.『올라퍼 엘리아슨: 세상의 모든 가능성』. 서울: 삼성미술관, 2016.

— 생태미학예술연구소.『지속가능한 도시_꽃』. 대전: 생태미학예술연구소, 2013.

— _____.『지속가능한 도시-꽃 II』. 대전: 생태미학예술연구소, 2014.

— _____.『지속가능한 도시_꽃 III』. 대전: 생태미학예술연구소, 2015.

— _____.『지속가능한 도시_꽃 IV』. 대전: 생태미학예술연구소, 2018.

— 서울거리예술창작센터.『만보객의 서울유람』. 서울: 서울거리예술창작센터, 2016.

— 서울대학교미술관.『푸른 유리구슬 소리, 인류세 시대를 애도하기』. 서울: 서울대학교미술관, 2021.

— 서울시립 북서울미술관.『2019 서울 포커스: 두 번의 똑같은 밤은 없다』. 서울: 서울시립 북서울미술관, 2019.

— 서울시립미술관.『일어나 올라가 임동식』. 서울: 서울시립미술관, 2020.

— 수원시립아이파크미술관.『자연스럽게』. 수원: 수원시립아이파크미술관, 2018.

— 스페이스몸미술관.『투명의 역설: 투명하게 존재하라 II—김보중 개인전 人乃地』. 청주: 스페이스몸미술관, 2020.

— 아르코미술관.『미장제색』. 서울: 아르코미술관, 2020.

— _____.『재활용 주식회사』. 서울: 아르코미술관, 2007.

— _____.『정재철: 사랑과 평화』. 서울: 아르코미술관, 2021.

— 안양문화예술재단.『제27회 마감뉴스 20주년 기념 초대전: 길에게 묻다』. 안양: 안양문화예술재단, 2012.

— 야투.『세계 자연미술의 현장』. 공주: 야투, 2014.

— ____.『2014 글로벌노마딕아트프로젝트: 코리아』. 공주: 야투, 2014.

— ____.『2015 글로벌노마딕아트프로젝트: 코리아II』. 공주: 야투, 2015.

— ____.『2016 글로벌노마딕아트프로젝트: 사우스아프리카, 코리아III, 이란』. 공주: 야투, 2016.

— ____.『2017 글로벌노마딕아트프로젝트: 유럽』. 공주: 야투, 2017.

— ____.『2018 글로벌노마딕아트프로젝트: 영국』. 공주: 야투, 2018.

— ____.『2019 글로벌노마딕아트프로젝트: 멕시코, 독일III, 이탈리아』. 공주: 야투, 2019.

— ____.『2020 글로벌노마딕아트프로젝트: 프랑스II, 몽골, 한국IV』. 공주: 야투, 2020.

— 야투자연미술연구회.『금강에서의 국제자연미술전 '95』. 공주: 야투자연미술연구회, 1995.

— _____.『1998 여름 금강에서의 국제자연미술전』. 공주: 야투자연미술연구회, 1998.

— 엄미술관.『대지의 연금술』. 화성: 엄미술관, 2020.

— 이영민.『임동식 80년대 함부르크 시절 드로잉부터 2018 오늘까지』. 대전: 대전터미널시티, 2018.

— 일민미술관.『디어 아마존—인류세에 관하여』. 서울: 일민미술관, 2021.

— 전혁림미술관.『김보중 KIM BO JOONG』. 통영: 전혁림미술관, 2019.

— 정재철.『분수령』. 서울: 금산갤러리, 2017.

— ____.『실크로드 프로젝트』. 서울: KC기획, 2005.

— ____.『정재철 작품집』. 과천: 터알, 2014.

— 제주현대미술관.『생태미술 2017 공존 순환』. 제주: 제주현대미술관, 2017.

— _____.『생태미술 2018 플라스틱 생물』. 제주: 제주현대미술관, 2018.

— 창녕우포늪생태관광협회.『2017 우포자연미술제』. 창녕: 창녕우포늪생태관광협회, 2017.

— _____.『2019 우포자연미술제』. 창녕: 창녕우포늪생태관광협회, 2019.

— _____.『2020 생태미술마을 프로젝트』. 창녕: 창녕우포늪생태관광협회, 2020.

— 창원국제조각비엔날레위원회.『2016 창원조각비엔날레, 억조창생』. 창원: 창원국제조각비엔날레위원회, 2016.

— 한국자연미술가협회-야투.『1999-2000 금강국제자연미술전』. 공주: 한국자연미술가협회-야투, 2000.

— _____.『2001 금강국제자연미술전』. 공주: 한국자연미술가협회-야투, 2001.

— _____.『2002 금강국제자연미술프로젝트전』. 공주: 한국자연미술가협회-야투, 2002.

— _____. 『2003 금강국제자연미술전
프레비엔날레』. 공주: 한국자연미술가협회-야투, 2003.

— _____. 『금강자연미술비엔날레』. 공주:
한국자연미술가협회-야투, 2004.
— _____. 『2005 금강자연미술프레비엔날레.
자연으로부터의 작업전』. 공주: 한국자연미술가협회-야투,
2005.
— 홍이현숙. 『폐경의례』. 서울: 복합공간 에무, 2012.

— Hiroshi Sugimoto. Hiroshi Sugimoto: Dioramas.
Bologna: Damiani, 2014.
— Joseph Beuys et al.. *Joseph Beuys*. New Haven:
Yale University Press, 2004.
— MAMbo-Museo d'Arte Moderna di Bologna.
BOLTANSKI-Souls, From Place to Place. Milan:
Silvana Editoriale S.p.A., 2017.
— Mangini, Elizabeth. *Seeing Through Closed Eyelids:
Giuseppe Penone and the Nature of Sculpture*.
Toronto: University of Toronto Press, 2021.
— Mylayne, Jean-Luc et al.. *Jean Luc Mylayne*.
New Mexico: Twin Palms Publishers, 2007.
— Olarfur Eliasson. *Take your time: Olafur Eliasson*.
ed. Madeleine Grynsztejn. London: Thames &
Hudson, 2007.
— Sugimoto, Hiroshi et al.. *Hiroshi Sugimoto:
Black Box*. Eastbourne: Gardners Books, 2016.
— Susan May. *Unilever Series: Olafur Eliasson—
The Weather Project*. London: Tate, 2004.

도움 주신 분들

김주리
김태균, 이철현, 김경현, 유형우, 김민정, 이경원, 정의혁, 함영훈, 김동언

나현
장즈산(張至善) 박사(국립대만선사박물관), 이미지원, 파주목공방

서동주
김예진(머신러닝 엔지니어 & 비주얼 아트), 김민재(3D 영상 그래픽), 캐롤라인 라이제(영상 그래픽 및 데이터 시각화), 언해피서킷(데이터 음향화 및 사운드 디자인), 편광훈(사운드 디자인), 김정인(시아노타입 프린트 및 사진 이미지 제작), (주)씨투아테크놀러지(기술 제공), (주)더디자인그룹(작품 설치), 곰디자인(공간 구현)

OAA(정규동)
권혁준(모노블럭 대표), 정민식(앤오즈 대표), 문재훈(플리츠마마 이사), 에이스폴리머, 일삼시스템, 임원택, 최종원, 많은 도움을 주신 소재/가공 업체분들, 그리고 함께 작업하고 있는 아내 배주희

이경호
봉다리를 직접 날리거나 작품 제작에 도움을 주신 분들: 성주영(갤러리 세줄), 강금실(지구와 사람), 이정숙(복실이 농산), 어스스튜디오, 이찬유, 송현주, 서영은, 김광진

장민승
서울대공원, 한국마사회, 서울랜드, 서울 영상위원회, 캐논 코리아

정소영
임동일 박사, 김지훈 연구원, 박준상 박사(한국해양과학기술원 남해연구소 해양시료도서관), 원은지 박사(한양대학교 해양대기과학연구소 해양융합공학과)

Special Thanks to

Chung Soyoung
Dr. Dhong Il Lim; Researcher Jihun Kim; Dr. Joon Sang Park (Korea Institute of Ocean Science & Technology, Library of Marine Samples) and Dr. Eunji Won (Hanyang University Institute of Marine & Atmospheric Science)

Jang Minseung
Seoul Grand Park, Korea Racing Authority, Seoul Land, Seoul Film Commission, and Canon Korea

Kim Juree
Taegyun Kim, Chulhyun Lee, Kim Kyung-hyun, Rhu Hyeong woo, Kim minjung, Lee kyoung won, Jeong Euihyuk, Ham Young Hoon, and KIM DONGEON

Lee Kyung Ho
Everyone who moved the plastic bags and helped with the art work production: Sung Ju-young (Gallery Sejul), Kang Kum-sil (People for Earth), Lee Jeong-suk (Boksili Nongsan & Food), UStudio, Lee Chanew, Song Hyun-joo, Seo Young-en, and Kim Kwang-jin

Na Hyun
Dr. Chang, Chi-Shan (National Museum of Prehistory, Taiwan), Image One, and PAJU Wood

OAA (Jung Kyudong)
Hyukjun Kwon (Director of Monoblock), Minsik Jung (CEO of Anodds), Jaehoon Moon (Director of FleetsMama), Acepolymer, Ilsam System, Lim Wontaek, Choi Jongwon, the material and processing companies, and my wife, my partner Joohee Bae.

Seo Dongjoo
Yejin Kim (Machine Learning Engineer and Visual Art), Minjae Kim (3D Motion Graphics), Caroline Reize (Motion Graphics and Data Visualization), Unhappy Circuit (Sonification and Sound Design), Ken Pyun (Sound Design), Jeongin Kim (Cyanotype Printing and Photography Image Making), C2 ARTECHNOLOZY (Technical Support), THE DESIGN GROUP (Installation), and GOM DESIGN (Construction)

대지의 시간

2021. 11. 25.-2022. 3. 27.
국립현대미술관 과천
1전시실 및 중앙홀

관장
윤범모

학예연구실장
김준기

현대미술2과장
강수정

학예연구관
조장은

도움 주신 분들
대안공간 소나무
마감뉴스
바깥미술
양구군립 박수근미술관
생태미학예술연구소
서울시립미술관
정익명(정길수)
(사)한국자연미술가협회-야투(野投)
주세페 페노네 스튜디오
히로시 스기모토 스튜디오
스튜디오 올라퍼 엘리아손
비타민 크리에이티브 스페이스
에바 알바란 앤 컴퍼니
갤러리 고야나기
스프루스 마거스

전시 기획
김경란

코디네이터
김유란

전시 디자인
김용주, 윤지원

그래픽 디자인
박휘윤

전시 조성
홍지원

운송·설치
박양규, 복영웅

작품 보존
범대건, 이남이, 윤보경

교육
황지영, 정윤혜, 김혜정

홍보·마케팅
이성희, 윤승연, 박유리, 채지연, 김홍조,
김민주, 이민지, 기성미, 신나래, 장라윤

고객 지원
이은수, 오경옥, 유중위

사진
김경태

영상
최기석

VR 기록 및 제작
테크캡슐

©2021 국립현대미술관

이 책은 국립현대미술관에서 개최된 《대지의
시간》(2021. 11. 25.-2022. 3. 27.) 전시
도록으로 제작되었습니다. 이 책에
수록된 작품 이미지 및 글의 저작권은 해당
저자와 작가, 소장처, 국립현대미술관에
있습니다. 저작권법에 의해 보호를 받는
저작물이므로 무단 전재, 복제, 변형, 송신을
금합니다.

발행처 국립현대미술관
경기도 과천시 광명로 313
02-2188-6000
www.mmca.go.kr
초판 발행 2021년 12월 26일

발행인
윤범모

편집인
김준기

제작 총괄
강수정, 조장은

글
김경란, 김용주, 박현선, 임지연, 장즈산, 최평순,
홍상지

편집 진행
김경란, 김유란, 필드워크

디자인
Plate

인쇄 및 제책
헤적프레스·으뜸프로세스

영문 번역
서울셀렉션

사진
김경태

ISBN 978-89-6303-309-9
가격 29,000원

Time of the Earth

November 25, 2021.– March 27, 2022.
National Museum of Modern and
Contemporary Art, Gwacheon, Korea
Gallery 1 and Main Hall

Director
Youn Bummo

Supervised by
Gim Jungi
Kang Soojung
Cho Jangeun

Curated by
Kim Kyoungran

Curatorial Assistant
Kim Yuran

Exhibition Design
Kim Yongju, Yoon Jiwon

Graphic Design
Park Hwi Youn

Space Construction
Hong Jiwon

Transportation · Installation
Park Yang-gyu, Bok Yeongung

Conservation
Beom Daegon, Lee Nami, Yoon Bokyung

Education
Hwang Jiyoung, Jeong YoonHye,
Kim Heijeong

Public Communication
Lee Sunghee, Yun Tiffany, Park Yulee,
Chae Jiyeon, Kim Hongjo, Kim Minjoo,
Lee Minjee, Ki Sungmi, Shin Narae,
Jang Layoon

Customer Service
Lee Eun-su, Oh Kyungok, Yu Joongwi

Photography
Kim Kyoungtae

Filming
Choi Kiseok

VR Production
TechCapsule

Special thanks to
Alternative Art Space Sonahmoo
MAGAMNEWS
Baggat Art
Park Soo Keun Museum in Yanggu
  County
Center for Eco Aesthetics and Art
  Research
Seoul Museum of Art
Jung Ik Myeong (a.k.a. Jung Gil Soo)
Korean Nature Artists' Association-
  YATOO
Giuseppe Penone Studio
Hiroshi Sugimoto Studio
Studio Olafur Eliasson
Vitamin Creative Space
Eva Albarran & Co.
Gallery Koyanagi
Sprüth Magers

Published by
National Museum of Modern and
Contemporary Art, Korea
313 Gwangmyeong-ro, Gwacheon-si,
Gyeonggi-do, 13829 Korea
T +82-2-2188-6000
www.mmca.go.kr

First Edition
26 December, 2021

Publisher
Youn Bummo

Editor
Gim Jungi

Supervisor
Kang Soojung, Cho Jangeun

Contributors
Chang, Chi-Shan, Choi Pyeong-soon,
Hong Sangji, Im Ji-yeon, Kim Kyoungran,
Kim Yongju, Park Hyeon-seon

Edited by
Kim Kyoungran, Kim Yuran, Fieldwork

Design
Plate

Printing and Binding
Hezuk Press · Top process

English Translation
Seoul Selection

Photography
Kim Kyoungtae

ISBN 978-89-6303-309-9
Price KRW 29,000